A DICTIONARY OF IOWA PLACE-NAMES

A BUR OAK GUIDE

A Dictionary of

IOWA (ī · ə · w ə)

Place-Names

TOM SAVAGE

University of Iowa Press
Iowa City

University of Iowa Press, Iowa City 52242

Copyright © 2007 by the University of Iowa Press

www.uiowapress.org

The University of Iowa Press is a member of Green Press Initiative and is committed to preserving natural resources.

Printed on acid-free paper

Library of Congress Cataloging-in-Publication Data

Savage, Tom, 1945–   .

  A dictionary of Iowa place-names / by Tom Savage.

    p.   cm.—(A bur oak guide)

  Includes bibliographic references.

  ISBN-13: 978-1-58729-531-7 (pbk.)

  ISBN-10: 1-58729-531-8 (pbk.)

  1. Names, Geographical—Iowa.   2. Iowa—History, Local.   I. Title.

  F619.S385 2007

  917.77—dc22   2006035801

07   08   09   10   11   P   5   4   3   2   1

This book is dedicated to Sharon, my wife.

CONTENTS

By Loren N. Horton

Ever since human beings communicated through language, they have assigned names to themselves and to the objects and conditions around them. With the development of written language, these names assumed the character of captions or labels, and gradually it came into common usage that all people in a cultural area used the same names for the same persons, objects, and conditions. Names became a means of identifying people and things. Names became very important. Names established a sense of place, a genealogical continuity, and a way of transmitting information and ideas. Without a name, a person loses identity, a community becomes a mere shadow, and there is no way of communicating social, political, economic, religious, or philosophical ideas. Names are important.

In the area that we know as Iowa, aboriginal inhabitants had names for their own clans and groups, names for the geographical features in which they lived and worked, and names for the artifacts with which they existed. With the coming of the Euro-Americans, many of these original place names were lost. Those original names were replaced with other names, either brought with the people from places of origin, chosen to give a certain importance by association with great people or events, or very occasionally created in imaginative ways. Whatever the source of the new names, they became permanent by being engraved upon maps of the area. Although changes did occur, for the most part the first Euro-Americans to reach a particular place assumed the right to name it, and usually that name became official. When the name of a person or place is recognized by the government, then it becomes as nearly permanent as something dependent upon language can be permanent.

Names of communities derive from many sources. Many relate to the natural features of the landscape and are recognizable as such. Whenever the words "lake," "river," "rapids," "falls," "creek," "springs," "grove," "hill," "field," or "bluff" occur in the name of a town, we can be reasonably sure that such a natural feature is present there or nearby. In some cases the names retain words from Native American languages. Sometimes the town name recalls the place from which the first inhabitant migrated, or the idea or whim of the most important person in the town at the time a name is chosen. Town names also come from the names of famous political and military figures and from events notable in the platting of the town itself. Iowa is rich in examples of all of these origins of town names.

Some town names in Iowa are unique in that they do not appear in any other state. For instance, Iowa is the only state with towns named LeMars, Delmar, or Primghar. At least the Iowa towns came to be called by those names by methods not duplicated in any other state. As far as can be determined, Iowa is the only state with a town named Keota. Very likely there are few other towns anywhere named What Cheer or Elkader. It is one of the beauties of Iowa that travel across the state brings a person in contact with so many wonderful names, some of which a traveler may understand immediately, but others that require a bit of investigation. Like the poet Stephen Vincent Benét, we have fallen in love with American names. They are part of our soul, be they family names, town names, or artifact names. We identify with them, are identified by them, and cannot live without them. This book will help us learn more about them and integrate them into our beings.

ACKNOWLEDGMENTS

This book would not have been possible without the help of officials from the secretary of state's office, county officials, and the many city clerks and mayors who took the time to answer my questions. I also have to thank the knowledgeable community residents who were kind enough to talk to me about their towns. Librarians in communities in every county in the state have been invaluable in assisting me in gathering information for this book. All of the county historical and genealogical societies have been most helpful. My cousin Alfred Savage and my sisters, Mary Alice and Margaret Savage, in southeastern Iowa have been helpful in locating information and offering suggestions. And finally, I must thank Loren Horton for his good advice and suggestions and for writing the foreword to this book.

I decided to compile this book when I found that there were no comprehensive guides to Iowa place-names in print. There are many community and county publications that record information about their local histories, and certainly information is in print about American Indian place-names in Iowa, but there is no central source for this information. Having spent many years working with students looking ahead and trying to assess what careers would be viable for them, I thought it would be refreshing to look back. I just didn't realize that it would take four years to complete this project.

The towns that I have included were drawn from the Iowa Department of Transportation (DOT) road map published in 2006. The DOT included all incorporated communities and all the unincorporated towns that met at least two of the following criteria: twenty-five residents or more; a retail business; an annual celebration or festival; a school, church, or cemetery; a building on the National Register of Historic Places; a zip-coded post office; or an association with a public recreation site. I used its list in determining which towns to include in the book, not only because it was expedient but also because many people have the DOT road map and could readily locate the towns listed. I have also included information about why the communities were named, when they were established, and when they were incorporated.

The names reflect the history and development of Iowa. American Indians were the inspiration for many names in Iowa, as they should be since they were the first residents of the area. The early French explorers left many names in the state as well. Many of the U.S. explorers and soldiers who traveled through the area have also been commemorated. Later, the influx of settlers from Europe and the eastern United States brought many new names. Place-names were applied to pay tribute to the hometowns from which they came. Other town names were drawn from the family names of the settlers and founders. Mining towns reflected the names of the companies that they sprang up around. With the railroads came many new towns. John Blair, who was heavily involved with the development of the railroads in Iowa, probably is responsible for the names of more towns in the state than any other individual.

While I was aware of the old coal mines along the Des Moines River and the extensive harvesting of timber in the forested areas of the state, I must admit that I did not understand the extent of the role those activities and others had played in the development of both the economy and the geography of the state. Although agriculture had been critical for the survival of the various American Indian tribes that had lived in the area, it did not become important economically for the settlers until after Iowa developed a strong rail system. The railroads were important in the location of towns throughout the state because of their policy of making sure that there were towns every seven to ten miles along their tracks. Those tracks were crucial for the development of Iowa's agricultural economy from the middle of the nineteenth century onward. On a lighter note, it was interesting to learn that Dewar has had a community pot-luck running for over sixty years and that the mayor of West Okoboji is the longest-serving mayor in the state of Iowa.

American Indians populated the upper Midwest for thousands of years before there was contact with Euro-Americans. There is little information recorded about the tribes before contact with the French. Most of the Iowa place-names derived from

Indian dialects are based on either the Siouan or Algonquian root languages, since those were the two language groups used by the Indian populations in Iowa. Some names are derived from the words used by Indians to describe an area. Ottumwa and Quasqueton are examples. Battles between tribes competing for space have been commemorated. While the term is French, Tete des Mortes Creek was named for the human skulls found in and by it, gruesome relics of an Indian battle. A town was named from the creek, Tete des Mortes, but later renamed St. Donatus. Another example was Battle Creek, named for a particularly vicious fight between tribes. Not all Indian names used in place-names in Iowa are from tribes that had direct connections to the region. Osceola and Pocahontas, for example, are both named to honor individuals who have no linkage to the places in Iowa that carry their names.

European interest in this part of the continent started around five hundred years ago. In 1493 the king and queen of Spain were granted rights to North America by Pope Alexander VI. In 1498 John Cabot and his sons claimed North America for England. For over a century the title over the territory encompassing Iowa was distributed in a variety of ways by English interests on the eastern coast of North America. In 1682 La Salle, who was the first representative of a European nation known to actually explore the region, claimed the territory from the headwaters of the Mississippi to the river's mouth for France. In this region the French had a policy of coexisting peacefully with the tribes they encountered. That, as well as their stronghold around the Great Lakes and the skill of the voyageurs with their canoes, allowed them to explore the center of the continent. The Portuguese, Spanish, and English strategies of attempting to conquer or kill the tribes they encountered made excursions into the interior very risky for them since the Indians would attempt to exact revenge on their attackers.

The French fostered relationships with the Indians living here and developed trade with them. The Indians were only too happy to trade pelts for new treasures. The first written records about what would become Iowa were the notes of Louis Jolliet, Father Jacques Marquette, and the voyageurs who traveled with them through this area in 1673, although assessments of the resources of the upper Mississippi valley were recorded as early as 1634. French traders and adventurers with French connections lived among and traded with the Indians in the area from the late 1600s onward, even after France sold its interest in the region to Spain in 1762. While France gave up its claim to the territory, its interests were still clearly represented. In the late 1700s French monks were reported to have established a Trappist mission near the mouth of the Des Moines River. In that same time frame individuals like Basil Giard, the namesake for the town of Giard, and Louis Honore Tesson gained permission from Spain to settle in what would become eastern Iowa. Julien Dubuque developed lead mines near the city that bears his name at approximately the same time.

Lead was mined by the Indians in the region for over a thousand years before Dubuque came on the scene. In fact, the Indians traded lead with the French from the beginning of the eighteenth century, and some of that lead was shipped to France as part of the treasure of the New World. These rich deposits in the upper Midwest furnished most of the lead for munitions in this country right up to and through the Civil War.

When the French lost Canada to Britain in 1763, the French, in order to limit British influence, gave Spain all the territory it had claimed west of the Mississippi River, including the land that now comprises Iowa. The Spanish then traded the territory back to France in 1800. France sold the territory to the United States as part of the Louisiana Purchase in 1803.

The United States and European claims to the territory were viewed as rights of oversight or governance. While it can be argued that the compensation offered to tribes may or may not have been appropriate, at least there was some payment for rights to the land. The Indian tribes living in the region had their own tribal claims, disputes, and wars over the land. The westward expansion of U.S. interests started to have a direct impact on the tribes at the beginning of the nineteenth century. The Indian tribes that lived in the territory were recognized as having rights of ownership. Although as we look back the United States tended to be fairly brutal in imposing its will on the indigenous populations, there typically was some compensation to the tribes. In fairness, the tribes themselves had struggled for the territories that they lived in, and wars between the tribes were not infrequent as they fought for space.

In the early 1800s U.S. interest in the West was expressed through the travels of Lewis and Clark, Zebulon Pike, and others. What would eventually become the western side of Iowa was explored when Lewis and Clark traveled through that area on their journey west. Shortly after that Zebulon Pike explored the upper Mississippi and then traveled west to the Rocky Mountains. Following Pike's exploration, U.S. dragoons explored the territory, initially to map and record information about the land and then to keep the peace between the tribes.

When a portion of the territory that would become Iowa was opened for settlement after the Black Hawk War of 1832, the first settlers set up near the waterways of the region, partially because of the comparative ease and safety of travel along the rivers and streams and partially because water power helped them grind grain and saw lumber. Dubuque had been developed as a mining camp in 1788, but when Julien

Dubuque died in 1810, the Indians burned the camp. Their stance was that they had granted Dubuque the right to mine lead and no one else, so they destroyed the buildings and reclaimed the territory. Mining did not commence again until the territory was opened to white settlement in 1833. A military outpost, Ft. Madison, was constructed in 1809, although it was abandoned in 1813. The fort had been an attempt by the United States to defend the region from British incursion. Settlement by immigrants from the United States officially started in the early 1830s.

Lieutenant Albert Lea, a dragoon assigned to the region, is credited with being the first person to record the term "Iowa." He referred to the area that he had explored as the "Iowa Territory." While the term was used among the pioneers who had moved into the area, Lieutenant Lea was the first to record it in writing in his 1836 book, *Notes on the Wisconsin Territory, with a Map*. The name was a reference to the Ioway Indians, who had emigrated from the Great Lakes in the late 1600s to the region west of the Mississippi River, roughly in the area that is now Van Buren, Davis, and Wapello counties in Iowa. They later moved up through central Iowa and eventually ended up on a reservation in Kansas. Since the Iowa tribe was associated with the area, the settlers used the name as a descriptive term for the region. Iowa was associated with a number of territories claimed by the United States between 1805 and its entry into the Union as the twenty-ninth state in 1846.

The popular view in the United States was that the territories that encompassed Iowa and the land to the west should be held in reserve for expansion as the population grew. The belief was that it would be a hundred years before the territory would ever be populated. The leaders could not envision the incredible changes in both society and technology that would influence western expansion. That belief had a lot to do with the shifting borders of the territory and the section denoted as Iowa. For a while there was no legal authority covering the area. This fact became quite clear when a lead miner in the mid 1830s murdered his partner. The community discovered that there was no legal structure to try the man for the act, so they formed their own court and dispensed justice. The U.S. government, made aware of the oversight by the lynching of the killer, quickly established a territorial authority.

Deteriorating conditions throughout Europe in the nineteenth century led to famine, economic upheaval, and a desperate need to escape from oppression. This caused waves of emigration from western Europe to the United States. The people were looking for a fresh start and opportunities for themselves and their families. They came with a variety of skills and education, with an interest in developing a more secure and prosperous life in the New World.

While subsistence agriculture had been a staple of the diet of the Indians in the region, it was critical to their survival but not to the overall economy of the region. Changing technologies led by innovators like John Deere and Cyrus McCormick were making it possible to break the thick sod that thousands of years of prairie grass had created and then efficiently harvest the crops. The explosion in agriculture really occurred in the 1840s and 1850s with the rapid influx of immigrants from the East and from Europe. The discovery of gold in California and the Mormon trek across the territory brought many people through the region, established some initial settlements, and helped to open the territory. Many who tried their hand in the goldfields headed back to take up farming when they were not able to get rich quickly in the West. Cheap fertile land, Iowa's statehood in 1846, and the development of the railroads through the region starting in the 1850s all contributed to Iowa's amazing agricultural development. The wealth created through the agricultural economy supported the many towns that dotted the Iowa landscape. Other communities sprang into being because of lumber, coal, gypsum, and the other resources that contributed to Iowa's development.

Iowa's names record the history of the Indians, the French, and the adventurers and explorers who came to the area. Names that the Indians applied to places and the names the French gave to sites are still the names used today in many locations. The names of the explorers and soldiers who had contact with the territory are also integrated into the Iowa landscape. But the history of Iowa's place-names extends beyond these inspirations. The imaginations, philosophies, and experiences of the new immigrants all played a role in the naming of Iowa's towns and places.

Optimism and hope were reflected time and time again in the naming of towns in Iowa. Many towns were named for other centers of commerce in the East and in Europe, both for sentimental reasons and in the hope that the name would work some magic for the new town. Towns were named for heroes drawn from history and for military men and politicians of the era in the hope that some of the luster of the name could benefit the enterprises in the new towns. Literary figures, Greek gods, and Norse gods have also lent their names to little towns all over the state of Iowa.

Many of Iowa's towns reflect the histories of the people who established them. Columbus City in Louisa County comes to mind. The founders of that town named it after Columbus, Ohio, from where they had traveled. Their hope was that the name would make their new town as successful and as much of a market center as its namesake. Lowell was named for Lowell, Massachusetts, as Cranston was named for Cranston, Rhode Island. Many other towns in Iowa were named for the hometowns of the settlers who helped found them. The ancestry of the immigrants is reflected in the names of many other towns in Iowa, with Germans, English, Welsh, Scots, Irish, Swedes, Norwegians, Dutch, and others contributing place-names in the state.

Towns were named for children, both to memorialize those who had not survived and to honor those who lived, like George and Edna, coincidentally named for a brother and sister who lived in the area of the two towns. Other towns were named for sweethearts or paramours. Nora Springs, for example, was named sadly for a young woman who never lived there. When her suitor went east to bring her back, she refused to return. He moved away from the town, just leaving the name. Valeria has a happier ending. Valeria was the name of a young woman who lived on a farm. One of the engineers laying track through the area became smitten with her, and somehow the track ended up going through her father's farm. A depot and town were established nearby, and the town was named in her honor, since it would not have existed if the romance had not blossomed.

Religion in one fashion or another played a part in the naming of many towns. Salem was named by the Street family for the biblical place of peace. Lourdes, Churchtown, Iconium, Amana, and many more towns owe their names to religions. In some instances, the fact that settlers founded gardens or established havens were included in the names given to the sites. The Amanas were named by a religious group that moved from New York to practice their religion here. Denmark was named for a visitor's favorite hymn.

Woden was named for the Norse god of war, because of the sound of the dynamite used by the track-laying crews as they neared the town site. The Norse god Thor and Greek Muse Clio were inspirations for the names of towns in the state. The arts were used for inspiration. Authors like Lydia Huntley

Sigourney, Lord Lytton, and Ralph Waldo Emerson inspired the names of towns, and Radcliffe, Waverly, and Amber all reflect popular works of the time.

Whimsy played a role in the names of some towns. Fonda was selected simply because the person naming the town liked the sound of the name. The same is true of Indianola. Other towns like Delmar, LeMars, and Primghar were constructed from initials of people either visiting or living in the towns. Madrid was named to spite the family of the deceased owner of the town site.

Other towns were given practical, descriptive names. Diagonal was located at a site along a rail line called the diagonal because the original plan was to extend the track diagonally through the state. Marysville was named because of the number of women named Mary in the area. Mechanicsville was named because of the skills of some of the settlement's residents. Cylinder was named after an engine that was dropped in a nearby creek. Fairfield was thought to be a descriptive name, as was College Springs.

People also named towns for their heroes or for battle sites and other historically significant events. The use of the term "Union" in naming towns was quite popular for obvious reasons in the 1850s. Palo was named for the battle of Palo Alto. Tripoli was of course named for the site of the marines' battle, and Waterloo was named for the famous battle site where English forces defeated Napoleon. Revolutionary War battle sites and heroes, Mexican War participants and sites, and Civil War leaders and sites were all inspirations for the names of towns.

While Iowans pride themselves on their educational system, some town's names are the results of misspellings. Centerville, for example, was named in honor of a senator from Tennessee, a Mr. Sentor. The town was called Sentorville, but it was misspelled when the town was registered. Another town that suffered at the hands of those who registered it was Oskaloosa. It was supposed to be called Ouscaloosa. Patterson was supposed to be Pattison, to honor the town's founder, but a slip of the clerk's hand changed that. Sand Mound became Grand Mound, and Missouri Dale became Modale as a result of faulty handwriting.

In all, I must say that the gathering of this material has been an adventure for me. I hope you enjoy reading this book as much as I have enjoyed pursuing this information.

Sources

Baldwin, Clarence W. *Historical Sketches: A Collection of Articles Prepared for Presentation to Various Clubs and Organizations and Now Assembled in Book Form.* N.p.: self-published, 1982.

Cole, Cyrenus. *History of the People of Iowa.* Cedar Rapids, Iowa: Torch Press, 1921.

Dilts, Harold E. *From Ackley to Zwingle: The Origins of Iowa Place Names.* 2nd ed. Ames: Iowa State University Press, 1993.

Fargo, O. J. *Agriculture.* Creston, Iowa: Green Valley AEA 14, 1985.

Gue, Benjamin F. *History of Iowa from the Earliest Times to the Beginning of the 20th Century.* Vol. 1. New York: Century History, 1903.

Harlan, Edgar R. *Narrative History of the People of Iowa.* Vol. 1. Chicago: American Historical Society, 1931.

Hickenlooper, Bourque B. "'Ioway' and Iowa in History." *Annals of Iowa* 31, no. 6 (October 1952).

Merry, Carl A. *The Historic Period*, June 30, 2005 http://www.uiowa.edu/~osa/learn/historic/hisper.htm (accessed March 31, 2006).

Nourse, Charles Clinton. *Iowa and the Centennial: The State Address.* Des Moines, Iowa: Iowa State Register Print, 1876.

Randall, William D. "Under Many Flags." In *Little Known Stories of Muscatine*. Vol. 1. Muscatine, Iowa: Friends of the Musser Public Library, 1980.

Richman, Irving B. *Ioway to Iowa: The Genesis of a Corn and Bible Commonwealth*. Iowa City: State Historical Society of Iowa, 1931.

Sabin, Henry. *The Making of Iowa*. 4th ed. Chicago: A. Flanagany, 1900.

Vogel, Virgil J. *Iowa Place Names of Indian Origin*. Iowa City: University of Iowa Press, 1983.

A DICTIONARY OF IOWA PLACE-NAMES

COUNTIES

The date in parentheses indicates the date that the county was established. The numbers in parentheses at the end of each entry indicate the number of the source listed at the end of the book.

A a ++++++++++++++++++++

Adair County (1851) was named for General John Adair. The general was a noted military man who fought in the Revolutionary War and the War of 1812. General Adair also served as a governor of Kentucky. The county seat is Greenfield. (4, 163)

Adams County (1851) was named after John Quincy Adams, who signed the Declaration of Independence and served as president of the United States. The county seat is Corning. (5, 163)

Allamakee County (1849) either was named for Allan Makee, an explorer and trapper who traded with the Indians in the area, or the name was derived from an Indian word. If drawn from an Indian dialect, it was probably the word *an-a-mee-kee*, meaning "thunder." The county seat is Waukon. (12, 163)

Appanoose County (1843) was named after a chief of the Sac and Fox Indians. The meaning of "Appanoose" in the Sac and Fox languages is "chief when a child." Appanoose was an important figure, because he attempted to peacefully end the Black Hawk War. The county seat is Centerville. (25, 163)

Audubon County (1851) was named after John James Audubon, the noted ornithologist. The county seat is Audubon. (31, 163)

B b ++++++++++++++++++++

Benton County (1843) was named after the Missouri senator Thomas Hart Benton. Senator Benton fought in the War of 1812 and was also a noted attorney. Vinton is the county seat. (39, 163)

Black Hawk County (1847) was named after the Sac chief Black Hawk, most remembered for his participation in the Black Hawk War. Waterloo is the county seat. (48, 163)

Boone County (1846) was named after Captain Nathaniel Boone, who explored the region. Captain Boone was the son of the famous Daniel Boone. The county seat is Boone. (50, 163)

Bremer County (1851) was named after the Swedish writer Frederika Bremer. Waverly is the county seat. (4, 163)

Buchanan County (1839) was named after James Buchanan, a noted politician. Buchanan later became the president of the United States. The county seat is Independence. (59, 163)

Buena Vista County (1851) was named after the battle in the Mexican War where Santa Anna was defeated by General Zachary Taylor. The county seat is Storm Lake. (63, 163)

Butler County (1851) was named after General William O. Butler, who fought in the Mexican War and was a prominent politician of the era. Allison is the county seat. (68, 163)

C c ++++++++++++++++++++

Calhoun County (1851) was first named Fox, for the Fox Indians who had lived in the region. The county was renamed by the legislature in 1853. It was named after John C. Calhoun, a prominent politician who served as vice president of the United States. The county seat is Rockwell City. (72, 163)

Carroll County (1851) was named after Charles Carroll, who signed the Declaration of Independence. Carroll is the county seat. (73, 163)

Cass County (1851) was named after Lewis Cass, a prominent Michigan politician. The county seat is Atlantic. (75, 163)

Cedar County (1837) was named after the Cedar River, which flows through the county. Tipton is the county seat. (76, 163)

Cerro Gordo County (1851) was named for the Mexican War battlefield where Santa Anna's troops suffered a defeat in 1847. Mason City is the county seat. (83, 163)

Cherokee County (1851) was named for the Cherokee Indians who lived in the southeast United States until they were forcibly relocated to the area that is now Oklahoma in 1838. Cherokee is the county seat. (86, 163)

Chickasaw County (1851) was named for the Chickasaw Indian tribe. The Chickasaws inhabited the southern United States until they moved to the area that is now Oklahoma after 1834. The county seat is New Hampton. (88, 163)

Clarke County (1846) was named after the governor of Iowa Territory at the time, James Clarke. Osceola is the county seat. (133, 163)

Clay County (1851) was named for Lieutenant Colonel Henry Clay Jr., who was killed in the war with Mexico. Clay was the son of the well-known politician Henry Clay. Spencer is the county seat. (134, 163)

Clayton County (1837) was named after Senator John Middleton Clayton of Delaware. Elkader is the county seat. (136, 163)

Clinton County (1837) was named after DeWitt Clinton, who built the Erie Canal and served as governor of New York. Clinton is the county seat. (137, 163)

Crawford County (1851) was named after a noted politician, William H. Crawford. Denison is the county seat. (144, 163)

D d ++++++++++++++++++++++

Dallas County (1846) was named after George Mifflin Dallas, who at the time was vice president of the United States. Adel is the county seat. (148, 163)

Davis County (1844) was named after Garrett Davis, a politician from Kentucky. Davis was involved in the establishment of the Iowa Territory. In its early days the county was known as "the Hairy Nation" because of the wild appearance and manners of the men who lived there. Bloomfield is the county seat. (150, 163)

Decatur County (1846) was named after Commodore Stephen Decatur, who fought in the War of 1812 and defended U.S. interests against Algerian pirates. Leon is the county seat. (154, 163)

Delaware County (1837) was either named after the state of Delaware or for a county in New York State. Manchester is the county seat. (156, 163)

Des Moines County (1834) was named for the Des Moines River. Burlington is the county seat. (160, 163)

Dickinson County (1851) was named after Senator Daniel Dickinson of New York. Spirit Lake is the county seat. (161, 163)

Dubuque County (1834) was named after Julien Dubuque, a French Canadian trader who mined lead in the area. The county seat is Dubuque. (163, 172)

E e ┼┼┼┼┼┼┼┼┼┼┼┼┼┼┼┼┼┼┼┼┼┼┼

Emmet County (1851) was named after the Irish hero and patriot Robert Emmet. Estherville is the county seat. (163, 183)

F f ┼┼┼┼┼┼┼┼┼┼┼┼┼┼┼┼┼┼┼┼┼┼┼

Fayette County (1837) was named after Marquis de La Fayette, the French general who fought in the Revolutionary War. The county seat is West Union. (163, 188)

Floyd County (1851) was named after Sergeant Charles Floyd, who was a member of the Lewis and Clark expedition. Floyd died and was buried in the region that would become Iowa. There is another, less credible explanation that the county was named for one of the signers of the Declaration of Independence. Charles City is the county seat. (163, 193)

Franklin County (1855) was named after Benjamin Franklin, the American statesman. Hampton is the county seat. (163, 198)

Fremont County (1847) was named after the soldier and explorer John C. Frémont. The county seat is Sidney. (163, 199)

G g ┼┼┼┼┼┼┼┼┼┼┼┼┼┼┼┼┼┼┼┼┼┼┼

Greene County (1851) was named after General Nathaniel Greene, who fought in the American War for Independence. The county seat is Jefferson. (163, 215)

Grundy County (1851) was named after Senator Felix H. Grundy, U.S. senator from Tennessee. Grundy Center is the county seat. (163, 219)

Guthrie County (1851) was named for Captain Edwin Guthrie, an Iowan who was a casualty in the war with Mexico. The county seat is Guthrie Center. (163, 222)

H h ++++++++++++++++++++++

Hamilton County (1856) was named in honor of William W. Hamilton, who was then president of the Iowa Senate. Webster City is the county seat. (163, 227)

Hancock County (1851) was named after the American patriot John Hancock. The county seat is Garner. (163, 231)

Hardin County (1851) was named after Colonel John J. Hardin, a soldier from Illinois who fought in the Black Hawk War and was a casualty in the Mexican War. Eldora is the county seat. (163, 232)

Harrison County (1851) was named after William Henry Harrison, the noted politician who served as the ninth president of the United States. The county seat is Logan. (163, 234)

Henry County (1836) was named for a participant in the Black Hawk War, but which participant in particular is subject to some controversy. It was possibly named after Henry Dodge, a veteran of the Black Hawk War and the governor of the Wisconsin Territory when the county was formed. The county was part of the Wisconsin Territory at that time. The other person reputed to possibly be the inspiration for the county's name is General James D. Henry, who had served with distinction in the Black Hawk War and had died two years before the county was established. The county seat is Mt. Pleasant. (163, 240)

Howard County (1851) was named after General Tilghman Ashurst Howard, a noted soldier and politician. The county seat is Cresco. (163, 308)

Humboldt County (1851) was named after a noted German scientist and explorer, Baron Alexander von Humboldt. Dakota City is the county seat. (163, 311)

I i ++++++++++++++++++++

Ida County (1851) was probably named after Ida Smith, the first settlers' child born in the area. Other stories attribute it to Mt. Ida in Greece or to someone's wife or friend back east. Ida Grove is the county seat. (163, 314)

Iowa County (1843) was named for the Iowa River, which runs through the county. The county seat is Marengo. (163, 319)

J j ++++++++++++++++++++

Jackson County (1837) was named for the seventh president of the United States, Andrew Jackson. Maquoketa is the county seat. (163, 322)

Jasper County (1840) was named after a Revolutionary War hero, Sergeant William Jasper. The county seat is Newton. (163, 325)

Jefferson County (1839) was named after Thomas Jefferson, who signed the Declaration of Independence and served as the third president of the United States. Fairfield is the county seat. (163, 326)

Johnson County (1837) was named after Richard Mentor Johnson, a veteran of the War of 1812 and a prominent politician. Iowa City is the county seat. (163, 329)

Jones County (1837) was named after George Wallace Jones, a surveyor and politician. The county seat is Anamosa. (163, 334)

K k ┼┼┼┼┼┼┼┼┼┼┼┼┼┼┼┼┼┼┼┼┼

Keokuk County (1843) was named after Sac chief Keokuk, or "watchful fox." The county seat is Sigourney. (163, 338)

Kossuth County (1851) was named after the Hungarian patriot Lajos Kossuth. It is the largest, in physical size, of all the counties in Iowa. The county seat is Algona. (163, 343)

L l ┼┼┼┼┼┼┼┼┼┼┼┼┼┼┼┼┼┼┼┼┼

Lee County (1836) has some controversy about the origin of the county name. The official county position appears to be that the county was named after William Elliot Lee, an eastern land speculator whose land company owned large tracts of land in the area. The other credible possibility is that the county might have been named after Lieutenant Albert M. Lea. Lieutenant Lea had explored the region, particularly the Des Moines River, the year before the county was established. Add to that the fact that Lea was reported to have said that the county was named after him. The original documents spelled the county's name as "Lea," which provides evidence that Lieutenant Lea was probably the source of the name. Lee County is unique in the state of Iowa in that it has two county seats, Ft. Madison and Keokuk. The county's population was deemed to be large enough that more than one seat of justice and county business was needed. The Iowa legislature passed a special act allowing two county seats in the county. (163, 354)

Linn County (1837) was named after a Missouri senator, Lewis Linn. Cedar Rapids is the county seat. (163, 362)

Louisa County (1836) has two potential explanations for its name. It could have been named in honor of a young woman who lived in Dubuque, Louisa Massey. Massey shot a man who had killed one of her brothers. The other story is that the county was named after Louisa County in Virginia. The county seat is Wapello. (163, 367)

Lucas County (1846) was named after the first territorial governor of Iowa, Robert Lucas. The county seat is Chariton. (163, 370)

Lyon County (1851) was first called Buncombe County. The name was later changed to honor General Nathaniel Lyon, a casualty in the Civil War. The county seat is Rock Rapids. (163, 372)

M m ++++++++++++++++++++

Madison County (1846) was named after the fourth U.S. president, James Madison. The county seat is Winterset. (163, 374)

Mahaska County (1843) was named after Mahaska, a chief of the Iowa tribe. The translation of the name is "White Cloud." Oskaloosa is the county seat. (163, 378)

Marion County (1845) was reportedly named after Revolutionary War general Francis Marion. There is another story that the county was named for one of the original settlers in the area. The county seat is Knoxville. (163, 383)

Marshall County (1846) was named after the U.S. Supreme Court justice John Marshall. The county seat is Marshalltown. (163, 387)

Mills County (1851) was named after Major Frederick Mills, an Iowan who died in the war with Mexico. The county seat is Glenwood. (163, 408)

Mitchell County (1851) was named for either the Irish patriot

John M. Mitchell or in appreciation for an area surveyor. The county seat is Osage. (163, 412)

Monona County (1851) was believed to be a name of Indian origin, but that appears to be a dubious explanation. There are two other explanations that are more reasonable. The county either was named after Monona, a town in Clayton County, or the name was possibly drawn from a created Indian name that eastern writers had used in works of fiction. Onawa is the county seat. (163, 415)

Monroe County (1843) was originally named Kishkosh County and was renamed in 1846 for the fifth president of the United States, James Monroe. Albia is the county seat. (163, 416)

Montgomery County (1851) was named after General Richard Montgomery, who fought and perished in the Revolutionary War. Red Oak is the county seat. (163, 418)

Muscatine County (1836) was named for an island in the Mississippi named Muscatine Island. The name was at one time thought to have been derived from the Mascoutin Indian tribe, thought to have lived on the island for a time. A more probable reason for the name is that it was drawn from the Fox word for a flat place or prairie. The county seat is Muscatine. (163, 427)

O o ++++++++++++++++++++

O'Brien County (1851) was named after the Irish patriot William Smith O'Brien. Primghar is the county seat. (163, 437)

Osceola County (1851) was named after Osceola, a well-known Seminole chief. Sibley is the county seat. (163, 446)

P p ++++++++++++++++++++

Page County (1847) was named after a casualty in the war with Mexico, Captain John Page. Captain Page died in the battle of Palo Alto. Clarinda is the county seat. (163, 450)

Palo Alto County (1851) was named for the first battle of the war with Mexico. The battle took place before the war was formally declared. The county seat is Emmetsburg. (163, 452)

Plymouth County (1851) was named after the Pilgrims' Plymouth Colony. The county seat is Le Mars. (163, 466)

Pocahontas County (1851) was named after the young Indian woman who was involved with the Jamestown Colony. The county seat is Pocahontas. (163, 467)

Polk County (1846) was named after James Knox Polk, who served as the eleventh president of the United States. Des Moines is both the county seat and the state capital. (163, 468)

Pottawattamie County (1847) was named for the Pottawattamie Indian tribe, who once controlled the area that became the Iowa Territory. Pottawattamie can be interpreted as meaning the "keepers or makers of the fire." Council Bluffs is the county seat, though the county has two courthouses, one in Avoca and one in Council Bluffs. (163, 479)

Poweshiek County (1843) was named after Poweshiek, a Fox chief. The area where the county is located was reportedly the hunting and fishing ground for Poweshiek and his followers. The county seat is Montezuma. (163, 473)

R r +++++++++++++++++++

Ringgold County (1847) was named after the soldier and inventor Major Samuel Ringgold, who was killed in the war with Mexico. Mt. Ayr is the county seat. (163, 496)

S s +++++++++++++++++++

Sac County (1851) was named for the Sac Indian tribe. "Sac" can be translated to mean "yellow earth." The county seat is Sac City. (163, 503)

Scott County (1837) was named after General Winfield Scott, the veteran of both the Black Hawk War and the war with Mexico. The county seat is Davenport. (163, 508)

Shelby County (1851) was named after the Revolutionary War veteran General Isaac Shelby. Harlan is the county seat. (163, 514)

Sioux County (1851) was named after the Dakotas, also known as the Sioux, an Indian tribe that inhabited the western prairies of Iowa. The name Sioux can be translated as "snakes." The tribe had lived in the region for many years. Orange City is the county seat. (163, 518)

Story County (1846) was named after the U.S. Supreme Court justice Joseph Story. Nevada is the county seat. (163, 533)

T t +++++++++++++++++++

Tama County (1843) was named after an Indian, but exactly which person is in dispute. There are advocates for the Fox chief Tama, or Taimah. Others believe that the name comes from the name of the wife of Poweshiek, Taomah. Still others believe that the county was named after Chief Potama. The county seat is Toledo. (163, 536)

Taylor County (1847) was named after Zachary Taylor, veteran of the war with Mexico and candidate for president of the United States when the county was established. Taylor served as the twelfth president of the United States. The county seat is Bedford. (163, 538)

U u ++++++++++++++++++++

Union County (1851) was named to reflect the interest of the citizens in the county in preserving the Union. The county was formed in the turbulent period before the Civil War. Creston is the county seat. (163, 549)

V v ++++++++++++++++++++

Van Buren County (1836) was named after Martin Van Buren, who was vice president of the United States when the county was established. Van Buren later served as the eighth president of the United States. Keosauqua is the county seat. (163, 556)

W w ++++++++++++++++++++

Wapello County (1843) was named after the Fox chief Wapello. The county seat is Ottumwa. (163, 561)

Warren County (1846) was named after General Joseph

Warren, who was killed in the Revolutionary War. The county seat is Indianola. (163, 565)

Washington County (1839) was named after the hero of the Revolutionary War and the first president of the United States, George Washington. The county seat is Washington. (163, 567)

Wayne County (1846) was named after General Anthony Wayne, a veteran of the Revolutionary War. Corydon is the county seat. (163, 571)

Webster County (1853) was named to commemorate the statesman and orator Daniel Webster, who died in 1852. The county seat is Ft. Dodge. (163, 574)

Winnebago County (1851) was named for the Winnebago tribe that had lived in the region. The word can be translated as "men of the bad-smelling waters." Forest City is the county seat. (163, 589)

Winneshiek County (1847) was named after the Winnebago chief Winneshiek. The county seat is Decorah. (163, 590)

Woodbury County (1851) was called Floyd County, but the name was changed to Wahkaw County before it was changed to Woodbury County in 1853 to honor the memory of Levi Woodbury. Woodbury, who died in 1851, had served as governor of New Hampshire and as a senator for that state. Sioux City is the county seat. (163, 592)

Worth County (1851) was named after General William J. Worth, a veteran of both the Black Hawk War and the war with Mexico. Northwood is the county seat. (163, 593)

Wright County (1851) was named after two men. It was named for Silas Wright, who had been governor of New York, and for Joseph A. Wright, who had been governor of Indiana. The county seat is Clarion. (163, 595)

TOWNS

In the section of this book dealing with towns, the terms "founded" and "established" are used interchangeably to indicate the date that either a plat of the town or a survey of the site was done. The intent is to indicate when the location was initially set up as a place where a community was intended to form. If the information about the registering of the plat is available and different than the initial platting of the town, the term "formally established" is used to indicate the date that an appropriate governmental agency recorded the site as a town. In any event, the dates cited are the earliest times that I could determine that a community was planned at the locations listed. Whether or not the community is incorporated (established as an independent entity with the rights to collect taxes and establish rules or laws and govern itself) or unincorporated (simply a collection of homes within a larger governmental structure, typically a county, and dependent on the county for civil assistance) is also listed. There appear to be no rules about the use of the terms "city," "community," "town," or "village" relative to the population. Those terms as used in this text are not an indication of the size of the community.

A a ┼┼┼┼┼┼┼┼┼┼┼┼┼┼┼┼┼┼┼┼┼

Abingdon, Jefferson County. Abingdon was founded by Colonel Thomas McCulloch on August 30, 1849. The colonel named the town for Abingdon, Virginia, where he had once lived. The town was informally known as Bogus since one of the early settlers was alleged to have been a counterfeiter. Abingdon is not incorporated. (477)

Ackley, Hardin County. The town was formally established on December 12, 1857, though there was little activity there until the advent of the railroad in 1865. Ackley was named for one of the founders, William J. Ackley. The post office near the site, established long before the town, was called the Fontaine Post Office. The post office was moved to Ackley and the name of the office changed to Ackley in 1865. Ackley was incorporated on August 28, 1869. (272, 438)

Ackworth, Warren County. The town was established as South River Meeting by Quakers in 1847. Ackworth Academy was established at the site in 1868. The name for the school was inspired by the largest Quaker school in England at the time, called Ackworth. The name of the town was probably changed when the post office at the site was opened as the Ackworth Post Office in 1871. Ackworth was incorporated on May 9, 1881. (315, 318, 423, 438)

Adair, Adair and Guthrie counties. Adair was established on August 20, 1872. The town was named for John Adair, a general in the War of 1812 who later became the governor of Kentucky. The town was incorporated on February 23, 1884. (163, 271, 438)

Adel, county seat, Dallas County. The present site of Adel was selected as the county seat and the survey for the town was completed on May 22, 1847. The town was originally called Penoach, but the name was reportedly changed to honor an attractive child. Another possibility for the name was suggested by A. T. Andreas, who indicated that it described the location of the town, in a dell. The town was incorporated on June 27, 1877. (6, 21, 522)

Afton, Union County. Afton was founded by E. A. Temple in 1854 and named by his wife for the Scottish river immortalized in the song "Flow Gently Sweet Afton." The town was incorporated on November 30, 1868. (45, 163, 438)

Agency, Wapello County. Initially known as Agency City, the town was established in 1843 at the site of an Indian agency. The Indian agency was in operation from 1838 until 1845, when the Indians were moved to Kansas. Agency was incorporated on January 6, 1859. (298, 438, 561)

Ainsworth, Washington County. Ainsworth was founded in October 1858 by D. H. Ainsworth. The town was named for him. It was incorporated on June 18, 1892. (299, 438)

Akron, Plymouth County. Akron was first established as Portlandville on June 5, 1871, by Edgar Sargeant and Lewis and Celina Crill. There was confusion between Portlandville and Portland in Cerro Gordo County, so the name was changed to Akron when the town was incorporated on September 7, 1882. It was renamed in honor of Akron, Ohio. (163, 294, 438)

Albert City, Buena Vista County. The town was established on property owned by George Anderson in 1890. It was initially named after Manthorp, a town in Sweden. The Post Office Department was concerned that there would be confusion between Manthorp and Marathon, so the name of the new village was changed. The town was named after Albertina Anderson, the founder's wife. Albert City was incorporated on December 9, 1900. (163, 438, 455)

Albia, county seat, Monroe County. Albia was surveyed by John Massey, as Princeton, in 1845. Dr. Anson Flint changed the name to Albia in honor of his prior home in New York. The town was incorporated as Albia in 1856. (244, 528)

Albion, Marshall County. Albion was founded in 1852, though it was not formally established until 1856. The town was initially called LaFayette, but the name was changed in 1858. Albion is a common name in English, meaning "Briton." Albion was also a character in William Blake's poetry. The first cabin was built at the location in 1853. The town was incorporated in 1870. (163, 285, 528)

Alburnett, Linn County. Albert Burnett established the town in the late 1870s. It was first called Burnett in his honor. Since there was confusion in deliveries between Bennett and

Burnett, the town was renamed to include part of Burnett's first name. The post office at the site was established as Trentham in May 1888. The post office's name was changed to Alburnett in May 1892. The town was incorporated on June 29, 1912. (125, 163, 438, 458)

Alden, Hardin County. Alden was named after its founder, Henry Alden. He established the town in 1855. The town voted to incorporate on February 14, 1879. (272, 414)

Alexander, Franklin County. Alexander started as a railroad station in 1881 and was apparently named for a Mr. Alexander who was affiliated with the railroad. The town site was established by Fred Wilks in 1883. Alexander was incorporated on March 25, 1902. (163, 270, 438)

Algona, county seat, Kossuth County. The town site was established by A. C. Call on December 2, 1856. The town was first named Call's Grove. The name was changed by Mrs. Call to Algona. The name Algona is drawn from Algonquin, the name of a Canadian Indian tribe. Algona was incorporated on January 31, 1872. (280, 438, 561)

Alleman, Polk County. Alleman was named after John Alleman, who donated the land. It was founded in 1890 and was incorporated in 1972. (90, 163)

Allendorf, Osceola County. The town was established in 1895 as a station on the railroad. It was initially called Oliver, but the railroad changed the name to Allendorf for one of the town's founders, Henry Allen. Allen had a stock farm in the area that was called the Allendorf Stock and Dairy Farm. Another story is that the town was named for Allendorf, Germany. Allendorf is not incorporated. (163, 548)

Allerton, Wayne County. Allerton was named after a Judge Aller, a railroad investor who had purchased some of the land used for the site. The town was initially called Aller Town, later abbreviated to Allerton. Allerton was planned by the Rock Island Railroad and established when the rail line reached the site in 1870. It was incorporated on October 1, 1874. (46, 438)

Allison, county seat, Butler County. Allison was platted by the Allison Town Company, a partnership of Dubuque capitalists, and named in honor of Senator William B. Allison of Dubuque in August 1870. It was incorporated on July 25, 1881. (254, 438)

Alpha, Fayette County. The town was named Alpha because it was the first settlement on Crane Creek. Alpha is the first letter in the Greek alphabet. The town was founded on May 23, 1871. Alpha is not incorporated. (163, 190)

Alta, Buena Vista County. The Iowa Falls and Sioux City Railroad Town Land and Lot Company founded Alta in 1872. There are two possible reasons for the naming of the town. One is that it was named after the daughter of John Blair, Altai. The other is that it was named for its altitude, since the town is located on the crest of the divide between the Mississippi and Missouri rivers. Alta was incorporated on October 11, 1878. (163, 302, 318, 438)

Alta Vista, Chickasaw County. The town was initially named Elk Creek. A military man, a Major General Jones, suggested the new name of Alta Vista, or "high view" in Spanish. Alta Vista was established and was incorporated on September 18, 1894. (17, 89, 163, 438)

Alton, Sioux County. Alton started as a depot at the head of a rail spur line to Orange City in 1872. It was called East Orange Station. The town was officially established on June 9, 1875, and was incorporated on March 8, 1883. (433, 438)

Altoona, Polk County. Altoona was founded in 1868 and initially called Petersburg. The name of the town was changed to Altoona, reflecting the fact that it was the highest point on the Des Moines Valley Railroad. The root of the name was the Latin term *altus*, which means high. For a time the railroad insisted on calling the station Yant after the landowner, but the post office established in 1868 was always known as Altoona. The community was incorporated on March 11, 1876. (18, 163, 438)

Alvord, Lyon County. Alvord was established by Mr. and Mrs. W. B. Park as Park on April 18, 1890. There was some concern that the name was similar enough to other towns' names in the area that deliveries might get confused. Mr. Park solved the problem by suggesting that the town be renamed Alvord for his brother-in-law. The community was incorporated on September 26, 1892. (163, 438, 464)

Amana, Iowa County. The community was founded in 1855. The name for the colony was brought to Iowa by members of the Amana Society, a communal group who had settled in Iowa County after initially establishing a colony in New York. The name is drawn from the Bible and means "to believe faithfully." Amana has special consideration in the Iowa Code and is treated as an incorporated community even though it is not. (19, 163, 320)

Amber, Jones County. Amber was called Blue Cut when it was founded in 1873, and in 1878 it was renamed Amber. The name change was suggested by J. C. Ramsey, for a character in a novel popular at the time. Amber is not incorporated. (20, 528)

Ames, Story County. The town was established in 1864 when Mrs. C. O. Duff deeded property over to John Blair. The Blair Town Lot and Land Company established the town that year. Ames was named in honor of Oakes Ames of Massachusetts, who had invested in the Cedar Rapids and Missouri River Railroad. He had also donated a bell to the first church built in the town. Ames was incorporated on December 20, 1869. (91, 163, 438)

Anamosa, county seat, Jones County. On June 28, 1840, Colonel Thomas Cox laid out a town called Dartmouth at the present site of Anamosa. The plat was never recorded. R. J. Cleaveland established the town of Lexington in 1846. The name was changed to Anamosa, apparently to avoid confusion with similarly named towns in the area. There are several versions as to why it was so named. One is that during the discussions about lost mail, there was a resolve to name the town so uniquely that confusion could not exist. The discussions were taking place at a boarding-house where the community mail was delivered. At the same time an Indian family from Wisconsin stopped at the site. The settlers inquired about the name of the family's young daughter and were told that it was Anamosa, meaning "White Fawn." While it is possible that the family might have chosen that name for a child, the translatable meaning appears to be "Little Dog." The second version is that the town was named for the daughter of a Winnebago chief named Nas-i-mus, who lived in the area. The problem with this story is that there is no record of any such girl, although the meaning of Anamosa is interpreted more appropriately in this story. The meaning was explained as a "litter of puppies or young foxes." In any event, a unique name of Indian derivation was selected for the community. Anamosa was incorporated on December 12, 1867. (142, 438, 528, 561)

Anderson, Fremont County. Anderson was first called Shiloh, then the name was changed to honor Major Albert R. Anderson, a representative of Fremont County who sponsored the railroad. The town was founded in 1878 and the name changed in 1879. Anderson is not incorporated. (200)

Andover, Clinton County. Andover was named by a railroad official for a town in Vermont. The town was established in

September 1886. The town was incorporated on January 12, 1910. (92, 438, 528)

Andrew, Jackson County. Andrew was, for a time, the county seat. The town was established as the county seat in 1841, and named in honor of Andrew Jackson. Andrew was incorporated on August 4, 1863. (21, 438)

Anita, Cass County. Anita was originally established in 1869 at the direction of Lewis Beason, who owned the property. He sold the property to Frank Whitney, B. F. Allen, and John P. Cook, who then registered the town site on November 10, 1870. In the summer of 1869 a number of railroad officials were eating dinner at Lewis Beason's home when the subject of the new station and its probable name was discussed. The railroad men proposed to call it Beason, but Mr. Beason modestly demurred. Mrs. Beason suggested that the town be called Anita, for her niece, Anita Cowles, of San Francisco. Anita was incorporated on June 10, 1873. (257)

Ankeny, Polk County. The town was named by John F. Ankeny after himself. John and Sarah Ankeny were the original owners of the town site. They established the town in April 1875. Ankeny was incorporated on February 28, 1903. (23)

Anthon, Woodbury County. Anthon was established on February 17, 1888, by the Cherokee and Western Town Lot and Land Company. Absalom Miller had donated the land for the town, and the plans were to name the town after his daughter, Anneta. There already was a town with that name, so the town was instead named for J. Q. Anthon, who was an engineer with the Illinois Central Railroad. Anthon was incorporated on July 25, 1890. (163, 294, 438)

Aplington, Butler County. Aplington was planned in 1857–1858 and established on February 2, 1858, by the proprietors, Thomas Nash, R. R. Parriott, Zenas Aplington, and Theodore A. Wilson. Zenas Aplington erected a store and stocked it, though he did not run it or even live in the town. The community was named for him. Aplington was incorporated on April 30, 1895. (163, 254, 438)

Arcadia, Carroll County. Arcadia was established by Isaac Voris in 1872 and originally called Tip-Top. Voris later suggested Arcadia, after the province in Greece, as the town's name. Arcadia was incorporated on November 3, 1881. (42, 163, 438)

Archer, O'Brien County. Archer was founded in 1888 by William Van Epps and Charles E. McKinney. The town was named after John H. Archer, who owned the land where the town was established. It was incorporated on May 5, 1902. (438, 460)

Aredale, Butler County. Aredale was founded in 1900. The name was created for the town with no other significance. Aredale was incorporated on June 5, 1920. (70, 438, 528)

Argyle, Lee County. The town, founded on February 7, 1885, was named for a county in Scotland. Argyle is not incorporated. (145, 163)

Arion, Crawford County. Arion was established on February 17, 1893 when the Northwestern Railroad and the Chicago, Milwaukee and St. Paul Railroad intersected at this point. The site was first known as Lydia but was renamed for a legendary musician of Lesbos in Greek history. Arion is also thought to be another name for the Greek god Apollo. The town was incorporated on May 31, 1894. (145, 440, 528)

Arispe, Union County. Arispe was founded on December 31, 1888, and was named for an Indian friend of Burr Forbes. Arispe was incorporated on October 21, 1904. (163, 438, 550)

Arlington, Fayette County. Arlington was settled in the 1850s. It was first called Moetown and later Brushtown, before it received its current name. The community thought that Brushtown was not as sophisticated a name as they would like, so Arlington was selected as an alternative. The name was probably a transfer name drawn from one of the Arlingtons in other states. Arlington was incorporated on April 30, 1895. (27, 189, 438)

Armstrong, Emmett County. Armstrong was named for an early hunter and trapper, Thomas Armstrong, who settled in the area in 1856. It was formally established on July 7, 1892, and was incorporated on March 30, 1893. (184, 438)

Arnolds Park, Dickinson County. The site was first developed by J. S. Prescott in 1857. He later sold the property to a Mr. Blake and a Mr. Arnold. Arnold started seriously developing a resort at the site in 1873. The town was named for him. Arnolds Park was incorporated on March 30, 1897. (438, 521)

Arthur, Ida County. Arthur was named for President Chester A. Arthur by I. S. Struble. Arthur was platted in 1885 and was incorporated on April 21, 1897. (32, 438)

Asbury, Dubuque County. Asbury was settled by Methodists in the 1830s. They named the town for Bishop Francis Asbury, the first Methodist bishop of America. After the Eighteenth Amendment was repealed, a number of the small, unincorporated towns feared they would not be permitted to have a tavern unless they were incorporated. The towns incorporated so that they could ensure the sale of beer in their communities. Asbury was incorporated on August 19, 1933. (171, 344, 438)

Ashton, Osceola County. Ashton was called St. Gilman when the Sioux City and St. Paul Railroad established the town in 1872. The name was changed to Ashton in 1882. The new name was selected to reflect the quantities of white ash trees in the area. There is another story that the town was named in honor of May Ashton, the daughter of a railroad official. The town was incorporated on March 28, 1885. (438, 462, 528, 548)

Aspinwall, Crawford County. Aspinwall was established when the railroad came through the area in 1880, though the town was not formally established until 1882. There are several versions of how the town came to be named. One is that there was a wall of aspen trees visible to the north of the town site, therefore an "Aspinwall." The second and more likely explanation is that it was named for someone affiliated with the railroad since this was a common practice when the railroad established stations. There were reports of a railroad employee named Aspinwall, which would effectively explain the naming of the town. Aspinwall was incorporated on November 10, 1914. (173, 407, 438)

Atalissa, Muscatine County. Atalissa was the name of a village in California, named after an Indian woman. Captain William Lunby, one of the founders of Atalissa, Iowa, was familiar with the western village and wanted to use the name for the new town. Atalissa was founded on January 31, 1856. Atalissa Davis, born after the naming of the town, was given a free lot because she was named after the town. Atalissa was incorporated on March 26, 1900. (438, 492)

Athelstan, Taylor County. The town's name was the name of the first king of England. Athelstan was established as a town along the Chicago Great Western Railroad line on September 26, 1897. The town is not incorporated. (29, 539)

Atkins, Benton County. Atkins was founded in 1881 as a station on the Chicago, Milwaukee and St. Paul Railroad. The town was first called Poker Flat, but when ownership of the town site passed to the railroad through the Milwaukee Land Company, the name was recorded as Atkins in honor of a railroad official. It was incorporated on June 15, 1917. (438, 551)

Atlantic, county seat, Cass County. Atlantic was founded in 1868. The town is roughly the same distance from both the

Atlantic and Pacific oceans, so the residents wanted to name the town after one of the two oceans. They decided to flip a coin to settle the name of the town. There was a complication since the railroad engineer planning the town called the town Avoca. The settlers intervened with the railroad, and the name of Atlantic was established. Atlantic was incorporated on November 26, 1869. (163, 257, 438)

Attica, Marion County. Attica was initially called Barkersville after James Barker, one of the sponsors of the town. The town was founded in 1847. The citizens wanted the name changed from Barkersville because they were upset by Barker's attention to his neighbor's wife. Since the town is located in Indiana Township, there appears to be an Indiana connection, and the town was possibly named after Attica, Indiana. Clearly the name is a transfer from another site. Attica is not incorporated. (594)

Auburn, Sac County. Auburn was established by the Western Town Lot Company on July 31, 1886. The town's name was drawn from Auburn, New York. Auburn was incorporated on January 10, 1887. (235, 438, 528)

Audubon, county seat, Audubon County. Audubon was planned by the Chicago, Rock Island and Pacific Railroad on September 23, 1878. Lots were sold in the town at an auction on October 15, 1878. Audubon was named for the county. The county was named in honor of John James Audubon, the noted ornithologist. The town was incorporated on December 2, 1880. (22, 438, 528)

Augusta, Des Moines County. Augusta started as a post office called Gibson's Ferry on April 19, 1836. The name was changed to Augusta, possibly for Augusta, Georgia, on September 22, 1837. The post office was closed on January 31, 1938, but the community has survived. Augusta is not incorporated. (65, 163)

Aurelia, Cherokee County. Aurelia was named in honor of John Blair's daughter. Blair controlled the Iowa Falls and Sioux City Railroad during its construction days. The town was founded on February 15, 1873, by J. H. McAlvin for the Iowa Falls and Sioux City Railroad Town Land and Lot Company. Aurelia was incorporated on December 27, 1879. (401, 438)

Aurora, Buchanan County. Aurora was founded in 1886 by the Chicago Great Western Railroad. The town was laid out on land donated by a Bishop Warren and his wife, Alice. Aurora was named after East Aurora, New York, where Bishop Warren had been born. The community was incorporated on May 25, 1899. (61, 85, 438)

Austinville, Butler County. The town was founded in 1897 and named for the original property owner. Austinville is not incorporated. (70, 163)

Avery, Monroe County. Avery was established when the Chicago, Burlington and Quincy Railroad line was laid through the area in 1868. The town draws its name from Avery Creek, which runs close by. The town was initially called Coffman, for the owner of the town site. Avery is not incorporated. (163, 246)

Avoca, Pottawattamie County. Avoca was founded in 1869 when the Rock Island Railroad reached the site. The town was first called Pacific, then it was named Botno. The name Avoca was finally settled on. Avoca was drawn from a description of an Irish site in Thomas Moore's "The Meeting of the Waters." The town was planned by a town company consisting of John Cook and Ebenezer Cook, John F. Tracy of the Rock Island Railroad, and B. F. Allen, a banker from Des Moines. Avoca was incorporated on December 2, 1874. (163, 191, 438)

Ayrshire, Palo Alto County. Ayrshire started as a railway depot in November 1882. The town was possibly named after Ayrshire, Scotland. Ayrshire was incorporated on September 20, 1895. (163, 398, 438)

B b ++++++++++++++++++

Badger, Webster County. Badger had its start when W. S. Fleming established a store and residence there in 1882. The town was named for the creek that runs nearby. The creek drew its name from a badger that soldiers had shot on its banks in frontier times. Badger was incorporated on December 28, 1899. (152, 438, 475)

Bagley, Guthrie County. Bagley was established on February 21, 1882, by the Milwaukee Land Company. The town was named for an unfortunate bartender who had died of diphtheria. Bagley was incorporated on June 16, 1891. (163, 271, 438)

Baldwin, Jackson County. Baldwin is the result of two adjacent villages combining: Fremont, established by Henry Haines in 1859, and Baldwin, established by Edward Baldwin and Joseph Skinner in 1871. When the railroad came through, the towns were combined, and the name Baldwin was maintained. Baldwin was incorporated on December 8, 1881. (323, 438)

Balltown, Dubuque County. Balltown was named for the Ball family who had settled in the area in the 1830s. Balltown was organized as a settlement in the 1840s. The town was incorporated on July 22, 1933. (171, 438)

Bancroft, Kossuth County. Bancroft was founded by A. C. Call and the Western Town Lot Company in September 1881. Call named the town in honor of George Bancroft, a noted historian. Bancroft was incorporated on December 16, 1884. (280, 438, 528)

Bangor, Marshall County. Bangor was established on August 17, 1854, by Abijah Hodgins. Bangor was a Quaker community that played a role in the Underground Railroad. It would seem likely that the township and the town were named for one of the other Bangors already established in the country. Bangor is not incorporated. (37)

Bankston, Dubuque County. Bankston was named for John Bankston, an early settler. The first settler was Willis Thompson, who made his home on Bankston's Prairie, later called Bankston, in 1835. After the Eighteenth Amendment was repealed, a number of the small, unincorporated towns feared they would not be permitted to have a tavern unless they were incorporated. The towns incorporated so that they could ensure the sale of beer in their communities. The town was incorporated on September 8, 1933. (171, 344, 438)

Barnes City, Mahaska County. The town was established when the railroad built a depot at the site in 1881 on land owned by James Barnes. The first railroad superintendent was also named Barnes, so the town was named Barnes Station in honor of both men. The name was later changed to Barnes City as the town's population grew. It was incorporated on April 20, 1899. (339, 438)

Barnum, Webster County. The Iowa Falls and Sioux City Railroad established Barnum on February 2, 1875. The town was named for a Connecticut senator who owned a great deal of land in the area. Barnum was incorporated on May 29, 1894. (163, 438, 475)

Bartlett, Fremont County. The town was named Bartlett for Annie Bartlett Phelps, the wife of the railroad engineer who established the town, Henry Phelps. Bartlett was founded on June 20, 1866. The town is not incorporated. (163, 226)

Bassett, Chickasaw County. Bassett was named after a Mr. Bassett of the firm of Bassett and Hunting, a wheat-buying firm. It was established and was incorporated on November 7, 1896. (89, 438, 472)

Batavia, Jefferson County. Batavia was established on September 26, 1846. It was originally called Creaseville for one of the town founders, Henry Crease. The name was changed to Batavia when the citizens of the town petitioned for the change on January 19, 1853. One explanation for the name could be that it was transferred from one of the other towns named Batavia in the East. Another possibility is that the name reflects the influence of the Dutch settlers in the area. An ancient Roman name for the Dutch was Batavi. Batavia was incorporated on January 6, 1868. (163, 277, 438, 557)

Battle Creek, Ida County. Battle Creek was named for the nearby creek. The stream was named because of a battle between Indian tribes on its banks. The town was established when the railroad placed a depot there in 1877. Battle Creek was incorporated on November 13, 1880. (32, 438, 528)

Baxter, Jasper County. Baxter developed at a site that was first set up as the Baxter Post Office. The town was established on October 24, 1883, by David and Amy Smith and was incorporated on December 13, 1894. Baxter's name was drawn from the name of the first postmaster, S. Baxter Higgins. (438, 573)

Bayard, Guthrie County. Bayard was founded on February 21, 1882, by the Milwaukee Land Company and was named for a Mr. Bayard, who was a senator from Delaware at the time. It was incorporated on June 14, 1883. (163, 271, 438)

Beacon, Mahaska County. Beacon was originally called Enterprise when it was founded in 1864. The town was also known as the Oskaloosa Station since Oskaloosa did not have a rail depot, and all shipping to and from Oskaloosa was handled by this station. The name was established as Beacon in 1874. There is a story that the town was supposed to have been called Brecon, but a misspelling occurred when the name was registered. There is a town in Wales called Brecon, in a range of hills called the Beacons, so the name was probably inspired by the location in Wales. Beacon was incorporated on February 7, 1874. (339, 438)

Beaconsfield, Ringgold County. The town was established on July 15, 1881, as a station on the Humeston and Shenandoah Railroad. It was named by Pete McCavett for a Lord Beaconsfield, or Beacon, of England. Beaconsfield was incorporated around 1885. (44, 163, 498)

Beaman, Grundy County. Beaman was originally called Wa-di-loupe, an Indian term reported to mean the "fork of the Wolf River." The town was established by H. H. Beaman on October 18, 1875. He named the town for himself. Beaman was incorporated on April 26, 1884. (55, 438, 528)

Beaver, Boone County. Beaver was founded on June 30, 1879, and named for the nearby Beaver Creek. Beaver was incorporated on October 5, 1912. (210, 438)

Bedford, county seat, Taylor County. The town site was selected by a board of commissioners appointed to locate a county seat for Taylor County in March 1853. The town was first called Beadforde. There are several possible reasons for the name of the community. One is that it was named for Bedford, Pennsylvania, since one of the engineers involved was from there. Another possibility is that it was named for a town in England, and since the original spelling of the town's name is the same as the English site's name, this is probably the correct version. One other very possible reason is that Thomas Bedford operated a trading post at the site before the town was established. The last possibility is that it was named for the home of one of the surveyors, Bedford, Indiana. The town was incorporated on July 28, 1866. (81, 293, 438)

Beebeetown, Harrison County. Beebeetown started as a post office named for the proprietor, Frederick Beebee, in 1880. The town is not incorporated. (312)

Beech, Warren County. Beech was established in 1911. Initially called New Sandyville, the name was changed to Beech to honor a railroad surveyor. The town is not incorporated. (566)

Belknap, Davis County. Belknap was established in 1871. It was possibly named for General William Worth Belknap, a major political figure from Iowa at that time. The town is not incorporated. (151)

Belle Plaine, Benton County. Belle Plaine was founded by John Blair in 1862. The town was named Belle Plaine, French for "beautiful plain," as a descriptive name for the location. Belle Plaine was incorporated on May 26, 1868. (246, 438, 528)

Bellevue, Jackson County. Bellevue was established by an act of Congress in 1836. The town was first called Bell's View, for an early settler named John Bell. The name was later altered to its current form. Bellevue was incorporated on February 5, 1851. (163, 276, 438)

Belmond, Wright County. Belmond was founded on October 20, 1856, by William Rogers, James Elder, and Archer Dumond. Dumond wanted to name the town Crown Point after his home in Indiana. The others wanted to call it Dumond, but he objected. As a compromise, Belmond was submitted and accepted. Another, more interesting story is that when the name Dumont was submitted, it was rejected because there was already a Dumont in the state. The story goes that Dumond's daughter was considered a "belle" of the community, so both father and daughter were honored with the name Belmond. The town voted to incorporate on October 21, 1881. (47, 163)

Beloit, Lyon County. Beloit was founded by James Carpenter on May 16, 1871. It was named for Beloit, Wisconsin. The town is not incorporated. (464)

Bennett, Cedar County. Richard Hill in 1884 deeded the land that was to become Bennett to Chester Bennett and H. C. Carr in equal half shares. Then Bennett deeded his half share to Carr, making Carr the sole trustee. The chief justice of the Iowa Supreme Court, Judge James Rothrock of Tipton, recommended that the town be named in honor of Chester Bennett. The president of the railroad agreed, and that is how the town came to be called Bennett. It was incorporated on December 26, 1896. (335, 438)

Benton, Ringgold County. Benton was established in 1898 on property owned by Samuel Irvin. Benton was named for Benton Township, before the county restructured and created Waubonsie Township, where the town is now located. It is probable that the township was named after Thomas Hart Benton, who was the inspiration for the names of Benton County and Bentonsport. The town was incorporated on July 3, 1900. (355, 438)

Bentonsport, Van Buren County. Bentonsport was established in 1839 and was incorporated in 1851, though it has since dropped its incorporation. The town was named in honor of Thomas Hart Benton. It was called both Port Benton and Benton's Port. The town eventually became known as Bentonsport. (336)

Berkley, Boone County. Berkley was established in 1883 by brothers Frances Carter and Charles Carter. The reason for the name of Berkley appears to be a mystery. There is no public record that would explain the name. Berkley was incorporated on October 11, 1912. (210, 438, 499)

Bernard, Dubuque County. Bernard was first called Melleray, for a monastery in Ireland. The name was changed in the 1870s to avoid confusion with the New Melleray Abbey and to honor the abbot of the New Melleray Monastery, Father Bernard. Bernard was formally established in 1896 and was incorporated on June 8, 1897. (163, 344, 438)

Bertram, Linn County. Bertram was established on April 19, 1858. It was named for Captain John Bertram, who was involved in establishing the first railroad in Linn County. The town was incorporated on January 17, 1914. (282, 438, 528)

Berwick, Polk County. Settlement had started in the area in 1846. On January 31, 1884, a post office was established at the site. The settlers wanted to name the post office Taylorville, for Henry Taylor, a popular resident. He declined, indicating that the name was too similar to Saylorville, another settlement in Polk County. Taylor suggested naming the post office for his hometown, Berwick, Maine. The town is not incorporated. (163, 400)

Bettendorf, Scott County. The site was first known as Lilienthal for a family who had a tavern there. The town site was formally established in 1858 and named Gilbert. The name was changed to Bettendorf on June 5, 1903, when the town was incorporated. Bettendorf was named for the Bettendorf brothers, who developed a rail car factory in the town. (438, 509)

Bevington, Madison County. A post office was established at the site and called Bevington on June 4, 1872. There are two possibilities for the name, either a court clerk named Bevington or a Dr. Bevington. The town was incorporated on February 1, 1916. (163, 438, 458)

Big Rock, Scott County. Big Rock was founded by Peter Goddard in 1855 and named for a nearby rock. The town is not incorporated. (509)

Birmingham, Van Buren County. The town was established in 1839 and named for Birmingham, England. Birmingham was incorporated around 1856. (297, 336)

Blairsburg, Hamilton County. Blairsburg was established by Robert Tinling in 1869. John Blair was involved in founding the town and named it for himself. The town was incorporated on December 21, 1900. (228)

Blairstown, Benton County. John Blair established the town as a railroad station on May 12, 1862. The town was named after him. Blairstown was incorporated in 1868. (246, 438)

Blakesburg, Wapello County. Blakesburg was established in 1852 by T. Blake and named for him. Blakesburg was incorporated on December 31, 1900. (298, 438)

Blanchard, Page County. Blanchard straddles the Iowa-Missouri border. Blanchard was founded when the Wabash Railroad established a depot there in 1880. The town was named for a railroad official. Blanchard was incorporated on June 11, 1880. (93, 438)

Blencoe, Monona County. Blencoe was established by the Missouri Valley Land Company in the summer of 1881 and named at the request of one of the settlers for a place in Canada. The town was incorporated on October 24, 1891. (287, 438, 528)

Blockton, Taylor County. Blockton was first called Mormon Town when it was founded in 1861. The name was later changed to honor the donor of the land for the town, a Mr. Block. The town was incorporated on March 28, 1890. (163, 421, 438)

Bloomfield, county seat, Davis County. Bloomfield was named by the county commissioners: S. W. McAtee proposed Jefferson; Adam Weaver proposed Davis; and Samuel Evans proposed Bloomfield. The names were placed in a hat, and Bloomfield was drawn. Bloomfield seems to be a descriptive term for the site. McAtee, Evans, and Weaver, acting as agents for the state legislature, planned the town on April 29, 1844. Bloomfield was incorporated on January 13, 1855. (264, 438)

Blue Grass, Scott County. Blue Grass was established in 1853. The site had been known as Blue Grass Point due to the color of the grass at the site. It was incorporated on December 10, 1893. (438, 509)

Bluffton, Winneshiek County. Bluffton was founded by the Morse brothers. They built mills that established the town. Henry Morse built a sawmill in 1852 and followed that with a gristmill in 1853. The town and the township were both named for the bluffs in the area. Bluffton is not incorporated. (33)

Bode, Humboldt County. Bode was established by the Cedar Rapids, Iowa Falls and Northwestern Town Lot Company in November 1881. Bode was reportedly named for either an early settler or a railroad employee. It was incorporated on February 20, 1892. (163, 275, 438)

Bolan, Worth County. Bolan was established in 1887 after a railroad track had been laid through the area. Anna Alexander owned the property on which the town was built. Matt Bolan, an official with the railroad, named the town for himself. The town is not incorporated. (138, 163)

Bonaparte, Van Buren County. Bonaparte was established in 1837 and called Meek's Mills. In 1841 the lots were resurveyed, and the name was changed to Bonaparte. There was a town site called Napoleon on the other side of the river that was never developed. William Meek was responsible for the names of both Bonaparte and Napoleon as he was an admirer of the French emperor. The town was incorporated on January 31, 1899. (163, 297, 336, 438)

Bondurant, Polk County. Bondurant was established by Alexander Bondurant in 1884 and named for him. It was incorporated on December 23, 1897. (49, 163, 438)

Boone, county seat, Boone County. Boone was originally named Montana, Latin for "mountainous region," because of the hills around the town site. Montana was established by John Blair on March 4, 1865. Boonesboro, at that time the county seat, was located about a mile away. Montana grew quickly and eventually absorbed Boonesboro. Montana's name was changed to Boone in 1866. Boone was named for the county, which was named for Nathan Boone, an explorer in the territory and a son of the legendary Daniel Boone. The town was incorporated on October 24, 1876. (210, 438, 528)

Booneville, Dallas County. Booneville was established on June 6, 1871, by A. J. Lyon. The property had belonged to William and Susannah Boone, so the community was named for them. Booneville is not incorporated. (263)

Bouton, Dallas County. Bouton was founded in 1881 and was named for the man who had owned the land. It was incorporated on September 27, 1911. (52, 163, 438)

Boxholm, Boone County. Boxholm was established on April 21, 1900. John B. Anderson had kept a store at that location for many years before the town was established. He named the town Boxholm to honor his birthplace in Sweden. The town was incorporated on September 29, 1913. (210, 438)

Boyden, Sioux County. Boyden was planned as Sheridan on January 14, 1879. The name was changed in 1881. The name Boyden was selected to honor J. C. Boyden, a railroad official. The town was incorporated on May 24, 1889. (433, 438)

Braddyville, Page County. Braddyville was named for James Braddy, who founded it in 1878. The town was incorporated on February 9, 1880. (163, 438, 523)

Bradford, Franklin County. The town was established in 1906 by the Bradford Land Company. While there is no confirmation of this, it seems likely that the name is a transfer from one of the other locations with that name in the United States or England. Bradford is not incorporated. (162, 406)

Bradgate, Humboldt County. Bradgate was founded by the Western Town Lot Company on March 7, 1882. The town was originally called Willow Glen, but the people in the community apparently were not happy with that name and changed it to Bradgate. There are several stories about the name. One is that Bradgate was an invented name for the town. A more plausible explanation is that it was named for Bradgate, England. A number of settlers in the area were from that area in England, so it seems very probable that Bradgate, England, was the inspiration. It was incorporated on June 20, 1893. (53, 275, 528)

Brandon, Buchanan County. In 1851 Thomas Brandon had started a trading post along Lime Creek. Brandon was founded by S. P. Brainard, Jacob Fouts, and E. C. Wilson in 1854. The men named the town after Thomas Brandon. It was incorporated on April 14, 1905. (61, 85, 438)

Brayton, Audubon County. Brayton was established in 1878 and named for a railroad employee. The town was incorporated on May 17, 1899. (22, 163, 438)

Breda, Carroll County. The Iowa Rail Road Land Company established Breda in 1877. The town was named after Breda in Holland by P. E. Hall, to honor one of the community's citizens who had emigrated from that town. It was incorporated on October 30, 1883. (42, 438, 528)

Bridgewater, Adair County. Bridgewater had its start when the Chicago, Burlington and Quincy Railroad built through that territory. The town was founded on October 13, 1885. The name was probably given to commemorate the fact that the railroad had considerable difficulty in bridging the Nodaway River. Bridgewater was incorporated on April 1, 1905. (249, 438)

Brighton, Washington County. Brighton was established in 1840 by Orson Kinsman and Thompson Dray. The town was named for Brighton, England, and was incorporated on July 26, 1870. (246, 299, 438)

Bristow, Butler County. Bristow was initially called West Point and then Boylan's Grove, before finally becoming Bristow. Bristow was founded by George Lash and H. A. Early, with the first store being opened there in 1860. The town was not formally established until 1876, when the name Bristow was applied. There is a story that the community was named for a prominent politician, though there is no written documentation. It was incorporated on December 15, 1881. (69, 254, 438)

Britt, Hancock County. Britt had its start in 1870 when the railroad put a depot and water tank at the location. The town was formally established on June 20, 1878, and was named in honor of a railroad employee. Britt was incorporated on June 23, 1881. (242)

Bronson, Woodbury County. Bronson was established by the Western Town Lot Company on November 23, 1901. Bronson was named for Ira D. Bronson, who had moved to the area from Kansas. It was incorporated on June 8, 1967. (304, 438, 528)

Brooklyn, Poweshiek County. Brooklyn was founded in 1849 by James Manatt, who called the town Greenville. A Dr. Sears suggested changing the name to Brooklyn, for

Brooklyn, New York. The town was incorporated on May 3, 1869. (290, 438)

Brooks, Adams County. The town was first called Canaan City when it was settled in 1853. The name was changed to Brookville in 1854 to reflect its location near a river. Since there was already a Brookville in Iowa, the post office was called Simpson. The names of both the town and the post office were changed to Brooks in 1871, apparently as an alternative to other proposed names. The town is not incorporated. (8, 163)

Brunsville, Plymouth County. Brunsville, established in 1911, was named for the owner of the town site, a Mrs. Brun. Brunsville was incorporated on July 18, 1911. (163, 208, 438)

Bryant, Clinton County. A post office was established at the town site on March 15, 1871. The town was named for William Cullen Bryant, the writer, by Isaac Howe, a civil engineer employed by the railroad. Bryant is not incorporated. (458, 528)

Buck Grove, Crawford County. Buck Grove was established in 1862 on the Milwaukee Railroad line. It was named because of the abundance of deer in the area. Buck Grove was incorporated on June 29, 1906. (62, 438)

Buckeye, Hardin County. Buckeye was founded by the Northern Land Company in September 1901. Since many of the settlers were from Ohio, it is possible that the town was named Buckeye to reflect that influence. Buckeye was incorporated on May 25, 1902. (414, 500, 576)

Buckingham, Tama County. When Buckingham was founded in 1900, it was first called Dennis. The town was renamed for a county in Virginia when it was discovered that there was already a town named Dennis in Iowa. The basis for the name of the county in Virginia was Buckinghamshire in England. There is another possibility for the name in that a Mr. Buckingham was an officer with the railroad that established the town. Buckingham is not incorporated. (36, 292, 528)

Buffalo, Scott County. Buffalo was founded in 1836 and named for Buffalo, New York. The town was incorporated on July 15, 1875. (438, 509)

Buffalo Center, Winnebago County. Buffalo Center was originally established on July 25, 1892. The town was replanned and was incorporated in 1894. Buffalo Center drew its name from its location in Buffalo Township. (303)

Burchinal, Cerro Gordo County. Burchinal was surveyed on July 8, 1887. T. P. Burchinal and his wife founded the town. The town was named for them. Burchinal is not incorporated. (84, 163)

Burlington, county seat, Des Moines County. The town was surveyed in 1834. John Gray, who had participated in the planning of the town, named it in honor of Burlington, Vermont. Burlington was incorporated on June 10, 1845. (24, 438)

Burnside, Webster County. Burnside was established on June 16, 1856, as Hesperion. The town was later named for General Ambrose Burnside, a Union army officer in the Civil War. Burnside is not incorporated. (152, 163, 196)

Burr Oak, Winneshiek County. Burr Oak was named for a grove of bur oak trees located nearby. The town was settled around 1850. The Burr Oak United Methodist Church was established in 1852. A post office was established there in September 1853. Burr Oak is not incorporated. (33, 458)

Burt, Kossuth County. Burt was established by the Western Town Lot Company on September 19, 1881. Burt was named for Horace Burt, who had been the chief engineer of the Chicago and North Western Railroad. It was incorporated on November 28, 1893. (280, 438, 528)

Bussey, Marion County. Bussey was founded in July 1875 by Jesse and Isabelle Bussey. The town was named for them. Bussey was incorporated on April 9, 1895. (438, 594)

C c ++++++++++++++++++++++

Calamus, Clinton County. Calamus was named after the post office, which was established in 1858. The post office was named after the nearby Calamus Creek, which in turn was named after the quantities of sweet flag, or calamus, growing along its banks. The town was established in 1860 by R. S. Dickinson and Colonel Milo Smith, owners of the property. It was incorporated on October 6, 1875. (438, 591)

California Junction, Harrison County. California Junction was founded by the Missouri Valley Land Company on September 9, 1880. The town was first called Yazoo, from the nearby Yazoo Landing on the Missouri River. John Blair was responsible for the name change. He thought that this would be a major transfer point for passengers going west, hence the name. California Junction is not incorporated. (312, 528)

Callender, Webster County. The town site started as a depot called Kesho on the Des Moines and Fort Dodge Railroad in 1869. James and Agnes Callender established the town on June 15, 1875, and it was named in their honor. Callender was incorporated on November 17, 1893. (438, 475)

Calmar, Winneshiek County. Calmar was established on November 21, 1854, as Marysville. The town's name was changed to Calmar because Alfred Clark, one of the founders of the town, was from Calmar, Sweden, and wanted to rename the town for his old home, a significant site in Swedish history. Calmar was incorporated on July 14, 1869. (33, 438)

Calumet, O'Brien County. Calumet was established by the Western Town Lot Company in November 1887. Calumet is the name the French gave to Indian peace or ceremonial pipes. Why that name was selected for this particular location is unknown, although the Big Sioux River in the region was also referred to as the Calumet or Red Pipe Stone River in the early days. It is therefore possible that it was an area where Indians collected the rock they used for their pipes. Calumet was incorporated on January 31, 1895. (438, 460, 546, 547, 561)

Camanche, Clinton County. Cammanche was established and named by Dr. George Peck in 1836. The town was named for the Comanche Indian tribe. The spelling of the name was altered so that it would, in the view of those christening the town, sound better when spoken. Camanche was incorporated by an act of the state legislature on January 28, 1857. (528, 591)

Cambria, Wayne County. A post office was established in this area on March 3, 1851. H. A. Nelson recorded a plan for a town he called Cambria in 1855. His town site was about a mile and a quarter away from the current site for Cambria. The name Cambria, an ancient term for Wales, probably reflected the influence of the Welsh settlers in the area. The current town site was established by the railroad in 1879, when the rail line was constructed through the area. Cambria is not incorporated. (46, 458)

Cambridge, Story County. Cambridge was laid out in November 1856 and was incorporated on December 6, 1881. The town was named for Cambridge, England. Another possibility is that a man by the name of Cambridge may have participated in the naming of the town. (16, 163)

Canton, Jones County. Canton was established in 1843. The naming of Canton is a mystery, but there were a number of settlers from Ohio in the area, so it was possibly named for Canton, Ohio. Canton is not incorporated. (596)

Cantril, Van Buren County. Cantril was platted in 1871. It was named for L. W. Cantril, the proprietor. The settlement was known as Nickleville in 1870, but the name was changed to Cantril in 1871. The town was incorporated on June 4, 1874. (336, 438)

Carbon, Adams County. The settlement was first called Walter's Mill, for Elijah Walters, who had established a sawmill there in 1849. When coal was found in the area in 1870, the village grew quickly and was renamed Carbon because of the coal deposits. Carbon was established in 1873 and was incorporated on July 18, 1903. (250, 438)

Carlisle, Warren County. Carlisle was established by Jeremiah Church in 1853. He named the town after Carlisle, Pennsylvania. Carlisle was incorporated on June 10, 1870. (438, 507)

Carmel, Sioux County. Carmel was started when a church was organized at the site on July 18, 1895. A Rev. TeSelle suggested Mt. Carmel as the name for the church because it was located on a slight hill. The town became known as Carmel. It is not incorporated. (442)

Carnarvon, Sac County. Carnarvon was established by George Pitcher on October 24, 1881. It was named after a town in Wales, the birthplace of a Mr. Hughes, an official with the railroad. The town is not incorporated. (235)

Carney, Polk County. Carney was an old mining town attached to the Carney Coal Mine. Apparently, the mine name was a phonetic spelling of the mine owners, the Kearney family. There was a post office in Carney for a while, starting in 1908, which would coincide with settlement there. That date is also consistent with the memories of the residents who were interviewed. Carney is not incorporated. (458, 598)

Carpenter, Mitchell County. Carpenter was reportedly named after a man by the name of Carpenter who worked on the building of the railroad track and lived in the hotel there. The town was founded in 1871 and was incorporated in 1879. (286)

Carroll, county seat, Carroll County. Carroll was established by the railroad in August 1867 and named for the county. The county and consequently the town were named in honor of Charles Carroll, a hero of the Revolutionary War and a signer of the Declaration of Independence. The town was first called Carroll City. Carroll was incorporated on September 27, 1869. (42, 438, 528)

Carson, Pottawattamie County. Carson was founded by the Burlington and Rock Island Railroad in 1880 and was incorporated on March 28, 1881. The town was named for a friend of one of the officials with the railroad. (256, 438, 471)

Carter Lake, Pottawattamie County. Settlement had started in the area when Edmond Jeffries claimed the property at the current site of Carter Lake in 1853. Carter Lake was named for the lake of the same name, although the lake went through several name changes before Carter Lake was settled on. The lake was created when the Missouri River carved out a new channel in 1877 and left a lake and a section of Iowa surrounded on three sides by Nebraska. The change in the riverbed did cause some litigation between Iowa and Nebraska, which was settled in Iowa's favor in 1892, and Carter Lake was officially an Iowa town. The lake was first called Cut-Off Lake, then Lake Nakomis, and finally Carter Lake for Selena Carter. The community was incorporated on July 5, 1930. (195, 438)

Cascade, Dubuque County. Cascade was founded by Caleb Bucknam and G. G. Banghart in 1842. The name comes from the cascading water of the North Maquoketa River, which borders the township. The town was incorporated on December 14, 1880. (266)

Casey, Guthrie County. Casey was founded by A. G. Weeks and R. H. Marshall on January 12, 1869. It was named in honor of a well-known contractor. Casey was incorporated on June 29, 1880. (271, 438)

Castalia, Winneshiek County. Castalia was known in its early days as Rattletrap, named for a particularly loquacious woman who lived there. The Castalia Post Office was established in 1851. There is a story that the name of the town is for a woman who ran a restaurant there. The name of the woman was supposed to have been Cass or Cast. Castalia was incorporated on August 16, 1901. (33, 163, 438)

Castana, Monona County. Castana was established by the Western Town Lot Company in July 1886. One story about the town's name was that a Mr. Day thought that the oak trees growing in the area resembled chestnuts, so he called the site Castana. He thought that was the Latin term for chestnuts. When the railroad established the town, the name was maintained. Another story is that the town was named for the springs near Delphi in Greece that were called Castalia. Yet another story is that the name came from a place in Asia Minor. The town was incorporated on March 3, 1891. (438, 528)

Cedar, Mahaska County. The name was selected by R. W. Moore when he applied for a post office at the site in 1868. He chose the name Cedar when he checked the list of post office names and saw that the name had not been used. The town is not incorporated. (339)

Cedar Bluff, Cedar County. The first settlement in the area was called Washington's Ferry. The post office established there carried that name, but it was later called Cedar River and then Gower's Ferry. The town was established by Robert Gower on property owned by his brother, Charles, in July 1851. Cedar Bluff was named for the bluffs along the Cedar River and is not incorporated. (258, 335)

Cedar Falls, Black Hawk County. Cedar Falls was first called Sturgis Falls, derived from the nearby waterfall on the Cedar River and the name of the first settler, William Sturgis. The town was established on April 26, 1853. The name was later changed to reflect the falls at the site on the Cedar River. Cedar Falls was incorporated on February 24, 1858. (236, 438)

Cedar Rapids, county seat, Linn County. When Cedar Rapids was first established in 1838, William Stone named the town Columbus. In 1841 it was resurveyed and renamed by N. B. Brown and his associates. They named the town Cedar Rapids, for the rapids in the Cedar River at the site. The river was named for the large number of red cedar trees that grew along its banks. Cedar Rapids was incorporated on January 15, 1849. (282, 438, 528)

Center Junction, Jones County. Center Junction was founded in October 1871. The town was so named by its founders because it was at the physical center of the county, and there was an intersection of railroads planned for the site. Center Junction was incorporated on March 26, 1885. (438, 528, 596)

Center Point, Linn County. Center Point was founded by Samuel Brice and Jesse Grubbs in January 1854. The location had been called McGonigle's Point, for an early settler at the location. "Point" came from the fact that there was a grove of timber that extended out onto the prairie at the site. "Center" came from the fact that it was the midpoint on the mail route between Cedar Rapids and Waterloo. Center Point was incorporated on February 6, 1875. (163, 282, 438)

Centerville, county seat, Appanoose County. Centerville was first called Chaldea by Jonathon F. Stratton, who founded the town in 1846. The county board of commissioners adopted the site as the county seat on October 6, 1846. Rev. William Manson opposed the name Chaldea and proposed the name Sentorville, in honor of a prominent Tennessee politician named Sentor. When the Iowa legislature approved the proposed name, the spelling was changed to Centerville. The citizens voted to incorporate on February 26, 1855. The first town charter was adopted on March 26, 1855, and the town was last incorporated on January 23, 1857. (26, 537)

Central City, Linn County. The town was platted on September 9, 1857. The town replaced one that had been planned the prior year and named Clarksford. Central City was named for its location in a farming area and location between rail lines. Central City was incorporated on July 6, 1889. (282, 438)

Centralia, Dubuque County. Centralia was founded in 1850 by Hardin Nowlin, who surveyed the site, and William Stratton, who owned the land. It was first known as Dacotah, but the name was changed to Centralia. It was possibly named because it is located in Center Township. After the Eighteenth Amendment was repealed, a number of the small, unincorporated towns feared they would not be permitted to have a tavern unless they were incorporated. The towns incorporated so that they could ensure the sale of beer in their communities. Centralia was incorporated on June 3, 1933. (266, 344, 438)

Chapin, Franklin County. The original Chapin was founded by Rev. J. B. Grinnell on December 6, 1858. The town was named in honor of Rev. Grinnell's wife, whose maiden name was Chapin. When the railroad came through the area, it located a station about two miles from the original town site and called it New Chapin. This town was established on July 29, 1871, by George Beed. The original town site died out, and the new location dropped the "New" in its name. Chapin is not incorporated. (270)

Chariton, county seat, Lucas County. Chariton was called Polk when it was founded in 1849, then it was called Chariton Point before its present name was established. Chariton was named for the Chariton River. Explorers believed the name to be of Indian origin. A more plausible explanation is that a Canadian trader, Joseph Chartran or Charitone, was closely linked with the river, and it was named for him. Chariton was incorporated on December 9, 1874. (21, 318, 438)

Charles City, county seat, Floyd County. Charles City has been renamed a number of times. It was first known as Freeman when Dr. Robert Freeman established the town in April 1854 and named it after himself. The town was next known as Charleston when Joseph Kelly renamed it for his son, Charles. When the townspeople learned that a Charleston already existed, the name was changed to St. Charles. When the community was incorporated as a village by the legislature, the name was recorded as St. Charles City. The local newspaper led a drive to drop the "St." in the name. The argument was that it made the name unnecessarily long. The name has been Charles City since 1860. Charles City was incorporated on May 1, 1869. (456)

Charlotte, Clinton County. A post office, which would indicate some settlement at the site, was established on July 26, 1853. The town was named in honor of Charlotte Gilman, who was married to the first settler in the area. Charlotte was incorporated on December 5, 1904. (94, 438, 528)

Charter Oak, Crawford County. Charter Oak was established by W. H. Crombie, who bought the property and created lots in 1869. The town was named after the well-known Charter Oak in Connecticut. Charter Oak was incorporated on February 6, 1891. (407, 438)

Chatsworth, Sioux County. Chatsworth was established on August 18, 1890. The town was named by railroad officials for Chatsworth Castle, a town in England. Chatsworth was incorporated on December 31, 1900. (433, 438, 442)

Chelsea, Tama County. Chelsea was established in 1864 by John Blair. The town was named Chelsea after Chelsea, Massachusetts. The location had originally been called Creek Station. Chelsea was incorporated on March 4, 1878. (21, 438, 528)

Cherokee, county seat, Cherokee County. The first town was planned as Cherokee Center near the current Cherokee site by Jay Sternburg, a Justice Townsend, and George Detwiler on November 19, 1856. There was little interest in settling the town, and it remained basically a "paper town." Next, Samuel W. Hayward planned a town, also near the current town and thought of as the "original Cherokee." He called the town Blair City in hopes of attracting the attention of John Blair, who was instrumental in establishing so many rail lines and towns. The hope was that the railroad would place a station there. New Cherokee was established by George W. Lebourveau and his wife, and Carlton Corbett and his wife, on March 21, 1870. Cherokee was named for the county, which was named for the Indian tribe. The town was incorporated on April 5, 1873. (401, 438)

Chester, Howard County. The original town was established in March 1858 by Artemus Eaton as Eatonville. In 1867 the railroad ran track through the area, missing Eatonville by two miles. Another settlement developed along the track, and the residents of Eatonville moved to the new settlement. The prevailing explanation for the new town's name is that while the Eaton families wanted the new town to be named Eatonville, Amos Kingsley, one of the settlers, wanted the town named for his older brother, Chester. Amos Kingsley was quite persuasive, and the town was named Chester, even though Chester Kingsley never lived in the area. Chester was formally established in 1873 and was incorporated on September 22, 1900. (8, 259, 310, 438, 459)

Chillicothe, Wapello County. Chillicothe was founded by A. J. Wicker in 1849. The town was named by settlers from Ohio for Chillicothe, Ohio. The name is of Indian derivation and was the name of one branch of the Shawnee tribe. Chillicothe was incorporated on December 22, 1881. (298, 438, 561)

Churchtown, Allamakee County. Churchtown was named for the church at the site. The church was incorporated on October 19, 1868, and the founding date of the town is probably close to this date. A post office operated at the location from 1897 to 1947. The town is not incorporated. (157, 163, 458)

Churdan, Greene County. Churdan was established in 1882 as a railroad track was being laid past the town site. The town was named after Joseph Churdan, one of the early settlers in the area. It was incorporated on March 25, 1884. (438, 531)

Cincinnati, Appanoose County. Cincinnati was established by J. F. Stratton, the surveyor, and John Overstreet in 1855. The town was probably named because a large number of the original settlers came from the vicinity of Cincinnati, Ohio. The town was incorporated on February 13, 1875. (26, 438, 537)

Clare, Webster County. Clare was founded in 1882 and named for Clare, Ireland, at the request of a priest, a Father Brazil. Clare was incorporated on March 29, 1892. (438, 475)

Clarence, Cedar County. The area was first known as Onion Grove, at least that is what the first post office in the area was called. That name was picked because of the profusion of wild onions growing in the region. When the Chicago and North Western Railway established a station at the site in 1858, it was known as Onion Grove Station. L. B. Gere, a local businessman, suggested changing the name to Clarence to honor Clarence, New York. The town was incorporated on February 26, 1866. (258, 438)

Clarinda, county seat, Page County. Clarinda was formally established in 1857. The town was named for the niece of the founder. Clarinda was incorporated on December 8, 1866. (21, 246, 438)

Clarion, county seat, Wright County. Clarion was named after Clarion, Pennsylvania. The planners had originally planned on calling it Grant, but at the time there was already a Grant Post Office in Iowa. The town had is start in 1865 when the county voted to move the county seat from Goldfield to a new location, which was purchased, surveyed, and platted as Grant. The town was established on November 1, 1865, and was incorporated on October 15, 1881. (47, 438)

Clarksville, Butler County. Clarksville was established in 1853. Thomas Clark and Jeremiah Clark assisted in planning the town and consequently had the town named after them. Clarksville was incorporated on May 11, 1874. (163, 254, 438)

Clayton, Clayton County. Clayton was established in November 1849. Clayton was named for the county that it is in. The county was named for a Senator Clayton from Delaware. Clayton was incorporated on November 23, 1856. (246, 261, 438)

Clear Lake, Cerro Gordo County. Clear Lake, founded in 1856, was named for the lake that is close by. The town was incorporated on May 26, 1871. (21, 438)

Clearfield, Taylor County. Clearfield was established on September 26, 1881. The name is both descriptive and commemorative since in the history of Taylor County there were a number of settlers from Clearfield County, Pennsylvania. Clearfield was incorporated on December 16, 1882. (293, 438)

Cleghorn, Cherokee County. Cleghorn was founded by Rev. Adam Cleghorn on March 12, 1890. It was incorporated on January 25, 1901. (87, 401, 438)

Clemons, Marshall County. Clemons was founded by William Clemons and named for him. Clemons was also known as Clemons Grove. The town was incorporated on May 25, 1903. (411, 438)

Clermont, Fayette County. Clermont was established by John Thompson and C. D. Carlson in 1851, though the town site was not recorded until 1855. The town was informally known as "Brick City" because of the brick-making business located there. Clermont was also once known as Norway. Clermont is thought to be named after a steamboat on the Hudson River in New York on which some of the settlers had ridden as they headed west. Another possibility is that the name was transferred from another location, as Claremont is a name used in New Hampshire and England. The community was incorporated on June 15, 1875. (95, 163, 269, 318, 438)

Climbing Hill, Woodbury County. The town's name came from the fact that it was at the top of a hill, and the only way to approach the town was to climb it. The town site was first settled by Cornelius Ostrander around 1867. Climbing Hill is not incorporated. (294)

Clinton, county seat, Clinton County. Clinton was originally named New York when the town was founded in 1838 by Joseph Bartlett. On January 26, 1857, the Iowa General Assembly conferred a city charter (incorporation) upon Clinton. (318, 591)

Clio, Wayne County. Clio was platted along the Rock Island Railroad track on April 16, 1874, by J. W. Tabler. The name Clio had been suggested by Marion Edgeman, for the Greek Muse representing history. The community was incorporated on February 20, 1882. (46, 246, 438)

Clive, Polk County. Clive was established on January 18, 1882, by the Union Land Company. There are several stories put forward to explain the name of the community. One is that Clive was named for Robert Clive, the British general who was involved in the British colonization of India. The second theory is that there was a railroad foreman named Clive working when the rail line was run through Clive. The story goes that when supplies were sent out to the rail crew, the instructions were to take the material out to Clive. The town was incorporated on October 9, 1956. (126, 438)

Clutier, Tama County. Clutier was founded in 1900 and named for B. F. Clutier. The village was incorporated on January 16, 1901. (292, 438, 528)

Coalville, Webster County. Settlement started in 1858, and the town was officially established in the late 1870s. Coalville was named for the many coal mines in the area. The town is not incorporated. (163, 577)

Coburg, Montgomery County. Coburg drew its name from a town in Germany. Coburg was established in 1870 when the Burlington and Missouri Railroad, later the Chicago, Burlington and Quincy Railroad, developed a branch line through the area. Coburg was founded by D. N. Smith, Justus Clark, and the Burlington and Missouri Railroad. The town is not incorporated. (213, 246)

Coggon, Linn County. Coggon was first known as Green's Mill and then Nugent and finally Coggon. The community was founded in 1857. The town was named by a railroad official for his cousin in England, William Coggon. It was incorporated on June 14, 1892. (139, 163, 318, 438)

Coin, Page County. Coin was founded by the Western Improvement Company at a railroad intersection on November 25, 1879. The town apparently was named because a coin had been unearthed when a foundation in the new town was being dug. Coin was incorporated on July 30, 1881. (163, 438, 440)

Colesburg, Delaware County. Coles Burgh was founded by Hiram Cole and Lawrence McNamee on August 4, 1848. The name was changed to Colesburg on April 3, 1849. The town was incorporated on February 21, 1893. (404, 438)

Colfax, Jasper County. Colfax was named in honor of Schuyler Colfax, a prominent politician. The town was founded in July 1867 by Abel Kimball. It was incorporated on August 10, 1875. (438, 573)

College Springs, Page County. College Springs was first known as Amity, but the name was changed to College Springs when a large spring was discovered in the area. The name Amity was drawn from Amity College, which was located in the town. The name College Springs reflected the college's presence as well as the presence of the nearby spring. College Springs was founded in June 1856 and was incorporated on January 19, 1875. (340, 438)

Collins, Story County. A Collins Centre post office was in operation from 1879 until 1881, when the post office was renamed Collins. The town of Collins was established at the site in February 1882. The names were drawn from the township in which the post office and town were located. The township was probably named for a Collins Township in New York. There is some speculation that Collins Township was named in honor of Rev. John Collins, a popular preacher in Ohio around the time the township was formed. Collins was incorporated on December 28, 1894. (16, 163, 438, 458)

Colo, Story County. John Blair named the town for a dog that had been killed when it was run over by a train. Colo was founded on May 22, 1865, and was incorporated on April 26, 1876. (16, 140, 528)

Columbia, Marion County. Columbia was surveyed by William Kent for Hugh and Rebecca Smith. The town was founded on May 2, 1857. Columbia took its name from the Columbia Post Office that was moved into the town from its location two miles away. The town is not incorporated. (594)

Columbus City, Louisa County. The original Columbus City was established as a midpoint on the road from Burlington to Iowa City. Due to land disputes, the town site was moved to its current location in 1841. The name was drawn from Columbus, Ohio, since some of the settlers were from there and hoped that naming their new town with the same name would yield success similar to that of the Ohio city. Columbus City was incorporated on November 26, 1870. (368, 438)

Columbus Junction, Louisa County. The site where Columbus Junction stands was initially known as Sand Bank. Columbus Junction's name was drawn from Columbus City, which is quite close. Columbus Junction was founded in 1869 by J. W. Garner and W. W. Garner when they saw an opportunity to develop a town on the rail line being constructed through the area. The town was initially known as Columbus City Junction due to its proximity to Columbus City, but when the town site was registered, it was listed as Columbus Junction. The town was incorporated on May 25, 1874. (368, 438)

Colwell, Floyd County. Colwell was named for James Colwell, who donated land for the school and built some of the first houses in the community. The town was established on September 15, 1915, and was incorporated on September 21, 1922. (438, 456)

Conesville, Muscatine County. Conesville was named after its founder, Beebe S. Cone. It was founded on November 26, 1870, and was incorporated on March 21, 1878. (438, 492)

Conrad, Grundy County. Conrad was established by the Iowa and Minnesota Town Lot Company on June 18, 1880. It was named in honor of one of its founders, I. W. Conrad. In 1881 the town's name was changed to Conrad Grove but was changed back to Conrad on March 30, 1896. Conrad was incorporated on November 15, 1886. (220, 438)

Conroy, Iowa County. Conroy was founded in 1884 when the Milwaukee Railroad came through the area. Railroad officials named the town in honor of James Conroy, for his assistance in establishing the rail line. The town is not incorporated. (164)

Conway, Taylor County. Conway was established in 1872 as a railway station. The original spelling was Conawa, but a "y" was added later. The name could possibly be for someone with the surname Conawa or possibly for the Muskogee Indian word *konawa*, meaning "money." There is no definitive information about the origin of the name. The town was incorporated on December 27, 1878. (163, 293, 438)

Coon Rapids, Carroll County. The location where the town was eventually established was purchased by a Mr. Winfred in 1861 as a site for a mill. There were some delays in the development of the town because of the Civil War. In 1863 a post office was established and called Fairview. The Post Office Department denied the name because a Fairview already existed in Iowa. After some discussion, Coon Rapids was suggested as the name by Jacob Cretsinger. The name was inspired by the town's location along the Middle

Raccoon River. Coon Rapids voted to incorporate on November 2, 1882. (42, 438)

Cooper, Greene County. Cooper was established in 1881 and named by a Mr. Hubbell in honor of his father-in-law, a Des Moines settler named Isaac Cooper. The town is not incorporated. (531)

Coppock, Henry, Jefferson, and Washington counties. Coppock was named for the man who donated the land for the town, John Coppock. Coppock was founded in 1882 and was incorporated on August 24, 1901. (245, 391, 438)

Coralville, Johnson County. Coralville was established in 1866. The name comes from the coral that was found there when the settlers started digging foundations. Coralville was incorporated on November 22, 1873. (278, 438)

Corley, Shelby County. Corley was started in 1878 when the Rock Island Railroad brought a rail line past the site. The town was named by the owner of the property, Thomas McDonald, in honor of his wife, whose maiden name was Corley. Corley is not incorporated. (587)

Corning, county seat, Adams County. Corning was founded in 1855 by D. M. Smith who named it for his friend Erastus Corning. Corning was incorporated on December 13, 1871. (318, 438)

Correctionville, Woodbury County. Correctionville was established on September 25, 1855, by the Henn, Williams, and Cook Company. Due to the curvature of the earth, surveyors would alter, or correct, their surveying line every sixty miles. Correctionville was established at one of those points, hence the name. The town was incorporated on October 3, 1882. (294, 304, 438)

Corwith, Hancock County. Corwith was founded on September 1, 1880. Corwith was named for a Mr. Corwith, an area landowner. The community was incorporated on June 1, 1886. (163, 242, 438)

Corydon, county seat, Wayne County. Corydon was once known as Springfield, but it was renamed as the result of a game of poker. The players agreed that the winner of the game would be given the honor of naming the town. The victor was a Judge Anderson, from Corydon, Indiana. He named the new town after his old home. The town was established in 1852 and was incorporated on April 27, 1867. (307, 318, 353, 438)

Cosgrove, Johnson County. Cosgrove was named in honor of Bishop Henry Cosgrove, who was the bishop of the Davenport diocese when the town was founded in 1890. The town is not incorporated. (330)

Cotter, Louisa County. Cotter was founded by Margaret E. Cotter on January 23, 1878, as Cotterville. The name was later changed to Cotter. The town was incorporated on April 27, 1867. (438, 526)

Coulter, Franklin County. The community was named for an official of the Chicago Great Western Railroad, a Mr. Colter. Coulter was founded in 1901 and was incorporated on April 24, 1909. (229, 438)

Council Bluffs, county seat, Pottawattamie County. The term "Council Bluffs" was introduced by Patrick Gass in the journal he kept on the Lewis and Clark expedition. He described a meeting between the members of the expedition and the Otoes and Missouris at a site he said was called Council Bluffs. While Council Bluffs is not at the exact location of this meeting, it draws its name from the conference site. In fact, there is strong evidence that the actual meeting place was on the Nebraska side of the Missouri River as well as some miles to the north. When the town was established on June 14, 1846, it was first called Miller's Hollow. Army officer Thomas Kane was sympathetic to the Mormons, so they renamed the town Kanesville. When the Mormons left in 1852, the remaining citizens called it Council Bluffs. The city was incorporated on January 19, 1853. (191, 318, 438)

Covington, Linn County. The community was established in October 1882. While the origin of the name is a mystery, there was an Isah Covington listed in the 1870 Linn County census, for whom the town could be named. The town is not incorporated. (363, 505)

Craig, Plymouth County. The town was named for Wright Craig, an attorney for the Northwestern Railroad. The town was incorporated on April 6, 1911. (163, 438)

Cranston, Muscatine County. Cranston, established in 1902, was originally called Madura. Since it was a loading point for livestock on the rail line, there was concern the name sounded a bit like "manure." Another and more credible explanation is found in the July 1949 *Annals of Iowa*. George Titus, who had been involved in railway development in the area, indicated that the railroad had changed the name to avoid confusion with another station on the rail line. One of the town's founders was from Cranston, Rhode Island, hence the name. Cranston is not incorporated. (313, 428)

Crawfordsville, Washington County. Crawfordsville was first known as Nealtown, for the Neal brothers who founded it on July 4, 1839. One reason for the change was that it helped induce a Dr. Crawford to practice there. An alternative reason for the name change could be the number of settlers named Crawford in the area. Crawfordsville was incorporated on March 26, 1891. (163, 299, 318, 438, 568)

Crescent, Pottawattamie County. Crescent was originally called Crescent City when it was established in 1856. The site was named by Brigham Young for the shape of the bluff that was near the village. Crescent was incorporated on October 16, 1959. (191, 318, 438)

Cresco, county seat, Howard County. Augustus Beadle, W. B. Strong, and B. H. Edgertown founded the town on June 12, 1866. Beadle named the town Cresco, Latin for "I grow." Cresco was incorporated on May 6, 1868. (8, 163, 438)

Creston, county seat, Union County. Creston was established by the railroad in 1869. The name comes from the fact that it is at the highest point on the Burlington and Missouri River Railroad through Iowa, so it was at the "crest." The town was incorporated on April 22, 1871. (45)

Cromwell, Union County. Cromwell was established as a station on the Burlington and Missouri River Railroad in 1868. Cromwell was probably named for Oliver Cromwell, a major figure in British history. The town was incorporated on November 24, 1893. (45, 246, 438)

Croton, Lee County. Croton was founded by Lewis Coon on July 3, 1849. The name is of Indian origin, specifically from the eastern United States since there are a number of sites in New York with Croton as part or all of their name. Croton is not incorporated. (281, 561)

Crystal Lake, Hancock County. Crystal Lake, established in 1897, was named for the nearby lake. It was incorporated on April 19, 1898. (146, 242, 438)

Cumberland, Cass County. Cumberland was established in 1884. There are several possibilities for the naming of the town. While it is possible that some of the area settlers came through the Cumberland Gap, a local historian thought that it is far more likely that some of the settlers were affiliated with one of the many towns in the South and East named

Cumberland. The community was incorporated on May 2, 1893. (127, 438)

Cumming, Warren County. Cumming was established in 1888. There is a story that the town drew its name from the response "it's coming" when a builder was asked about the progress in constructing the new town. It is probable that the town was named for an individual by Frazer Callison, the town's founder. Cumming was incorporated on April 23, 1925. (315, 438)

Curlew, Palo Alto County. Curlew was named by the president of the Des Moines and Fort Dodge Railroad, Charles E. Whitehead. An avid hunter, Whitehead named the town for the bird that he had hunted in the area. He also named Mallard and Plover. Curlew was established in 1882 and was incorporated on May 22, 1902. (398, 438)

Cushing, Woodbury County. Cushing was platted by the Blair Town Lot and Land Company on May 10, 1883, and was first named Penrose. The town was later named for a Bostonian named L. Cushing Kimball, whose brother was a director of the Chicago and North Western Railroad. Cushing was incorporated on November 21, 1892. (294, 438, 528)

Cylinder, Palo Alto County. Cylinder started with a large hay barn constructed in 1885. The railroad company built a siding in order to load hay. In 1890 the railroad built a depot and named the stop after Cylinder Creek, which runs nearby. The stream got its name from an attempt by early settlers to carry an engine across the stream when the water was high. The machine sank into the mud. The cylinder became detached and was never recovered. Cylinder was incorporated on April 5, 1900. (398, 438)

D d ++++++++++++++++++++++

Dakota City, county seat, Humboldt County. Dakota City was planned by Edward McKnight in 1855, though it was not officially set up until June 7, 1858. McKnight named the town for the Dakota (Sioux) Indians. Dakota City was incorporated on June 22, 1878. (163, 275, 438)

Dallas Center, Dallas County. A firm known as Percival and Hatton established the town in 1869 as Dallas Center. The town was named for the county that it is in and its location near the physical center of the county. The county was named for a politician, George Dallas. Dallas Center was incorporated on March 22, 1880. (163, 246, 263, 438)

Dana, Greene County. Dana was named after Samuel Dana, an early settler at the site that would become the town. The first house in the town was constructed in 1880. Dana was incorporated on July 22, 1907. (438, 531)

Danbury, Woodbury County. Danbury was founded on November 1, 1877, by Daniel Thomas and his wife. They named the town by combining "Dan" from Daniel's name with "bury" from Woodbury County. Danbury was incorporated on October 1, 1881. (163, 294, 438, 528)

Danville, Des Moines County. Danville was founded by Alonson Messenger and Harriet Messenger, brother and sister, in 1854. They named the town after Danville, Illinois. Danville was incorporated on September 27, 1902. (24, 163, 438)

Davenport, county seat, Scott County. Davenport was established as a town in 1839. The town was named in honor of Colonel George Davenport. Davenport was incorporated on February 5, 1851. (438, 509)

Davis City, Decatur County. Davis City was founded by W. H. Cheever in 1855. It was named for William Davis, who had established a sawmill at the site the prior year. Davis City was incorporated on May 19, 1877. (44, 438)

Dawson, Dallas County. Dawson was first called Undine. It was founded in 1882. In 1884 the community voted to honor Clark Dawson, a man who was in part responsible for populating the town. He had an interest in the nearby Neola elevator and was an agent for the railroad. Dawson was incorporated on April 25, 1908. (163, 438)

Dayton, Webster County. Dayton was founded in November 1856 by B. F. Allison. Allison originally called the town West Dayton after Dayton, Ohio, but "West" was eventually dropped. The town was incorporated on July 8, 1881. (438, 475)

De Soto, Dallas County. The land for the site of De Soto was donated by Thomas Hemphill, J. J. Van Meter, and H. G. Van Meter to the Chicago, Rock Island and Pacific Railroad. The town was established in 1868 and named for a railroad official. De Soto was incorporated on April 28, 1875. (263, 438)

De Witt, Clinton County. De Witt was named for De Witt Clinton, fifth governor of New York State. The town was founded on July 6, 1841, and was the original county seat. It was originally called Vandenburg for a Miss Vandenburg, who was engaged to one of the county commissioners. The territorial legislature changed the name to De Witt on February 17, 1842. De Witt was incorporated on September 20, 1858. (438, 591)

Decatur City, Decatur County. Decatur City was established in 1851 and was the original county seat, hence the name Decatur City. The county was named for Commodore Stephen Decatur, the naval hero. The town was incorporated on July 8, 1875. (153, 246, 438)

Decorah, county seat, Winneshiek County. William Day and William Painter founded Decorah in 1853 and named the town for a Winnebago chief, Waukon Decorah. The town was incorporated on June 30, 1857. (33, 438)

Dedham, Carroll County. Dedham was founded in 1882. It was named for Dedham, Massachusetts, by a Captain Collins. Dedham was incorporated on April 2, 1884. (74, 373, 438)

Deep River, Poweshiek County. Deep River was established as a post office in 1852. The town was named for the nearby river. The river was descriptively named. The community was incorporated on June 15, 1887. (290, 438, 528)

Defiance, Shelby County. Defiance was established by the Milwaukee Land Company on February 20, 1882, and named Marmon. The town's name was reportedly changed because the townspeople, mainly settlers who had relocated from a settlement called Willow Creek, were unhappy that the railroad had not laid track by that community. The people called themselves "defiers" and the town Defiance. Defiance was incorporated on December 4, 1882. (233, 438, 587)

Delaware, Delaware County. Delaware was founded in 1852 by the families of John Hefner, W. M. Hefner, J. P. Ball, John P. Fear, and D. M. Smith. The town was named for the county. The county was named for the state of Delaware. The village was incorporated on July 22, 1915. (246, 380, 438)

Delhi, Delaware County. Delhi was established as the county seat when it was surveyed in 1842. It was named for Delhi, the county seat of Delaware County in New York. The town voted to incorporate on January 15, 1855, and was last incorporated on April 26, 1909. (163, 404, 438)

Delmar, Clinton County. Delmar was planned in 1871 and formally established in 1872. The name of the town was drawn from the initials of six women who were on an excursion train from Clinton that opened the rail line to the town site in 1870. The town was incorporated on June 10, 1876. (438, 528, 591)

Deloit, Crawford County. Deloit was first called Mason's Grove, then Boyer Valley, then Bloomington, and then Beloit. The town was founded in 1899 by the Western Town Lot Company and finally named Beloit, for Beloit, Wisconsin. It was suggested that the name be changed again to avoid confusion with other towns with the similar names, so "D" was substituted for "B" in the name. Deloit was incorporated on May 15, 1900. (407, 438, 528)

Delphos, Ringgold County. The town, first known as Borneo, was founded in 1880 as a rail station. The current name was derived from the Greek word *adelphos*, meaning brother. Delphos was incorporated on April 3, 1920. (44, 158, 438, 497)

Delta, Keokuk County. Delta was established in 1875. G. W. Fay, chief engineer with the Rock Island Railroad, was given the honor of naming the new town. When Fay looked at the town site on the map, he noticed that it was shaped like the fourth letter in the Greek alphabet, delta. Delta was incorporated on March 22, 1877. (279, 438, 516)

Denison, county seat, Crawford County. Denison was established in 1856 and named for one of the founders, J. W. Denison. The town was incorporated on October 2, 1875. (407, 438)

Denmark, Lee County. The settlement was established in 1836 and first called Haystack because of a large stack of prairie grass gathered by the settlers. The town of Denmark was founded in 1837. The community was named by John Edwards, who was visiting the area, for his favorite hymn, "Denmark." The town is not incorporated. (519)

Denver, Bremer County. Denver was founded as Jefferson City in 1855, but the name was later changed to Denver. There appears to be no record as to why the name Denver was chosen. It could have been named for Denver, Colorado, which was founded in 1858, but it is just as likely that it was named for the governor of the Kansas Territory, General James Denver. Denver was incorporated on June 30, 1896. (159, 438)

Derby, Lucas County. Derby was founded on May 1, 1872, by a Mr. Perking and a Mr. Manchester. The location had been known as Tinkletown before the establishment of the town. It is presumed that the name Derby came from the settlers of English ancestry near the site. It was incorporated on February 4, 1901. (283, 438)

Des Moines, state capital, county seat, Polk County. Des Moines was founded as Ft. Des Moines, at the site of an army fort of the same name, in 1846. The army had selected the name due to the proximity to the Des Moines River. The name of the river can be traced to the French explorers and cartographers who initially named the river for a branch of the Illinois Confederacy called the Moingwenas, whom they found in the area in the late 1600s. The name was altered over time, with many changes in pronunciation and spelling, until it was finally widely known as the Moins. Des Moines was incorporated on October 18, 1851. (289, 438, 561)

Dewar, Black Hawk County. Dewar was first called Emert for John and Elizabeth Emert, who donated the land for the town. The name was later changed to DeWar so there would be less confusion with the mail going to Emmetsburg. DeWar was named for a railroad surveyor, though the spelling has been altered to its current usage. The town was established in October 1880 and is not incorporated. (178, 390)

Dexter, Dallas County. Dexter was founded in June 1868 by M. J. Marshall and A. Kimball. The year before the town was established, a horse named Dexter had set a record for the mile as a trotter and was quite well known. The town was named for the racehorse. Dexter was incorporated on January 7, 1871. (163, 263, 438)

Diagonal, Ringgold County. Diagonal was originally going to be called Goshen, after a nearby post office. Diagonal was established in 1881 as a rail depot. The name Diagonal came from the fact that the depot was a central station on a rail line that was called the Diagonal. That name came from the proposed path of the rail line across the state, from northeast Iowa through southwest Iowa into Nebraska. Diagonal was incorporated on March 6, 1896. (44, 163, 438, 497)

Dickens, Clay County. The area was first settled in the early 1880s. The name apparently was drawn from a large barn on a farm owned by the Dickenson brothers. The barn, a distinctive landmark, was known as the Dickenson barn. As more people moved into the area, the reference to the landmark was dropped and the settlement name shortened to Dickens. Another story about the naming of the town was that a woman involved said "dickens" when she learned that the name that had been proposed was already in use in the state, so it was suggested that her reaction be the name of the town. One other possibility is that Dickens was named for a worker on a railroad crew. Dickens was incorporated on April 7, 1909. (163, 260, 438)

Dike, Grundy County. Dike was established around 1900, with a post office that was opened on July 27, 1900. The town was named by C. T. Dyke, for himself. The town was incorporated on January 16, 1901. (36, 438, 458, 528)

Dinsdale, Tama County. Dinsdale was a station on the Chicago, Rock Island and Pacific Railroad. Dinsdale was named for L. P. Dinsdale, since the town was located on property owned by the Dinsdale family. The town was officially established in 1891, though a settlement had been in existence since the 1870s. Dinsdale is not incorporated. (71, 292)

Dixon, Scott County. Dixon was founded in 1854 by Rudolphus Dickinson. The town was named for him, with some modification. The town voted to incorporate on May 12, 1909. (438, 509)

Dolliver, Emmett County. Dolliver was named for Senator Jonathan P. Dolliver, a politician from the area. The town was established by the Western Town Lot Company in 1899. It was incorporated on April 16, 1902. (184, 268, 438)

Donahue, Scott County. In 1870 the Davenport, Rock Island and Northwestern Railroad established a station on the farm of Phineas Curtis. The station was named in honor of Michael Donahue, a prominent citizen of Davenport and an investor in the railroad. It was incorporated on May 9, 1909. (438, 509)

Donnan, Fayette County. Donnan was founded in 1878. The community was named for an existing post office named Donnan. The Donnan Post Office had been named for W. G. Donnan, who had been a Civil War hero and who later had a career in Iowa politics. Donnan is not incorporated. (167)

Donnellson, Lee County. Donnellson was founded on May 21, 1881. The town was named for the Donnell family, early settlers in the area. Donnellson was incorporated on October 25, 1892. (96, 265, 438)

Doon, Lyon County. Doon was founded by G. W. Bowers and A. H. Davison on September 6, 1889. The town was named by H. D. Rice for the "Bonnie Doon" in Robert Burns's poem "Ye Banks and Braes o' Bonnie Doon." It was incorporated on March 8, 1892. (438, 464, 528)

Dorchester, Allamakee County. Dorchester was originally settled by Edmund Bell and Harvey Bell. The name was inspired by Dorchester, England. The town was founded on November 27, 1873, and is not incorporated. (13, 15, 246)

Douds, Van Buren County. Douds was founded in 1866. Eliah Doud and David Doud Jr. planned the town, and it was named in their honor by the railroad officials who ran a rail line through the area. The town is not incorporated. (336)

Dougherty, Cerro Gordo County. Dougherty was established on June 30, 1900, and named for an area farmer. The town was incorporated on December 29, 1900. (84, 528)

Dow City, Crawford County. Dow City was named for an early settler, S. E. Dow. It was first called Crawford when it was founded in October 1869. The name was then changed to Dowville and finally to Dow City. The community was incorporated on February 22, 1892. (407, 438, 517)

Downey, Cedar County. In 1853 Hugh D. Downey purchased the town site. Once the Chicago, Rock Island and Pacific Railroad had laid track through the area, he founded the town and named it for himself. The town is not incorporated. (258)

Dows, Wright County. Dows was originally called Otisville. The town was established by the Burlington, Cedar Rapids and Northern Railroad's town lot company on September 28, 1880. It was named in honor of one of the railroad's officers. The town was incorporated on May 3, 1892. (47, 438)

Drakesville, Davis County. Drakesville was established on February 12, 1847. It was named after the township that it is in. The township was named after J. B. Drake, an early settler. Drakesville was incorporated on May 5, 1866. (264, 438)

Dubuque, county seat, Dubuque County. Dubuque was named for Julien Dubuque, who established a trading post in the area in 1788. A lead deposit was discovered, and he petitioned the French authorities to mine the metal. He received this permission in 1788. He also petitioned the Spanish government, since the land he wanted to mine was under Spanish rule. He received permission from Spain in 1796. Julien Dubuque died in 1810 and was buried on a bluff over the river. Dubuque was formally established as a town in 1833 and was incorporated on January 28, 1857. (172, 266, 438)

Dumont, Butler County. Dumont was founded by Samuel Dumont in 1879 on property that he owned. It was incorporated on January 24, 1896. (254, 438)

Dunbar, Marshall County. Dunbar was established on February 3, 1882, by the Milwaukee Land Company and named for an area landowner. The town is not incorporated. (214, 246)

Duncan, Hancock County. Duncan was initially called Hancock. It is thought that the town was named in honor of a railroad employee. The Duncan Post Office was established in 1893, which should be an indicator of settlement in the area. The town is not incorporated. (242, 458)

Duncombe, Webster County. Duncombe was named after John F. Duncombe, who owned the property where the town was located. The first house was erected at the site in 1866. The town was incorporated on January 25, 1893. (438, 475)

Dundee, Delaware County. Dundee started as a station on the Chicago Great Western Railroad in 1887. The story put forth about the name is that a landowner who donated land to the railroad asked that the town be named for Dundee, Scotland. The community was incorporated on August 30, 1977. (163, 404, 438)

Dunkerton, Black Hawk County. Dunkerton was established on land provided by James Dunkerton in 1866. He had settled in the area in 1853. It was incorporated on March 18, 1899. (365, 438, 494, 570)

Dunlap, Harrison County. Dunlap was founded by John Blair on June 26, 1867, and named in honor of George Dunlap, a railroad official. It was incorporated in 1871. (312)

Durango, Dubuque County. A town named Durango was originally established at another location in the county. When the Chicago and North Western Railroad did not pass near the town, the settlers moved the town to a site known as Timber Diggings, which had been settled since 1834 as a lead-mining camp. The name Durango is a Spanish surname. After the Eighteenth Amendment was repealed, a number of the small, unincorporated towns feared they would not be permitted to have a tavern unless they were incorporated. The towns incorporated so that they could ensure the sale of beer in their communities. Durango was incorporated on June 5, 1933. (163, 344, 438)

Durant, Cedar County. Durant was established in 1854 on the Chicago, Rock Island and Pacific Railroad route through Cedar County. The town was named for Thomas Durant, a railroad official who owned some of the property at the town site. The community was incorporated on July 1, 1867. (258, 438)

Dyersville, Dubuque County. The town was named for the Dyer family who founded it in 1848. It was incorporated on November 9, 1872. (266, 267, 438)

Dysart, Tama County. Dysart was established as a depot on a rail line that ran past the location. Dysart came into being in 1872 and was named for an area resident, Joseph Dysart. It was incorporated on May 30, 1881. (71, 438)

E e ++++++++++++++++++++

Eagle Center, Black Hawk County. Eagle Center was probably named for its central location in Eagle Township. The township was named for the eagles that nested in an old oak tree located there. There was an Eagle Centre Post Office established in 1879, which would indicate that settlement had begun. The spelling was changed to Eagle Center a few years later. The town is not incorporated. (435, 458)

Eagle Grove, Wright County. Eagle Grove was originally platted as Eagle Grove Junction on April 5, 1881. The name was altered to Eagle Grove when the first post office was established. Eagle Grove was named from an eagle's nest in a large tree that all the settlers called the "Eagle Tree." The town was incorporated on October 16, 1882. (47, 438)

Earlham, Madison County. Earlham was named for a Quaker college in Richmond, Indiana. The town was established in 1869 with the advent of the railroad in the area and was incorporated on April 26, 1870. (375, 438)

Earling, Shelby County. Earling was named for the president of the Chicago, Milwaukee and St. Paul Railroad, a Mr. Earling. Earling was founded as Marathon by the Milwaukee Land Company on August 21, 1882, but the name was soon changed to Earling. It was incorporated on June 1, 1892. (438, 587)

Earlville, Delaware County. Earlville was established in October 1857 by the Iowa Land Company. The town was first known as Nottingham, but the name was changed to honor George M. Earl, the property owner. It was incorporated on June 12, 1882. (404, 438)

Early, Sac County. Early was platted by the Blair Town Lot and Land Company on October 4, 1882, and named in honor of a Judge Early. It was incorporated on June 22, 1883. (235, 438)

East Amana, Iowa County. Established in 1859 by members of the Amana Society, the village was named East Amana because it is east of the main colony of Amana. The name Amana was drawn from the Bible and means "to believe faithfully." East Amana is not incorporated. (19)

East Peru, Madison County. East Peru was established on November 7, 1888. When the railroad laid tracks through the area, it passed one mile south of the town of Peru. When a new town was built near the tracks, it was called East Peru. The community was incorporated on March 31, 1897. (376, 424, 438)

Eddyville, Wapello County. Eddyville was founded by J. P. Eddy, an Indian trader, in 1843. He named the town after himself. Eddyville was incorporated on February 22, 1900. (298, 438)

Edgewood, Clayton County. The site was first established as Yankee Settlement in 1856 at the site of a post office of that name that had been in existence since 1848. In 1874 the town was surveyed again. The town was not officially called Edgewood, but that it is what the people in the area called the community. Why that name was selected appears to be a mystery. The name did become official when the railroad named its station at this location Edgewood when it was established in 1876. Edgewood was incorporated on April 6, 1899. (163, 176, 438)

Edna, Lyon County. Edna was established on May 29, 1888, by the Cherokee and Western Town Lot and Land Company. The town was named for a girl who lived in George. Her brother was the inspiration for the name of George. Edna is not incorporated (163, 464)

Elberon, Tama County. Elberon was established on February 1, 1882, by the Milwaukee and St. Paul Railroad. The town was first called Halifax, but the name was changed to Elberon in honor of the location in New Jersey associated with President James Garfield. Elberon voted to incorporate on October 28, 1893. (71)

Eldon, Wapello County. Eldon was called Ashland Crossing by the railroad, Williamsburg by the Post Office Department, and Eldon by the people in the settlement. The town was founded in 1870 by Judge J. M. Love, Edward Johnston, William Leighton, and George Williams. Eldon was named for a British lord, John Scott, Lord Eldon, who served as chancellor in England from 1801 to 1827. Eldon was incorporated on April 29, 1872. (177, 298)

Eldora, county seat, Hardin County. A commission was appointed by the Iowa legislature to establish a county seat in 1853. The town was named by Mrs. S. R. Edgington. There is some confusion about why she named the town Eldora. One story says that she named the town for a heroine in a religious story that she had just read. Another story indicates that she had just read a book where that term was used and explained as Spanish for "the gilded." Yet another story is that she named the town for her daughter. The story about naming the town for her daughter seems very plausible as her young daughter, named Eldora, died in 1853. The town was established in July of that year. There is yet another suggestion as to the name. The area where the town is located had been the focus of gold hunters in 1851, and it is at least remotely possible that the name was an abbreviation of El Dorado to commemorate that failed adventure. Eldora was incorporated on July 1, 1895. (163, 272, 438, 528)

Eldorado, Fayette County. Eldorado was founded on November 5, 1852. The founders clearly thought that it was a special place since they used the Spanish term meaning "land of gold" for the site. The town is not incorporated. (163, 269)

Eldridge, Scott County. Eldridge was founded as Eldridge Junction by Jacob Eldridge in 1871. Eldridge was incorporated on June 1, 1900. (438, 509)

Elgin, Fayette County. Elgin, founded in 1849, was named for Elgin, Illinois. Elgin was incorporated on March 14, 1892. (269, 438)

Elk Horn, Shelby County. Elk Horn was founded on November 2, 1901. Elk Horn was named for the nearby Elk Horn Creek. The creek was named for an elk skeleton with a large set of antlers discovered when the area was being explored. The community was incorporated on February 28, 1910. (438, 515, 587)

Elk Run Heights, Black Hawk County. When it was founded in 1951, Elk Run Heights was named for the nearby Elk Run Creek. Elk Run Heights was incorporated on May 31, 1951. (97, 179, 438)

Elkader, county seat, Clayton County. Elkader was established in 1845 by John Thompson, Chester Sage, and Timothy Davis. The town was named by Timothy Davis for Abd El Kader, an Algerian emir who was widely known for his resistance to the French invasion of his country. Elkader was incorporated on May 1, 1891. (261, 438)

Elkhart, Polk County. The name Elkhart moved around Polk County before settling in its current location. The first Elkhart was established in October 1853. The town gradually faded away, but the post office, maintaining the name Elkhart, was moved to a little town, now gone, called Ottawa. Finally, Elkhart was established at its current location. The name was drawn from Elkhart, Indiana. Elkhart was incorporated on July 27, 1904. (289, 438)

Elkport, Clayton County. Elkport was founded on March 30, 1855. Situated at the mouth of Elk Creek, the town was named for its location. The community was incorporated on February 24, 1896. (261, 438)

Elliott, Montgomery County. The town was established on October 31, 1879, by the Chicago, Burlington and Quincy Railroad. Elliott was named for Charles Elliott Perkins, a vice president of the railroad. It was incorporated on March 14, 1882. (98, 403, 438)

Ellston, Ringgold County. First called Wirt, the community was established in 1881. In 1895, after the railroad established a station there, the town was required to change its name because it was thought that the name was too similar to Van Wert, another town in the state. The name was changed to honor a railroad employee named Eliston, but the name was adopted as Ellston. The town is incorporated, though it has been difficult to establish the date that occurred. (82, 181, 498)

Ellsworth, Hamilton County. The town was founded in October 1880 by John Blair for the Western Town Lot Company. Ellsworth was named in honor of Colonel Elmer Ellsworth, who died in the Civil War. It was incorporated on October 12, 1893. (182, 438, 528)

Elma, Howard County. Elma was founded in 1886 as a railroad town. Elma was named for the daughter of Lemuel Potter. He had owned the land where the town was established. The community was incorporated on July 11, 1891. (438, 542)

Elvira, Clinton County. Elvira was established on October 30, 1854, by the county surveyor, Amos Mathews. The name was given by W. H. Gibbs, the owner of the site, in honor of his wife. The town is not incorporated. (591)

Elwood, Clinton County. Elwood was founded by Kinsey Elwood and Barnabas Clark and their wives on November 26, 1873. The town was named for Kinsey Elwood. Elwood is not incorporated. (591)

Ely, Linn County. Ely was established on June 5, 1872, on property controlled by John Ely. The town was incorporated on August 12, 1903. (282, 438)

Emerson, Mills County. Emerson was named for Ralph Waldo Emerson by a railroad official according to a plan to name the towns from Red Oak to Glenwood for noted authors. The official plat of Emerson was filed on September 17,

1879, by Atkinson, Russell and Cushing, a town lot company. Emerson was incorporated on December 2, 1875. (409, 438)

Emmetsburg, county seat, Palo Alto County. The town was established when a group of farmers settled there in July 1856. It was named in honor of the Irish hero Robert Emmett. Emmetsburg was incorporated on November 11, 1877. (21, 163, 438)

Epworth, Dubuque County. Epworth was established on March 1, 1855, by Otis Briggs, Zephaniah Kidder, and Hezekiah Young, who were the property owners. The town was named in honor of the birthplace of John Wesley. Epworth was incorporated on October 20, 1879. (266, 438)

Essex, Page County. Essex was founded in 1872. The town was named Essex because Robert Wood, one of the founders, was from Essex, Massachusetts, and his parents were from Essex County in England. It is believed that Wood named the town for his former home in Massachusetts. Essex was incorporated on January 20, 1876. (128, 186, 438)

Estherville, county seat, Emmett County. Estherville was established when Robert and Esther Ridley built a house at the site in 1858. The town was named for Esther Ridley to honor the birth of her daughter, who was the first settlers' child born in the area. Estherville was incorporated on October 4, 1881. (187, 438)

Evans, Mahaska County. Evans was first known as Elida, for the Elida Coal Company. It was later known as Knoxville Junction and then finally as Evans when it was named in honor of D. J. Evans, a well-known resident of the town. The town was established around 1879. Evans is not incorporated. (339)

Evansdale, Black Hawk County. The community, an amalgam of several smaller, unincorporated settlements, actually came into existence when Evansdale was incorporated on November 13, 1947. The "Evans" in the town's name came from the name of the judge whom the citizens petitioned for incorporation, Judge William Evans, and the "dale" in the town's name came from the name of the attorney who represented them, Dale Van Eman. The settlements in the area that combined to form Evansdale had their beginnings around 1900. (202, 438)

Everly, Clay County. Everly was platted in 1884 and named Clark in honor of an area farmer. Another town in the state was already named Clarke, so the name was changed. There is no definitive proof, but the belief is that Everly was the name of the conductor on the railroad that brought many of the settlers to the area and that the town was named in his honor. Everly was incorporated on April 7, 1902. (99, 260, 438)

Exira, Audubon County. Exira was established on June 1, 1857, by Peoria Whitted on land owned by David Edgerton. Judge Daniel M. Harris is also credited with a great deal of involvement in the town's development. It was first proposed that the town be called Viola after one of Edgerton's daughters, but Judge John Eckman, from Ohio, a relative of a family living in the area, offered to buy a lot in the town if the town would be named after his daughter, Exira. The community was incorporated on December 13, 1880. (22, 438, 543)

Exline, Appanoose County. Exline was founded in 1874 by David Exline on land that he had purchased from Bob Benefield. The town was first called Bob Town in honor of the prior owner. It was later called Caldwell City in honor of a prominent local family. When a post office was established at the site in 1877, the postal department required that the village have an official name. The citizens decided to honor

David Exline. The town was incorporated on June 20, 1904. (26, 438)

F f ++++++++++++++++++++++

Fairbank, Buchanan County. Fairbank was founded in 1854 by F. J. Everett and C. W. Bacon. The name was suggested by Bacon, as that was his grandmother's name. Fairbank was incorporated on May 12, 1891. (85, 163, 438)

Fairfax, Linn County. The town was established as a railroad station in 1863. Fairfax was first called Vanderbilt in honor of the owners of the property where the town was located. The name was changed to Fairfax, a transfer name from Fairfax County, Virginia. The Forfax Post Office was established in 1852 and operated under that name until the name was changed to Vanderbilt in 1862. In 1863 the post office name was changed to Fairfax. Fairfax was incorporated in August 1930. (294, 456, 476)

Fairfield, county seat, Jefferson County. Fairfield's location was established on the first Monday in March 1839 by a legislative commission. The commissioners called it Fairfield, apparently because they thought that the site was attractive. It was incorporated on May 14, 1875. (277, 438)

Fairport, Muscatine County. Fairport was first established as Salem on April 20, 1839. The town site was then reestablished as Wyoming. It was informally known as "Jug Town" because of the clay deposits nearby and the potteries that operated at the site for many years. John Feustel and Elijah Sells were among the enterprising businessmen who established potteries at the site. At one time there were five potteries operating to meet the needs of stores and liquor houses up and down the river. The name was changed to

Fairport to denote a safe harbor on the Mississippi River and to reflect the name of John Feustel's boat, which he had used to deliver jugs and pots up and down the river, the *Fairport*. The town is not incorporated. (288, 318)

Farley, Dubuque County. Farley was established by the Iowa Land Company in 1856. The town was named for Jesse Farley, who had been instrumental in the railroad development in the area. Farley was incorporated on March 1, 1879. (266, 438)

Farlin, Greene County. Farlin was established in 1886 and named in honor of a Des Moines grain buyer, a Mr. Farlin, who hosted a long-remembered oyster supper to celebrate the naming of the town. The town is not incorporated. (531)

Farmersburg, Clayton County. Norman Hamilton surveyed the town in March 1858. The post office started at the site in 1854 had been called National. The name selected for the town clearly reflects the focus of the community, though it easily could have been transferred from towns with the same name farther east. Farmersburg was incorporated on June 1, 1902. (261, 438)

Farmington, Van Buren County. Farmington was founded in 1839. There were a number of early settlers in the area from Connecticut, so the name was probably drawn from Farmington, Connecticut. The community was incorporated on January 11, 1841. (163, 336, 438)

Farnhamville, Calhoun County. Farnhamville was established by Wilford Farnham and the Western Town Lot Company on August 15, 1881. The railroad that named the town indicated that it was named for a civil engineer, R. E. Farnham, although it should be noted the landowner was also named Farnham. In the original records, the name was Farnham. Farnhamville was incorporated on April 1, 1893. (528, 532)

Farragut, Fremont County. Farragut was platted along a Chicago, Burlington and Quincy Railroad track for John

Dennison in 1870. Dennison had purchased the town site. The town was originally called Lowland. Then it was called Lawrence. Finally, it was suggested that it be called Coyville, in honor of the man who had sold the property to Dennison, a Major Coy. The major demurred and suggested that it be named Farragut, in honor of Admiral David Farragut, a naval hero he admired. Farragut was incorporated on January 21, 1878. (438, 523)

Farrar, Polk County. The community was developed in 1902–1903 when the railroad ran track past the site. The Farrar Post Office was founded in 1904. Farrar was named in honor of one of the railroad employees involved in establishing the track past the town site. The town is not incorporated. (295, 458)

Farson, Wapello County. Farson was founded in 1903, after the Chicago, Milwaukee and St. Paul Railroad established a track through the area. The town was located on property owned by George Dickins, and the streets in the town were named after members of his family, so it can be assumed that the name Farson had some family meaning to him, unless it was a name associated with the railroad. The town is not incorporated. (34, 529)

Fayette, Fayette County. Fayette was founded in 1855 by Samuel Robertson and was incorporated on March 14, 1874. The town was named for the county. The county was named in honor of the Marquis de Lafayette, who participated in the Revolutionary War. (246, 269, 438)

Fenton, Kossuth County. The Western Town Lot Company established Fenton in 1899. It was named for a New York politician, R. E. Fenton. The town was incorporated on June 10, 1903. (438, 528)

Ferguson, Marshall County. The Milwaukee Land Company established Ferguson on February 1, 1882. The town was named for one of the settlers in the area. Ferguson was incorporated on December 4, 1906. (163, 438)

Fernald, Story County. Fernald was founded when a railroad laid track by the site. The Fernald Post Office was registered on February 28, 1903, shortly after the town was established. Fernald was named in honor of one of the first settlers in the area. The town is not incorporated. (371, 429)

Fertile, Worth County. Fertile was established on August 21, 1877, though the area had been settled since William Rhodes built a house there in 1856. The location was once known as Rhodes Mill for the original settler. Before Fertile was created, a land speculator created a fictional town, very close to the site for Fertile, that he named Fontanelle. The local population called his "paper town" Putsey. Fertile was named for the quality of the soil in the valley where the town was located. Fertile was incorporated on April 10, 1908. (138, 163, 438)

Festina, Winneshiek County. A house of entertainment was established at the location of the present-day Festina in the early 1850s. When a Catholic church was built at the site around 1853, replacing a nearby church that had been the victim of arson, the name Twin Springs was applied. The Twin Springs Post Office was established in 1856. The town was officially established on October 17, 1856. The name was eventually changed to Festina. The inspiration for the new name was from a Latin term used in Catholic vespers, *festina*, meaning "make haste slowly." The town is not incorporated. (155, 296, 458)

Finchford, Black Hawk County. Finchford was first called Newell's Ford, for Sam Newell, who owned the land where the ford was located. The area was first settled by Sam Newell's brother, David, in 1846. Sam joined him there in 1849, with other settlers joining them in the early 1850s. The name was later changed to Finch's Ford, for Josiah L. Finch, who constructed a mill at the location in 1867. Sullivan and Hannah Day founded the town of Finchford on September 27, 1871. The town is not incorporated. (36, 324, 405)

Floris, Davis County. Floris was established on July 7, 1854. The town's name was supposed to demonstrate the fertility of the area. The town was named by Dr. O. C. Udell and was incorporated on May 12, 1913. (151, 163, 438)

Floyd, Floyd County. Floyd was founded in July 1855 by James Griffith and Henry C. Tatum. The town wanted to be the county seat but lost out to Charles City in a court decision in 1859. Floyd was named for the county. The county was named either for William Floyd, one of the signers of the Declaration of Independence, or for Sergeant Charles Floyd, one of the men with the Lewis and Clark expedition. Floyd was incorporated on February 26, 1899. (246, 438, 456)

Folletts, Clinton County. Settlement started when William Follett established a ferry at the site in 1837. The Folletts Post Office was established in 1884. Service was transferred to Camanche in 1933. Folletts is not incorporated. (262, 458)

Fonda, Pocahontas County. Fonda was platted by John Blair, acting as an agent for the railroad, on September 10, 1870. The town was first called Marvin to honor Marvin Hewitt, then superintendent of the Illinois Central Railroad. There was some confusion in deliveries with the town of Manson, so in 1874 A. O. Garlock and George Fairburn took a post office directory and selected the name Fonda. There was only one entry in the nation for that name, and they liked it. Fonda was incorporated in 1884. (192, 194)

Fontanelle, Adair County. When Adair County was organized in 1855, three commissioners—George B. Hitchcock, Elias Stratford, and John Buckingham—were appointed to locate the seat of county government. They initially named it Summerset but later changed the name to Fontanelle. The name Fontanelle was used to commemorate the Omaha Indian chief Logan Fontanelle. The community was incorporated on August 23, 1871. (249, 438, 561)

Forest City, county seat, Winnebago County. Forest City was founded in September 1856 by Robert and Rebecca Clark, who owned the property. The town was called Big Brush and Hill City before the name was changed to reflect the amount of timber growing in the area. It was incorporated on June 14, 1878. (163, 303, 438, 449)

Ft. Atkinson, Winneshiek County. Ft. Atkinson was named for a nearby fort that had played a role in the early history of the area and in fact remained an army post until 1853. The fort was named for a hero of the Black Hawk War, General Henry Atkinson. The town of Ft. Atkinson was founded when the railroad laid a track and located a town near the original fort site in 1869. Ft. Atkinson was incorporated on June 5, 1895. (33, 438)

Ft. Dodge, county seat, Webster County. Ft. Dodge was established as a military post in 1850. The fort was named in honor of Colonel Henry Dodge. The community was incorporated on October 26, 1869. (129, 246, 438)

Ft. Madison, county seat, Lee County. The town was founded at the location of Ft. Madison, a military outpost that was erected in 1808. The first settlers at the town site arrived in 1832. Ft. Madison was incorporated by an act of Congress on July 2, 1836. It was last incorporated on February 5, 1851. (21, 438)

Fostoria, Clay County. Fostoria was established as a railway station in 1882. The town was named for Isaac Foster, who owned the land where the town was located. It was incorporated on January 30, 1912. (260, 438)

Franklin, Lee County. Franklin was first called Franklin Center when it was founded on March 21, 1840. The town site was located as a county seat by a legislative commission and possibly named for a town in Tennessee. It was incorporated in 1874. (163, 281)

Frankville, Winneshiek County. Frankville was founded by Frank Teabout, who settled in the area in 1851. The town is not incorporated. (33)

Fraser, Boone County. Fraser was established on September 21, 1893, by the Fraser Coal Company, represented by Hamilton Brown. The town was incorporated on February 8, 1904. (210, 438)

Fredericksburg, Chickasaw County. Fredericksburg took its name from that of Frederick Padden, its first settler and founder. The town was founded in 1856. Padden was one of the original proprietors. Fredericksburg was incorporated on December 18, 1894. (8, 438)

Frederika, Bremer County. Frederika was established on property owned by John Henry in 1868. The town was named after Frederika Bremer, the writer for whom the county had been named as well. Frederika was incorporated on March 28, 1896. (163, 253, 438)

Fredonia, Louisa County. Fredonia was at one time two towns, Fredonia and an adjacent village called Alimeda, which eventually became part of Fredonia. Fredonia was established as a ferry landing in 1836. Alvin Clark founded the town in 1836 just below the point where the Cedar River feeds into the Iowa River. It is thought that the town was named for Fredonia, New York. Fredonia was incorporated on May 30, 1874. (368, 438)

Fremont, Mahaska County. Fremont was founded by William Morrow on July 4, 1848. He named the town in honor of

General John C. Frémont. It was incorporated on March 14, 1883. (339, 438)

Froelich, Clayton County. Froelich was named for a family that had settled in the area. The town was established around 1882 after a railroad track was laid between Elkader and Beulah. Froelich is not incorporated. (180)

Fruitland, Muscatine County. Fruitland was first called Island. The town was established as a railroad depot in 1880. The current name reflects the large amount of produce grown there. Fruitland was incorporated in 1972. (203, 318)

Frytown, Johnson County. Frytown was also called Williamstown. The town was founded in 1854 by E. R. Williams. The name Frytown came from the Fry family who had settled there. The town is not incorporated. (330)

Fulton, Jackson County. Fulton was founded in 1851 by William Morden, an early settler. The reason for the name remains a mystery, although there are so many places in the country named for Robert Fulton that it is possible that it was a transfer name. The town is not incorporated. (323)

G g ++++++++++++++++++++++

Galesburg, Jasper County. Galesburg was founded by William Burton and his wife on August 22, 1853. There is no information on the origin of the name, though it seems reasonable to assume that it was transferred from Galesburg, Illinois. The town is not incorporated. (573)

Galt, Wright County. Galt was originally founded as Norwich on January 4, 1881, by a town lot company. The post office located there in 1882 was called Galtville to honor a man named Galt. The town's name was changed to Galt on April 18, 1888. Galt was incorporated on January 2, 1913. (47, 163, 438)

Galva, Ida County. Galva was named after Galva, Illinois, by Samuel Eldridge, who had moved to the area from that location. The town was founded in 1882 and was incorporated on September 26, 1889. (32, 438)

Garber, Clayton County. Garber was initially established as East Elkport in 1873 by John Garber. The name was changed to reflect the name of the town's founder. Garber was incorporated on November 18, 1907. (163, 261, 438)

Garden City, Hardin County. Garden City was founded as a station on the Des Moines, Iowa Falls and Northern Railroad in November 1901. The town was probably named descriptively. Garden City is not incorporated. (414)

Garden Grove, Decatur County. Garden Grove was established as a restocking point for Mormon travelers heading west. The first groups planted gardens there so later travelers would have supplies. The town was incorporated on November 14, 1879. (44, 438)

Garnavillo, Clayton County. Garnavillo was established as Jacksonville in 1844. The name was changed to Garnavillo in 1846, at the suggestion of Samuel Murdock, for an Irish town of that name. Garnavillo was selected as the county seat by popular vote in 1849. The community was incorporated on November 21, 1907. (261, 318, 438)

Garner, county seat, Hancock County. Garner was founded on August 23, 1870, and named for a railroad employee. It was incorporated on November 19, 1901. (242, 318, 438)

Garrison, Benton County. When the town was established in 1872, it was called Benton. In 1877, to avoid confusion with another town named Benton, the name was changed to Garrison. Garrison was the name of a family living in the area on whose property the town's post office was located. The town was incorporated on June 9, 1893. (438, 440)

Garwin, Tama County. Garwin was named for one of the original settlers in the area when it was established in 1879. It was incorporated on June 5, 1890. (292, 438, 528)

Gaza, O'Brien County. Gaza was originally established as Woodstock on April 18, 1888. The name was changed since there was another town in the state called Woodstock. Gaza was named after the biblical Gaza. The town is not incorporated. (460)

Geneva, Franklin County. Geneva was established in September 1871 by William McVey of Dixon, Illinois. The town was named for an area resident, Geneva Clock. Geneva was incorporated on April 7, 1903. (163, 270, 438)

George, Lyon County. George was founded by the Western Town Lot Company on November 28, 1887. The town was named for the son of one of the early residents. The man's daughter was the inspiration for the name of the nearby town of Edna. George was incorporated on March 27, 1890. (163, 438, 464)

Georgetown, Monroe County. There were two nearly adjacent towns, Georgetown and Stacyville. The original Georgetown was abandoned, and the name of Stacyville was changed to Georgetown. The name probably came from Curtis George, who had operated a post office in the area since 1852. Georgetown is not incorporated. (417, 425)

Germantown, O'Brien County. Germantown was founded on June 10, 1901, by Fred Kluender, George Eggert, and Edward Beerman. The town was named because many of the settlers in the area were from Germany. Germantown is not incorporated. (460)

Giard, Clayton County. Giard was established in May 1871. The town was named in honor of Basil Giard, who laid claim to some of the land in the area in 1795. Giard Township, Clayton County, was also named in his honor. Giard is not incorporated. (261)

Gibson, Keokuk County. Gibson started in the late 1880s as a railroad town. The town was initially called Nassau, but the name was changed in 1903 to avoid confusion with Nashua. Gibson was incorporated on December 14, 1954. (279, 438)

Gifford, Hardin County. Gifford was founded in 1875 by C. T. Gifford. The town was named for him. Gifford is not incorporated. (272)

Gilbert, Story County. Gilbert was first known as Gilbert Station when it was established in 1879. The town was named for one of the property owners, Hezekiah Gilbert. The community was incorporated on July 15, 1882. (28, 438, 528)

Gilbertville, Black Hawk County. Gilbertville was originally called Frenchtown. The town was founded in 1854, but when the community was formally recorded in 1856, the name registered was Gilbertsville. There are two reported possible explanations for the name. One is that since there were a number of settlers from France, the town could have been named for Gilbert, France. The other explanation is that the town was named by one of the founders, one of the Felten brothers, for his girlfriend's last name. When the town was incorporated on April 9, 1917, the name listed was Gilbertville. (201, 206, 236, 438)

Gillett Grove, Clay County. Settlers moved into the area starting in 1856. The town was named for the township, which was named in honor of the Gillett brothers who lived in the area. Gillett Grove was incorporated on May 13, 1874. When the town was moved from the west side of the Sioux River to the east side in 1899, the name traveled with the town. (260)

Gilman, Marshal County. Gilman was established on January 24, 1872. It was named for the chairman of the Iowa Central Railroad. Gilman was incorporated on April 24, 1876. (285, 438)

Gilmore City, Humboldt County. Gilmore City was founded on July 15, 1882, by E. L. Garlock and L. L. Taylor. It was named in honor of C. N. Gilmore, a railroad official. The community was incorporated on April 16, 1887. (163, 275, 438)

Gladbrook, Tama County. The name is an invented one, created by an official with the Chicago and North Western Railroad. The story is that the town was named in a roundabout way for nearby Wolf Creek. When the promoters were talking to the railroad officials in Chicago about the advantages of the site, they told the railroad representatives that Wolf Creek was at the site and that they were glad about the brook. No name had been proposed for the site, so Gladbrook was invented. Gladbrook was founded in 1880 and was incorporated on December 20, 1880. (292, 392, 438, 528)

Glenwood, county seat, Mills County. Glenwood was settled by Mormons in 1848. It was established by Dr. L. T. Coon and was originally known as Coonville. The name was apparently changed to reflect the wooded areas around the town site. Glenwood was incorporated on January 17, 1857. (163, 409, 438)

Glidden, Carroll County. Glidden was founded in 1867 and named for Captain W. Glidden, an advocate for railroads in Iowa. Glidden was incorporated on August 22, 1873. (74, 373, 438)

Goldfield, Wright County. Goldfield was established on February 5, 1858, by a Mr. and Mrs. Melrose, a Mr. and Mrs. Hanna, and O. W. McIntosh. It was the original county seat from 1855 to 1866. Goldfield was named in honor of a man named Brassfield. The citizens changed "Brass" to "Gold," thinking that it added more luster to the town's name. The town was incorporated on March 24, 1885. (47, 438, 528)

Goodell, Hancock County. Goodell was founded on December 16, 1884. The town was initially called Cashman after an area businessman. The name was changed to Goodell to honor a railroad financier, John Goodell. The community was incorporated on February 3, 1893. (242, 438)

Goose Lake, Clinton County. The first post office in the township was known as Boone Springs, or Boon Spring, when a post office was set up in December 1853. In 1871 the post office was moved to O'Brian's, a town that had been established along the railroad. O'Brian's was named for the first settler to build a house at the town site. When the post office was moved to the site, the name was changed to avoid confusion with Bryant, a nearby town. The name Goose Lake was drawn from the nearby lake, which was a favorite stopping spot of migrating geese. Goose Lake was incorporated on December 26, 1908. (438, 458, 528, 591)

Gowrie, Webster County. E. A. Lynd gained title to the land the town is located on in October 1870. He built a home and a store there. The town was named by a stockholder in the Des Moines and Fort Dodge Railroad in honor of Gowrie, Scotland, his hometown. Gowrie was incorporated on March 18, 1881. (438, 475)

Graettinger, Palo Alto County. The owner of a large tract of land in Walnut Township offered the railroad company a half interest in the location on his property where the railroad right-of-way passed on the condition that it place a town there. This was done in 1882, and the town was named after him. Graettinger was incorporated on September 30, 1893. (163, 398, 438)

Graf, Dubuque County. Graf was built on land given for that purpose by Christian Graf. A post office was established there in 1898 and remained in operation until the 1950s. After the Eighteenth Amendment was repealed, a number of the small, unincorporated towns feared they would not be permitted to have a tavern unless they were incorporated. The towns incorporated so that they could ensure the sale of beer in their communities. Graf was incorporated on August 30, 1933. (344, 438, 458)

Grafton, Worth County. Grafton was established in 1878 by the Chicago, Milwaukee and St. Paul Railroad. The station was named Grafton, for a person associated with the railroad. Grafton was incorporated on April 10, 1896. (138, 436, 438)

Grand Junction, Greene County. Grand Junction was founded in August 1869. The town was named for a railroad intersection at the site. Grand Junction was incorporated on May 6, 1872. (211, 438, 531)

Grand Mound, Clinton County. Grand Mound was created when a railroad station was established at the site in 1858. The intention was to call the site Sand Mound, for a sand hill in the region. When the name was recorded in 1866, there was a misspelling, and the name has been Grand Mound ever since. The town was incorporated on February 11, 1884. (438, 528, 591)

Grand River, Decatur County. Grand River was founded by E. C. Perkins in 1881. Grand River was named for the river of the same name that flows by the town. Grand River was incorporated on December 21, 1899. (44, 163, 438)

Grandview, Louisa County. Grandview's name came from the commanding view the site offers of the surrounding prairie. There was a post office established at the site in 1838. Grandview was founded by Alvin Clark and Robert

Childers in 1841 and was incorporated on February 18, 1901. (368, 438)

Granger, Dallas County. Granger was named for a railroad official, Ben Granger, when it was founded in 1885. The town was incorporated on September 6, 1905. (163, 212, 438)

Grant, Montgomery County. The town at this location was founded as Milford on June 29, 1858. There were two Milfords in Iowa for many years. Eventually, the Montgomery County Milford decided to change its name. To avoid confusion in the mail, the post office in the community had been named the Grant Post Office, in honor of General U.S. Grant of Civil War fame. Therefore it was logical that Grant finally became the name of the town. Grant was incorporated on February 27, 1912. (163, 403, 438)

Granville, Sioux County. Granville was named for either Lord Grenville, an English lord who had invested in the Northwestern Railroad Company, or for Sir Richard Grenville, a British adventurer who investigated the eastern coast of North America in the sixteenth century. The railroad company that named the town indicated that it was named for the explorer, so that seems the more credible explanation. The town was established on May 4, 1882, as Grenville. In 1884 the post office at the site was renamed Granville. It had been called the Ricker Post Office, so the change of the town's name was probably accomplished at the same time the post office's name was changed. Grenville had not been considered for a post office's name since it was thought that there would be confusion with the already established Greenville Post Office. The town voted to incorporate on May 22, 1891. (433, 438, 458, 528)

Gravity, Taylor County. Founded in 1881, Gravity drew its name from an area landmark, the Old Gravity Post Office, which was about a mile and a half west of the town. The

Gravity Post Office was possibly named because it was the "center of gravity" for the township. The town was incorporated on May 26, 1882. (163, 438, 520)

Gray, Audubon County. The town was named after its founder, George B. Gray. The community was founded on August 10, 1881. Gray was incorporated on November 10, 1894. (22, 438)

Greeley, Delaware County. The post office established at the site in 1854 was called Plum Spring. The town that was founded on February 24, 1855, was also called Plum Spring. In 1863 both the town and post office changed their names to Greeley in honor of journalist and politician Horace Greeley. The community was incorporated on July 8, 1892. (318, 404, 438)

Green Island, Jackson County. The Wickliffe Post Office was established at this site in 1847. The post office was renamed Green Island in 1874. The town was first known as Clarkstown because James Clark had donated some land for the town when the Milwaukee Railroad laid track in the area. The railroad later changed the name of the town to fit the terrain. When the area would flood, the only land to be seen for miles was the town site since it was located on a rise. Green Island is not incorporated. (323, 438, 458)

Green Mountain, Marshall County. The original Green Mountain was established on November 1, 1855. When the railroad came through the area in 1883, the town was moved so that it would be on the rail line. Green Mountain was named for Green Mountain, Vermont. The town is not incorporated. (163, 386)

Greene, Butler County. Greene was established some time between 1877 and 1879. The town was named in honor of Judge George Greene. The community was incorporated on July 15, 1879. (70, 163, 438)

Greenfield, county seat, Adair County. Greenfield was founded in September 1856 by Milton C. Munger. In 1875 Greenfield became the county seat of Adair County. The town is supposed to have been named for the quality and quantity of the vegetation in the area. Greenfield was incorporated on June 22, 1876. (163, 249)

Greenville, Clay County. The town was named Greenville because of the number of families named Greene living in the area. Greene was the first choice for a name, but there already was a town with that name. A post office was established there in 1871, but the town was not formally established until November 3, 1899. Greenville was incorporated on December 30, 1916. (135, 260, 438)

Grimes, Polk County. Grimes was named in honor of James W. Grimes, governor of Iowa from 1854 to 1858 and U.S. senator from 1859 to 1869. Grimes was founded in 1880 and was incorporated on June 7, 1894. (318, 438, 530)

Grinnell, Poweshiek County. Grinnell was named for its founder, J. B. Grinnell. With some partners, he established the town site in May 1854. Grinnell was incorporated on April 28, 1865. (290, 438)

Griswold, Cass County. The farm of John Rezner was purchased for the town of Griswold in November 1879. The town was named in honor of J. N. A. Griswold, one of the directors of the Chicago, Burlington and Quincy Railroad. Griswold was incorporated on December 13, 1885. (257, 438)

Grundy Center, county seat, Grundy County. Grundy Center is located near the geographical center of the county. The county was named for Felix Grundy, a prominent Tennessee politician. Grundy Center was founded on July 2, 1856, by Thomas G. Copp and John Overdeer. The county seat was located there in the fall of 1856. The name of the town was once changed to Orion, but for some reason the name Orion was never recognized in any official paper or documents. Grundy Center was incorporated on April 17, 1877. (246, 438)

Gruver, Emmett County. Gruver was named after Bert Gruver, an employee of the railroad. The town was initially called Luzon, but since there was already a Luzon in Iowa, the name was changed. The town was founded in 1899. Gruver was incorporated on February 4, 1913. (184, 220, 438)

Guernsey, Poweshiek County. Guernsey was named by the owner of the land, a Mr. Morton, who named it after his home county in Ohio. The town was founded in 1884 and was incorporated in 1906. (56, 474)

Gunder, Clayton County. Gunder was named for Gunnel Svenson. Svenson was from Norway, and his first name pronounced in English was Gunder. His family settled in the area in the mid 1860s. Gunder is not incorporated. (180)

Guthrie Center, county seat, Guthrie County. Guthrie Center was founded by E. B. Newton and William M. Tracey on May 6, 1856 and was named for the county. The town voted to incorporate on June 25, 1880. (271, 438)

Guttenburg, Clayton County. Guttenburg was named in honor of Johannes Gutenberg, the inventor of printing from movable type. The town's name was originally established with one t in the name, but the residents of the area were spelling it with two t's. As a consequence, it is now officially spelled with two t's. The town was called Prairie La Porte when it was founded on December 4, 1839. It was the original county seat of Clayton County. Guttenberg was incorporated on January 27, 1857. (261, 438)

H h ++++++++++++++++++++++

Halbur, Carroll County. Halbur was named for Bernard Anton Halbur, who came to Carroll County in 1872 after leaving Germany to escape military service. Halbur was established in 1882 and was incorporated on April 22, 1902. (74, 438)

Hale, Jones County. Hale was started in 1872 as a railroad station and post office and was named for J. P. Hale. It was initially called Hale Village and then shortened to Hale. The town was founded in April 1876 and is not incorporated. (142, 458)

Hamburg, Fremont County. The town was founded in 1857 by Augustus Borcher, who named the town for his hometown, Hamburg, Germany. Hamburg was incorporated on April 1, 1867. (221, 438)

Hamilton, Marion County. Hamilton was founded in 1849. At that time the town was known as "Jake's Ruin" because the surveying crew that laid out the town had been drinking as they worked. Jake Hendricks, a chain carrier, became so unsteady that he had to crawl and hold on to the tall grass to maintain his balance. Hendricks was the original owner of the land on which the town was built. He apparently became quite enthusiastic about strong drink after the surveying. His wife, who was distressed at her husband's behavior, told visitors one day that the town would be Jake's ruin. The name stuck as an informal name for the town. Most of the people involved in creating the town were from Hamilton County, Ohio, so the town was named after their home county rather that the more entertaining name of Jake's Ruin. The town was incorporated on April 11, 1900. (438, 594)

Hamlin, Audubon County. Hamlin Station was established in Hamlin Township on November 10, 1890. The township and the town were named for the Hamlin family. Hamlin is not incorporated. (22)

Hampton, county seat, Franklin County. The town site was selected as the county seat in March 1856. Hampton was founded by George and Harriet Ryan and James B. Reeve on June 2, 1856. When the town was established, R. F. Platt suggested naming the town for Hampton Roads in Virginia. Hampton was incorporated on November 19, 1870. (163, 270, 438)

Hancock, Pottawattamie County. Hancock was established by F. H. Hancock when the Carson branch of the Rock Island Railroad was completed in 1880. It was incorporated on May 16, 1891. (191, 438)

Hanlontown, Worth County. Hanlontown was founded on October 9, 1899, when the Chicago and North Western Railroad was built across the southwestern corner of the county. The town was named for the property owner, James Hanlon. Hanlontown was incorporated on January 18, 1902. (138, 436, 438, 528)

Hanover, Allamakee County. Hanover was started as a post office in Hanover Township. The post office was open from 1875 to 1885. It would seem reasonable to assume that the name was a transfer from Hanover, Germany, since there were a number of settlers in Allamakee County from Germany and some specifically from the Hanover region. Hanover is not incorporated. (1, 458)

Hansell, Franklin County. Hansell was established by George W. Hansell in 1881 and was named after its founder. It was incorporated on May 7, 1918. (270, 438)

Harcourt, Webster County. Harcourt was established by the Western Town Lot Company in 1881. The town was named for a British statesman. Harcourt was incorporated on February 11, 1896. (438, 528)

Hardy, Humboldt County. Hardy was established by the Cedar Rapids, Iowa Falls and Northwestern Town Lot Company on February 20, 1882, and was named after a railroad employee who had been killed in a derailment. Hardy was incorporated on April 13, 1915. (275, 438, 528)

Harlan, county seat, Shelby County. Harlan was founded by Dr. A. T. Ault in August 1858 and became the county seat in 1859. The town was named in honor of James Harlan, a prominent politician from eastern Iowa, and was incorporated on April 25, 1879. (438, 587)

Harper, Keokuk County. Harper was named after the magazine *Harper's Weekly* by Levi Whistler, who admired the magazine. The community was founded in June 1872 by John and Matilda Yerger. Harper voted to incorporate on November 17, 1879. (279)

Harpers Ferry, Allamakee County. The village was platted as Vailsville in 1851. The name was changed to Winfield in 1852 and changed by an act of the state legislature in 1860 to Harper's Ferry. David Harper had been active in business enterprises and had added operating a ferry to his interests. The apostrophe in the name was dropped in 1894. Harpers Ferry was incorporated on December 24, 1901. (230, 438)

Harris, Osceola County. Harris was built on property owned by A. W. Harris and Philip Proper. They established the town in 1889 and named it Harris, for the property owner. The community was incorporated in 1903. (438, 460)

Hartford, Warren County. Hartford was founded by John Hartman in 1846. The town was named both for him and for a ford across a nearby stream. Hartford was incorporated on June 29, 1913. (507)

Hartley, O'Brien County. Hartley was founded on April 18, 1881, by E. N. Finster, J. S. Finster, and Mr. and Mrs. Horace E. Hoagland. The town was named for the Hartley family from southeastern Iowa. The Hartleys would buy cattle in the area and drive them to a stockyard at that location for shipment. The railroad referred to the site as the Hartley Siding. There is another story that the town was named for a railroad employee. Hartley was incorporated on July 24, 1888. (163, 245, 273, 438, 460)

Hartwick, Poweshiek County. Hartwick was founded by the property owners, a Mr. and Mrs. Ostrom, on April 9, 1885. The town was named after Hartwick, New York, where Mr. Ostrom had been born. The town was incorporated in 1912. (474)

Harvey, Marion County. Harvey was established on December 12, 1876, by James Harvey and Mrs. J. H. Mitchell. It would appear that the town was named after James Harvey. The town was incorporated on December 12, 1903. (438, 594)

Hastings, Mills County. Hastings was situated at the intersection of the Chicago, Burlington and Quincy and the Sidney and Avoca Branch Railroad. It was established in the summer of 1870 and named for a railroad employee. Hastings was incorporated on May 26, 1879. (318, 409, 438)

Havelock, Pocahontas County. Havelock was founded and registered on November 23, 1881, by the Western Town Lot Company. The town was named for the British general Sir Henry Havelock and was incorporated on February 16, 1892. (192, 438)

Haven, Tama County. The town was founded as Eureka in 1854. The name was changed to Haven in 1874. In 1872 the Post Office Department had required a name change since there was another Eureka in the state. There is a clue to the reason for the name in that the Union Church located there was open to all Christians, and not restricted to members of any particular denomination, so in a sense it was a haven for all. Haven is not incorporated. (71, 292)

Haverhill, Marshall County. The town was founded on February 1, 1882, by the Milwaukee Land Company. It is believed that Haverhill was named for Haverhill, England. Haverhill was incorporated on July 12, 1968. (163, 238, 438)

Hawarden, Sioux County. Hawarden was founded in 1882 by the Western Town Lot Company. It was named for the estate of the British prime minister William E. Gladstone. Hawarden was incorporated on March 18, 1887. (438, 528)

Hawkeye, Fayette County. Hawkeye was established in 1879 by Charles Packwood. Since the nickname for Iowa is the Hawkeye State, it is reasonable to assume that the town was named with that in mind. The origin of the nickname is somewhat murky. It either could be from the 1826 novel *The Last of the Mohicans* or named for the noted Sac chief Black Hawk. There is some evidence that the proponents of the nickname intended it to be a tribute to Black Hawk. The town voted to incorporate on April 9, 1895. (189, 438, 561)

Hayesville, Keokuk County. Hayesville began as a store operated by Joel Winthrop Hayes in the 1860s, with a post office commencing operation in 1869. The town was named for Hayes. It was incorporated in 1916. (279)

Hayfield, Hancock County. Hayfield was founded on April 10, 1891. Madison was proposed as the name of the town, but the postal department requested that the town be renamed. Hayfield was selected because of the agricultural focus of the area. The town is not incorporated. (242)

Hazleton, Buchanan County. In 1853 E. W. Tenney opened a store at the site. A post office was soon established at the location and given the name Hazelton, because the settlement was in a hazelnut grove. When the railroad came through the area, it missed the original town site. The town was moved a mile to be by the railroad. The current site of the town was established on December 10, 1873. Hazleton was incorporated on July 12, 1892. (85, 239, 393)

Hedrick, Keokuk County. Hedrick was built on land owned by J. T. Brooks and W. H. Young. Hedrick was probably named after John Morrow Hedrick, a Civil War general from Iowa. The town was founded in August 1882 and was incorporated on April 23, 1883. (246, 279, 438)

Henderson, Mills County. In 1881 Joel Woods and his wife donated forty acres to establish a village, initially called Potter. Since there was already a town named Potter in Iowa, the citizens renamed the town Henderson. There are several possible explanations for the name. One is that it was named for Henderson, Illinois, where some of the settlers were from. Another possibility is that it was named for a Colonel Henderson who worked for the railroad. Dave Henderson allowed the railroad work crews to camp in his yard, so it is possible that the town was named for him. Another reason put forth is that it was named for David B. Henderson, who was a prominent politician, though he was not elected to national office until two years after the town was renamed. Henderson was incorporated on May 18, 1893. (207, 409, 438)

Hepburn, Page County. Hepburn was founded on December 9, 1872. The town was named in honor of an area politician, Colonel William Hepburn. It was incorporated on January 13, 1883. (438, 451)

Hesper, Winneshiek County. Hesper was founded by Russell Tabor and Ed Pew in 1857. Tabor, the property owner, gave the land for the town with the provision that liquor never be produced or sold there. The name is of Greek origin, meaning "evening" or "evening star." Hesper is not incorporated. (33)

Hiawatha, Linn County. Hiawatha was named from Longfellow's poem *The Song of Hiawatha*. Hiawatha was an actual person who lived in the late 1500s. He was a Iroquois sachem who united a number of tribes. The meaning of "Hiawatha" appears to be in dispute among scholars. Hiawatha lists its founding date as 1950, the year it was incorporated. (2, 438, 561)

High Amana, Iowa County. The community was founded in 1857 as one of the Amana Colonies. The name for the colonies was brought to Iowa by members of the Amana Society. The name is drawn from the Bible and means "to believe faithfully." High Amana is a physical description of its location in relation to the original colony. The town is not incorporated. (19, 163)

Highland Center, Wapello County. The Highland Centre Post Office was established in 1869. The site was a stagecoach stop. In 1882, when the Chicago, Milwaukee and St. Paul Railroad established a rail line through the area, a depot near the original Highland Centre was established, and the town was moved to the new site. The name was changed to Highland Center in 1892. The name was probably applied because of the town's location in Highland Township. Highland Center is not incorporated. (34, 458)

Highlandville, Winneshiek County. The town was established in Highland Township as a post office in 1868. Records indicate that settlement started in the area around 1851. The town appears to have been named for the township that it is in. The township name was a descriptive one for the geology of the area. Highlandville is not incorporated. (33, 155, 163)

Hills, Johnson County. Hills was originally called Hill's Siding due to a railroad siding being established in that location in 1876. The site was named for an area farmer, Thomas Hill.

The town of Hill's was established in 1900, and the name was altered to Hills when the community was incorporated in 1906. (100, 330)

Hillsboro, Henry County. Hillsboro was once known as Washington, but when it was decided to locate a post office at this point, the name was changed to Hillsborough because another town in the state was called Washington. Eventually, the spelling was altered to its current form. The town was founded in February 1840 and was incorporated on July 19, 1916. (273, 438)

Hinton, Plymouth County. The town was established in 1883 as Hinton Station and was named by one of the early settlers named Hinton. He was also responsible for naming Hinton, West Virginia. Settlement had started at the site by at least 1875, with a post office in service since 1870. Hinton was incorporated in June 1908. (294, 438, 458, 528)

Hiteman, Monroe County. Hiteman was founded on September 1, 1890, and named for an area landowner, John Hiteman. The town is not incorporated. (246, 426)

Holbrook, Iowa County. The Holbrook Post Office was established at the site of the present-day Holbrook on January 28, 1885. The town was named for Norman Holbrook, who was deeply involved in getting mail delivery to the area. Holbrook is not incorporated. (382)

Holland, Grundy County. Holland was established in August 1877 on land owned by Elias Marble. The town was named for the pastor of the German Presbyterian Church, who was a native of Holland. The community was incorporated on June 29, 1897. (220, 438)

Holly Springs, Woodbury County. The town was named after Holly Springs, Mississippi, by a Mr. Newell, who was from there. Newell established a store at the site in 1881. Holly Springs is not incorporated. (304)

Holmes, Wright County. Holmes was founded on March 11, 1895, by a Mr. and Mrs. Fraser. It was named for a congressman who had been helpful in establishing a post office at the site. The town is not incorporated. (47, 132)

Holstein, Ida County. Holstein was named after the province in Germany from which many of the settlers came. The town was founded in 1883. Holstein was incorporated on April 25, 1883. (32, 438)

Holy Cross, Dubuque County. The location was originally established as the Pin Oak Post Office. In 1856 George Gallon donated some land so that a town could be established. The town was first called Georgetown in his honor. The church at the site was called Holy Cross, for a large wooden cross that Bishop Mathias Loras had used to mark the church site. The town's name was changed in 1899 to the name of the church. Holy Cross was incorporated on August 20, 1898. (318, 344, 438)

Homestead, Iowa County. The Homestead Post Office was established in 1852. The site was purchased in 1860 by the Amana Society so that the colonies would have access to the railroad. A railroad track was being laid past what was a location with the simple descriptive name, Homestead. This is the only one of the seven colonies that does not have Amana as part of its name. Since it was an established site, albeit barely, the original name was maintained. It was probably simply a descriptive term for the site. Homestead is not incorporated. (19, 163)

Honey Creek, Pottawattamie County. Mormons driven out of Nauvoo, Illinois, were the original settlers of Honey Creek. When it was established in 1846, the town was named for the nearby creek. The creek was named for the large number of bees in the area. Honey Creek is not incorporated. (318, 528)

Hopeville, Clarke County. Hopeville was established in western Clarke County in 1851 as a commune first known as the Hopewell colony. The name probably reflected the founders' optimism in the venture. Hopeville is not incorporated. (43, 163, 348)

Hopkinton, Delaware County. Hopkinton was founded on December 29, 1851, on property owned by Leroy Jackson and Henry A. Carter. Carter had lived in Hopkinton, Massachusetts, and wanted the new town to carry that same name. Hopkinton was incorporated on March 3, 1874. (163, 404, 438)

Hornick, Woodbury County. Hornick was established by the Milwaukee Land Company on April 4, 1887. The town was named for an area landowner named Hornick. The town was incorporated on June 23, 1896. (163, 294, 438)

Horton, Bremer County. When the town was founded in 1856 by C. A. Lease, the names of three settlers were considered for the town's name, Allen, Lease, and Horton. George Horton was selected for the honor. The town is not incorporated. (252, 253)

Hospers, Sioux County. Hospers was established in 1872 by H. G. Randall for the St. Paul and Sioux City Railroad Company. The town was named in honor of Henry Hospers of Orange City, a successful banker and area landowner. Hospers was incorporated on December 6, 1890. (433, 438, 528)

Houghton, Lee County. Houghton was founded as a station on the St. Louis, Keokuk and Northwestern Railroad in 1880. The town was named for John Hough. Houghton was incorporated on February 19, 1962. (438, 519)

Hubbard, Hardin. Hubbard was established by the Chicago and North Western Railroad on October 12, 1880. The town was named in honor of Judge N. M. Hubbard, the attorney for the railroad. Hubbard was incorporated on November 1, 1881. (272, 438)

Hudson, Black Hawk County. Hudson was established on June 15, 1857. The town was first known as Greenfield, but the name was changed to avoid confusion with another Greenfield in Iowa. A number of settlers in the area were from New York State and wanted to name the town for the Hudson River. The village was incorporated on July 1, 1893. (163, 236, 438)

Hull, Sioux County. The town was originally called Pattersonville to honor the memory of John G. Patterson, who had been killed in a railroad accident. The citizens of Pattersonville signed a petition to change the name of the town to Hull in 1887. The name was selected to honor John A. T. Hull, a popular politician and Iowa's lieutenant governor at the time. The railroad officials wanted the name to be Winland but eventually accepted the name Hull. The community was incorporated on May 15, 1886. (433, 438)

Humboldt, Humboldt County. Humboldt was founded in 1863 and named Springvale because of the springs in the area. Since there was already a town with a very similar name in Iowa, the citizens looked for an alternative. The town was renamed for the county, which was named after an eminent German scientist and writer, Baron Alexander von Humboldt. Humboldt was incorporated in 1869. (101, 246, 275)

Humeston, Wayne County. Humeston was named after Alva Humeston, who had once owned some of the land used for the town site. Alva Humeston had also been an enthusiastic backer of the railroad that ran by the town. The town started when the rail line was completed in 1872. Humeston was incorporated on March 4, 1881. (46, 438)

Hurstville, Jackson County. Hurstville developed around a pottery built by Alfred Hurst in 1871. The town is not incorporated. (276)

Hutchins, Hancock County. Hutchins was named in honor of John Hutchins, who settled in the area in the 1880s. It was established on January 13, 1893, on land belonging to J. N. Inman and L. G. Inman. The town is not incorporated. (242)

Huxley, Story County. The town was initially called Bullards Grove. Huxley was named for a British scientist, Thomas Henry Huxley. It was incorporated on August 27, 1902. (163, 438)

I i ++++++++++++++++++++

Iconium, Appanoose County. There was a post office at the location called Iconium from 1853 until service was transferred to Mystic. The town was founded in 1854 and was named for the post office. The town was reestablished in 1857. The name Iconium was drawn from the Bible. Iconium is not incorporated. (163, 251, 458)

Ida Grove, county seat, Ida County. Ida Grove developed as a successor to a town named Ida. Ida had the bad fortune to miss being on a rail line. When the railroad passed by Ida, a new town was established on the rail line and called Ida Grove. Ida Grove was founded in June 1877. Most of the buildings in the old town were moved to the new location. The name Ida was drawn from the name of the county, which has several plausible explanations for its name. It could be named for Mt. Ida in Greece; it could be named for Ida Smith, the first settlers' child born in the area that would become Ida Grove; or it could be named for someone's wife or friend left in the East. It seems most plausible that it was named for Ida Smith. The "Grove" in the town's name apparently refers to the number of trees in the area. Ida Grove was incorporated on May 31, 1878. (32, 163, 438, 528)

Imogene, Fremont County. Imogene was founded in 1879 and named for the daughter of a Captain Anderson, one of the town's founders. It was incorporated on February 18, 1881. (226, 318, 438)

Independence, county seat, Buchanan County. In June 1847 three commissioners appointed by the state legislature visited the county. On June 15, they located the county seat and called it Independence, probably because of the proximity to the Fourth of July. It was incorporated on October 15, 1864. (85, 438)

Indianola, county seat, Warren County. Indianola was founded on November 17, 1849. The town was named for Indianola, Texas. P. P. Henderson suggested the name after he saw a newspaper article mentioning the Texas town. Indianola was incorporated on October 5, 1863. (438, 507)

Inwood, Lyon County. The town site was first called Warren and later Pennington. When the town was established in 1884, it was named Inwood by Mr. and Mrs. Jacob Rogers. While the reason for the name appears to not be recorded anywhere, one of the citizens of the community recalls seeing something in his great-grandfather's journal that indicated the town was given that name because the trains would stop to "put in wood." Inwood was incorporated on April 25, 1893. (102, 316, 438, 464)

Ionia, Chickasaw County. Ionia was founded as Dover, but there was confusion with a town in the area called Devan, so the name was changed to Chickasaw Station. Then there was confusion between the town of Chickasaw and Chickasaw Station, so the name was changed to Ionia. There is no definitive information about the naming of the town. Harold Dilts speculated that Ionia was possibly a transfer name from Michigan, with origins in Asia Minor. The local folk tale about the naming of the town goes like this: Around 1883 the railroad, which came through Chickasaw Station but not Chickasaw, said the town had to have a unique name. A railroad man came to town to talk to business owners about a new name, and one of them said to him, "I don't care what you call it, I own the lumberyard, I own that land, I own that building." And thus the railroad man declared, "We'll call it Ionia!" Ionia was incorporated on April 23, 1891. (8, 163, 317, 438)

Iowa Center, Story County. Iowa Center was established in 1854 and so named because of its physical location in the state. The town is not incorporated. (21, 163)

Iowa City, county seat, Johnson County. The town site was located in May 1839 by a commission charged with locating a territorial capital for Iowa. Chauncey Swan, one of the commissioners, oversaw the planning of the town during the summer of that year. The town was named Iowa City, as it was to be the capital of the Iowa Territory. It was incorporated on January 24, 1853. (318, 331, 438)

Iowa Falls, Hardin County. A town was organized at the site in 1854 and called Rocksylvania. The cofounder of the town, a Mr. Talbott, was adamant about the name for the town, though people settling there did not like it. Talbott sold his claim to his partner and moved to another location, where he started another Rocksylvania. The property was sold again in 1855, and the new owners established the town of Iowa Falls on June 28, 1856. Iowa Falls was named for the falls on the Iowa River near the town site. Iowa Falls was incorporated on May 14, 1869. (272, 438, 528)

Ira, Jasper County. The town was founded by William Rippey and his wife on December 3, 1883. Ira was originally called Millard. The town was renamed for someone named Ira. There is controversy as to whether Ira was a settler in the area or someone employed by the railroad. The town is not incorporated. (476, 573)

Ireton, Sioux County. Ireton was named in honor of the British general Henry Ireton. It was founded in 1882 and was incorporated on December 6, 1890. (433, 438)

Irving, Benton County. Irving was founded by Samuel Huton on October 10, 1855. The town was named by Levi Marsh for the writer Washington Irving. Irving is not incorporated. (246, 528)

Irvington, Kossuth County. The original town of Irvington was established in 1856 by George Smith, Lyman Treat, and Kendall Young. The town was either named in honor of Washington Irving or for Irving Clarke, the first settlers' child born in Kossuth County. The most probable explanation is that the town was named for Irving Clarke. In 1881 the Western Town Lot Company established a town on a rail line adjacent to the original Irvington. The new town was named for the old town of Irvington. Irvington is not incorporated. (163, 280, 528)

Irwin, Shelby County. Irwin was established by the Western Town Lot Company on May 30, 1881, and was named for the property owner, F. W. Irwin. Irwin was incorporated on May 20, 1892. (438, 528)

Ivester, Grundy County. Ivester was founded in 1871. The town was named for Charles Ivester Keiter, the popular editor of the Grundy Center newspaper, the *Atlas*. Ivester is not incorporated. (141)

J j

Jackson Junction, Winneshiek County. Jackson Junction was established as the New Alba Post Office in 1861. The Jackson Junction Post Office was established in 1883, so the renaming of the community was probably around that time. The town was named for the Jack family who had settled in the area. It was incorporated on October 9, 1897. (163, 438, 458)

Jacksonville, Chickasaw County. Jacksonville was founded in 1854. J. H. Dickens named the town for his former home, Jacksonville, Illinois. The town is not incorporated. (8, 472)

Jamaica, Guthrie County. Jamaica was first known as Sedalin, but the town was registered as Van Ness on February 21, 1882, by the Milwaukee Land Company. Reportedly, there was another town named Van Ness, and therefore another name needed to be chosen. The local story is that people could not agree on an alternative, so the mayor, wearing a blindfold, faced a map and placed his finger on the West Indies, specifically Jamaica. Another suggested explanation is that it could possibly be a transfer name from New York. The town was incorporated on January 4, 1901. (271, 561)

Janesville, Bremer County. Janesville was established by John Barrick in 1853 and named by him for his wife, Jane. It was incorporated on October 29, 1895. (21, 438)

Jefferson, county seat, Greene County. Jefferson was originally called New Jefferson. Lots in the town went on sale in 1856. The founders had wanted to call it Jefferson, to honor Thomas Jefferson, but the Post Office Department refused the name since there was already a Jefferson in Iowa. The "New" in the name was never really used by the community, and in 1868, when the Jefferson in Dubuque County changed its name, "New" was dropped. Jefferson was incorporated on November 20, 1871. (438, 531)

Jerico, Chickasaw County. The brothers Tolaf Johnson and Peter Johnson established a blacksmith shop at the site in 1869. A post office was established in the small settlement in 1887. Francis Dane, a pioneer in the area, named the post office Jerico for the Jericho mentioned in the Bible. The town is not incorporated. (58)

Jerome, Appanoose County. Jerome was named for Jerome Lyon, the son of Horace Lyon, a well-known citizen in the area. The town was probably established around 1855 when a Methodist church was organized there. The town is not incorporated. (170, 537)

Jesup, Buchanan County. When the Illinois Central Railroad built a track through the territory in 1860, the village of Jesup was created. The new town was named Jesup in honor of a railroad official. Jesup was incorporated on December 21, 1875. (85, 318, 438)

Jewell, Hamilton County. Jewell was founded in 1880 and originally known as Jewell Junction. Jewell was named for the property owner, David Jewell. It was incorporated on October 22, 1880. (228, 438)

Joetown, Johnson County. Joetown is another name for the village of Amish. Amish came from a family living there of that name. Joetown, the alternative and current name, came from a hotel operator named Joe Hollaway. The town grew from a hotel and livery built in the late 1840s or early 1850s. Joetown is not incorporated. (330)

Johnston, Polk County. The area has been settled since September 1846 when a Mr. and Mrs. Hunt founded Huntsville. Ridgedale was another community established at the site. When the Interurban Railway placed a depot at the site in 1907, it was named Johnston Station, for the station agent,

John Johnston. Johnston was incorporated on September 19, 1969. (333, 438)

Joice, Worth County. The Joice Post Office was established in 1900. Joice was named in honor of a banker, R. M. Joice. The town was incorporated on June 4, 1913. (438, 458, 528)

Jolley, Calhoun County. Jolley was established by James McClure for the Union Land Company in 1883. The town was named for an attorney working for the railroad, O. J. Jolley. The town was incorporated on November 16, 1895. (163, 438, 532)

K k ++++++++++++++++++++

Kalo, Webster County. Kalo was created when coal was being mined nearby at the Kalo Coal Mines in the 1870s. The town was located at the site of an earlier settlement called Hart's Ford, established in the 1850s. The name was drawn from the Greek word for "beautiful." Kalo is not incorporated. (196, 306, 475)

Kalona, Washington County. Kalona was established on August 6, 1879. The town was named Kalona at the suggestion of a Mr. Myers. The railroad officials who christened the town were not aware that Kalona was the name of a Shorthorn bull owned by Myers. Kalona was incorporated on May 22, 1890. (163, 299, 438)

Kamrar, Hamilton County. Kamrar was established as a rail depot in 1881 by the Western Town Lot Company. The town was named in honor of Judge J. L. Kamrar. The town was incorporated on June 6, 1896. (228, 438)

Kanawha, Hancock County. Kanawha was founded in May 1899. The first choice for a name was Luzon, but postal authorities declined the name, saying it was too close to

Luzerne in spelling. A railroad engineer suggested the name Kanawha, the name of a river in West Virginia. Kanawha was incorporated on April 18, 1902. (242, 438)

Kellerton, Ringgold County. The town was named in honor of Judge Isaac Keller of Mt. Ayr. It was founded in 1879 and was incorporated on December 3, 1881. (44, 438)

Kelley, Story County. A post office was established at the site in 1875. The town was named for J. T. Kelly, the owner of the town site. At first the town was called Hubbell in tribute to a railroad man, but the name was changed to Kelley. The current spelling of the town's name was done at the insistence of the Post Office Department. Kelley was incorporated on January 31, 1900. (16, 438, 528)

Kellogg, Jasper County. Kellogg was founded by Enos Blair and Dr. Abraham W. Adair on September 12, 1865, at a location that had been known as Manning's Station. The town was first called Jasper City. The railroad named the station at the site Kellogg for Judge Abel Avery Kellogg, and the post office was known as Kimball, named for the Iowa superintendent of the Chicago, Rock Island and Pacific Railroad, A. Kimball. The citizens of the community wanted to name the town for Kimball, but he demurred and the town was named in honor of the judge. The town was incorporated on February 6, 1874. (337, 438, 573)

Kendallville, Winneshiek County. The site was originally called Twin Springs. When S. G. Kendall opened a mill there in 1862, the settlement that developed was called Kendallville. The town is not incorporated. (33)

Kensett, Worth County. Kensett was founded on October 11, 1872. It was located on property owned by James Thompson, C. C. Gillman, and J. L. Sherman. Kensett was named for a Baltimore oyster packer who promised the town a church if the town was named it after him. He reportedly never built the church. The town retained the name, however. Kensett was incorporated on February 10, 1894. (138, 438)

Kent, Union County. Kent was established by the Burlington Town Site Company in 1869 as a railroad station. The town was named after a man who owned a nearby farm, a Mr. Kent. Kent is not incorporated. (163, 369)

Keokuk, county seat, Lee County. Keokuk was named after a chief of the Sac Indians. The name was first applied to the site on July 4, 1829. A Dr. Muir was the first settler, building a cabin at the site in 1820. A Dr. Galland actually founded the town when he planned it in 1837, though the town site was not registered until July 23, 1840. Keokuk was incorporated on December 13, 1848. (281, 438)

Keomah Village, Mahaska County. The community was established and was incorporated in 1973. The town was named for Lake Keomah. The lake, created in 1934, was given that name since it rests on the border between Keokuk and Mahaska counties. (339, 481)

Keosaqua, county seat, Van Buren County. Keosaqua was first settled in 1836. The town was founded in 1839. The name is of Indian derivation, but the meaning is in dispute. Keosaqua was incorporated on February 5, 1851. (318, 336, 438, 561)

Keota, Keokuk County. Keota was founded in 1872 by J. P. Yerger and C. H. Achard. The town was incorporated in December 1878. A Rev. Smock, a settler in the area, suggested the name Keoton from Keokuk and Washington counties. Either the railroad or the Post Office Department altered the name to Keota. (279, 438)

Kesley, Butler County. Kesley was founded in 1900. The town was named for a local farmer named Kesley Green. Kesley is not incorporated. (70, 528)

Keswick, Keokuk County. Keswick was established as a station for the Burlington, Cedar Rapids and Northern Railroad on October 16, 1879. A Mrs. Cameron, at whose home members of the railroad's track-laying crew had stayed, was given the honor of naming the new town. She named the town for her former home, Keswick, England. Keswick was incorporated on July 5, 1912. (341, 438)

Keystone, Benton County. Keystone was founded in 1881 and was incorporated on December 15, 1893. There are two possible explanations for the name of the town. One possibility is that the town was the midpoint between Chicago and Omaha on the rail line and was therefore a key or keystone on the line. The other possibility is that when the town was being established by the railroad, railroad officials mistook the German settlers for Pennsylvania Dutch and named the town for Pennsylvania, the Keystone State. (103, 438)

Kilduff, Jasper County. Kilduff was founded by Timothy Kilduff and his wife on January 5, 1884. The town was named after the founders. Kilduff is not incorporated. (573)

Kimballton, Audubon County. Kimballton was founded by Hans Jensen Jorgensen in 1883 when he opened a post office at the site. The town was not officially established until June 22, 1888. It was named for Edward Kimball, a railroad employee. The town was first named Kimballtown. The name has been abbreviated over time. Kimballton was incorporated on June 5, 1908, (163, 342, 438)

Kingsley, Plymouth County. The town site was founded in 1880 as Quorn. The town was established as Kingsley by the Blair Town Lot and Land Company in 1884 and was incorporated that same year. The town was named for Henry Kingsley, who sold the town site to the land company. (294, 528)

Kingston, Des Moines County. Kingston was founded in 1853 by W. King. The town was initially called Kings Town. Kingston is not incorporated. (24, 65)

Kinross, Keokuk County. Kinross was organized in March 1854. The town was named for a township in Henry County, Indiana, by William J. Watkins. Watkins had once lived in that township in Indiana. Kinross was incorporated on September 10, 1898. (279, 438)

Kirkman, Shelby County. Kirkman was established on October 22, 1880, by the Western Town Lot Company. It was named for a railroad official, M. M. Kirkman, and was incorporated on July 6, 1892. (438, 528, 587)

Kirkville, Wapello County. The first house in Kirkville was erected between 1852 and 1853. The town was named after John Kirkpatrick, who founded the town. Kirkville was incorporated on December 2, 1883. (163, 298, 438)

Kiron, Crawford County. Old Kiron was founded by A. Norelius in 1868. The town was first informally called both Swedeboy and Swedeburg, but the residents were not comfortable with those names. The town was named for a community in Manchuria by Lars Olson and A. Norelius. The reasons were not recorded. When the railroad came through, a new town site was established by the Western Town Lot Company in 1899. There was an exodus from the original site to the new location. Kiron was incorporated in 1900. (407)

Klemme, Hancock County. Klemme was named for Harmon J. Klemme, owner of the land where the town was located. The town was established on October 18, 1889. Klemme was incorporated on February 9, 1899. (242, 438)

Knierem, Calhoun County. Knierem was founded on November 16, 1899, by William and Wilhelmina Knierem, and the town was named after its proprietors. Knierem was incorporated on May 13, 1901. (438, 532)

Knoxville, county seat, Marion County. Knoxville was created by a commission appointed by the state legislature to locate a county seat for Marion County. Isaac B. Power established the town in September 1845. In 1847 the postmaster, a Mr. Babbitt, who did not like the name Knoxville, approached the legislature with a suggestion for a name change to Osceola. The legislature, under the assumption that this change was favored by the citizens of the area, passed a bill changing the name. When the community residents got wind of this action, a petition was raised and signed by almost everyone in the town. A bill to rescind the name change was hastily constructed and passed. The only problem was the legislation did not reinstate the name Knoxville, so for a few days the town was officially nameless. The legislature quickly corrected that oversight. The name Knoxville is drawn from a hero of the American Revolution, General Henry Knox. Knoxville was incorporated on January 24, 1855. (163, 438, 594)

L l ++++++++++++++++++++

La Motte, Jackson County. The town was named for one of its founders, Alexander La Motte. La Motte was platted on November 10, 1873. The town voted to incorporate on May 24, 1879. (276)

La Porte City, Black Hawk County. La Porte City was first called La Porte, but the name was changed because of another La Porte in the state. The town was established on July 16, 1855. One of the founders, a Dr. Watson, named the town after his old home in Indiana. La Porte City was incorporated on February 11, 1871. (236, 347)

Lacona, Warren County. Lacona was founded by Samuel Myers and Willis Clevenger in 1856. It probably was named by J. C. Lally for his prior home in Greece, Lacona Prairies. Another possibility is that the town's name is a contraction of the name of the nearby Lake Ona. Lacona was incorporated on November 25, 1881. (163, 438, 507)

Ladora, Iowa County. Ladora was founded on October 25, 1867, by James A. Paine. It was incorporated on December 27, 1879. The town was named by a Mrs. Scofield, a music teacher, who suggested using the musical syllables la, do, and ra (re). (164, 438)

Lake City, Calhoun County. Lake City was named for the nearby Lake Creek. The creek earned its name because it flowed out of a lake. The town was established by the Western Town Lot Company in 1885 and was incorporated on March 14, 1887. (438, 528)

Lake Mills, Winnebago County. Lake Mills was founded on December 31, 1869, by the property owners, Charles and Janet Smith. The site was originally called Slaunchville. The town's name was changed when a post office was established. The residents did not want Slaunchville as an address. Slaunchville apparently was applied to refer to the swamp surrounding the town. Lake Mills was suggested because there was both a mill and a lake at the site. The community was incorporated on June 7, 1880. (303, 438, 528)

Lake Park, Dickinson County. Lake Park was incorporated on June 7, 1880. The town site was first a post office called Austin, established in 1872. The name was changed to Lake Park in the early 1880s to reflect the town's location on Silver Lake. (438, 521)

Lake View, Sac County. The town was first called Fletcher. The name was changed to Lake View to reflect the view of Wall

Lake from the site. Lake View was established by the Blair Town Lot and Land Company on August 2, 1877. The community was incorporated on October 29, 1887. (235, 438, 528)

Lakeside, Buena Vista County. The town site was originally part of a farm called Lakeside Stock Farm. A post office was established there in 1878, which would correspond with the development of the settlement. The assumption is that the town drew its name from the farm. Lakeside was incorporated on July 15, 1933. (163, 438, 458)

Lakota, Kossuth County. The town was called Germania when it was founded on October 10, 1893. The name was changed during World War I when there were strong sentiments about Germany and all things German. The name reflects the fact that the town site was once part of the Sioux territory and means "allies" in the Teton dialect. Lakota was incorporated on October 1, 1918. (10, 318, 438, 561)

Lambs Grove, Jasper County. The community was established in 1927 by E. C. and Jennie Ogg. Lambs Grove was named for Jennie Ogg's father, Richard Lamb. Lambs Grove was incorporated on December 29, 1952. (349, 438)

Lamoille, Marshall County. Lamoille was founded in 1867 by John Stevens. The town was named for the Lamoille River in Vermont. Lamoille is not incorporated. (285, 528)

Lamoni, Decatur County. Lamoni was established in 1879 by Mormon settlers when a railroad ran track through the area. Lamoni was named after a king recorded in the Book of Mormon. The community was incorporated on October 15, 1885. (44, 318, 438)

Lamont, Buchanan County. Lamont was originally called Erie. A post office was established at the site in 1875 with that name. Seymour Whitney deeded the land where the village stood and built the first house. A Mr. Ward was established as postmaster, and he changed the name to Wards Corners in honor of himself. When G. M. Foster became postmaster in 1883, he apparently changed the name. Some authorities claim the railroad changed the name, but others attribute the change to Foster. Lamont was established as a town on December 14, 1886, and was incorporated on December 10, 1891. No credible information about the reason for the name change was located, but Lamont is a Scottish surname, and there were Lamonts living in northeastern Iowa at that time. There were also other places named Lamont in existence at the time, so the name could be a transfer. (85, 104, 438)

Lanesboro, Carroll County. Lanesboro was founded in 1901 when a rail line was established in the area. The town was named for Julius Lane, an early area settler and Civil War veteran who owned the land on which the town was built. Lanesboro was incorporated on April 30, 1903. (74, 373, 438)

Langdon, Clay County. The town was founded in 1899 and named for the first president of the Minneapolis and St. Louis Railroad, Robert Bruce Langdon. Langdon is not incorporated. (260)

Langworthy, Jones County. Langworthy was founded by Colonel W. T. Shaw on January 2, 1858. The town was named in honor of a former president of the Dubuque Western Railroad, Lucius Langworthy. Langworthy is not incorporated. (142, 163)

Lansing, Allamakee County. Lansing was first occupied in 1848 by a man named Garrison. He named the new site after the town that he was from, Lansing, Michigan. The town was established in 1851 and was incorporated on July 1, 1867. (9, 14, 230, 438)

Lanyon, Webster County. Lanyon was named for a railroad surveyor named Lanyon. Lanyon was a Swedish settlement, part of the migration from Knox County, Illinois. Settlers started moving into the area in 1860, with the bulk of the settlement taking place after 1866. Lanyon is not incorporated. (457)

Larchwood, Lyon County. Larchwood was founded by J. W. Fell in 1870 and was named because of the number of larch trees planted by Fell. Larchwood was incorporated on January 6, 1892. (318, 438)

Larrabee, Cherokee County. Larrabee was founded on November 25, 1887, by A. H. Meservey and J. P. B. Primrose. The town was named in honor of William Larrabee, who was governor of Iowa at the time. Larrabee was incorporated on July 25, 1896. (318, 401, 438)

Latimer, Franklin County. Latimer was founded by J. F. Latimer on property owned by C. L. Clock in 1883. The town was named for its founder. It was incorporated on April 17, 1901. (197, 270, 438)

Laurel, Marshall County. The first Laurel in the area was located about two miles from where Laurel is now located. That town was named by Rufus H. Archerd for Laurel, Ohio. Archerd came to Iowa from that location. The current town was established on December 30, 1880, along the Iowa Central Railroad and was incorporated on April 23, 1903. (328, 351, 438)

Laurens, Pocahontas County. Laurens was established in 1881 by the Western Town Lot Company. The town was named in honor of Henry Laurens and John Laurens, a father and son who were heroes of the Revolutionary War. It was incorporated on April 30, 1890. (192, 438)

Lawler, Chickasaw County. The early records of the establishment of Lawler were lost in a fire. There is a newspaper account of a group planning to build a railroad depot at the site on November 14, 1868. The town was named for John Lawler, who was affiliated with the McGregor and Sioux City Railroad. The depot was established in July 1869. Lawler was first incorporated in 1871, but because those records were lost, the town was reincorporated on April 28, 1873. (8, 438)

Lawton, Woodbury County. Lawton was established in 1901 by the Western Town Lot Company. The town was first called Truxton but was renamed by Joseph Law, for Lawton, Michigan. It was incorporated in 1906. (438, 528, 575)

Le Claire, Scott County. Le Claire was founded in 1837 and named for Antoine Le Claire, an important figure in Iowa's history. He was one of the owners of the property where the town was located. Le Claire was incorporated on January 13, 1855, combining Middletown, Parkhurst, and Le Claire under one municipal government called Le Claire. (438, 509)

Le Grand, Marshall County. M. Webb and James Allman founded the town in 1850. The town was named for Le Grand Byington, a lawyer from Iowa City. Le Grand was incorporated on May 9, 1891. (285, 438)

Le Mars, county seat, Plymouth County. Le Mars was established by John Blair on June 4, 1870. The town was named in September 1870 when a party made up of Blair and his family, W. W. Walker, Mrs. John Weare, a Mrs. Reynolds, a Miss Underhill, a Mrs. Swain, a Mrs. Parsons, Mrs. George Weare, Mr. and Mrs. William Smith, Mrs. John Cleghorn, a Colonel Wayne, and a Mr. Anable came by special train to the town site. The town was named by having the women write down the initials of their names, and then combining and arranging them for possible town names. Lemars was selected. Usage has changed the format to Le Mars. It was incorporated on May 25, 1881. (294, 438)

Le Roy, Decatur County. Le Roy was established as a station on the Humeston and Shenandoah Railroad in 1880 and initially spelled Leroy. The town was named for the man who donated the land for the town, Leroy Buffman. It was incorporated on June 6, 1904. (44, 394, 438)

Leando, Van Buren County. The town was established in 1838, though it was not formally registered until 1847. There is some controversy about the evolution of the name. Some sources indicate that the original post office was established as Portland as early as 1838, though post office records indicate that the office was established in 1840. The story then goes that the postal department requested that the name be changed, and the name was changed to Leando in 1840. Post office records indicate that the Leando Post Office was not established until January 1883, and the Portland Post Office ran from 1840 until 1864. There is some information that indicates the name was initially Leander and that it was altered to Leando over time, though the records of the post offices do not confirm that. The origin of the name is still a mystery. The town is not incorporated. (217, 487)

Ledyard, Kossuth County. Ledyard was founded in 1884 by the Western Town Lot Company. The town was named for a town in New England. It was incorporated on April 16, 1895. (318, 438, 528)

Lehigh, Webster County. Lehigh was established by Oliver Tyson, who operated a sawmill at the site. The town was originally called Slabtown because of the sawmill. The name was changed to honor the Lehigh coal fields in Pennsylvania. Coal was mined in this area of Iowa starting in 1858. The town was incorporated on February 10, 1883. (438, 475)

Leighton, Mahaska County. Leighton was founded in 1865 by William Leighton, John Carver, and W. A. Burt and was named for William Leighton. It was incorporated on September 21, 1909. (339, 438)

Leland, Winnebago County. Leland was established on July 15, 1887. The town had been founded under the sponsorship of John D. Leland. The community was incorporated on February 28, 1895. (303, 438)

Lenox, Taylor County. Lenox was founded in 1871 as Summit, when a branch line for the Chicago, Burlington and Quincy Railroad was completed through the county. The town was renamed for the daughter of an officer of the railroad. Lenox was incorporated on July 2, 1875. (163, 293, 438)

Leon, county seat, Decatur County. Leon was first named Independence when it was founded in 1853. There already was an Independence in Iowa, so the name was altered to South Independence to avoid confusion. The town's final name was suggested by George Moore, who had been in California, where he had become familiar with that name. Leon was incorporated on June 2, 1867. (44, 438)

Lester, Lyon County. Lester was originally going to be called Cleveland, but when a man was killed in a snowstorm, the town was named in his memory. Lester was established by a Mr. and Mrs. Thomas on November 29, 1889, and was incorporated in 1892. (356, 464)

Letts, Louisa County. Letts, originally called Ononwa, was founded by Joseph A. Green on October 6, 1855. In April 1868 S. C. Curtis presented a petition to the board of supervisors to change the name of the town to Lettsville because of the similarity in names of Ononwa to another Iowa town, Onawa. Lettsville was officially adopted in June 1868. The post office was named Letts, the name the town carries today. Letts was incorporated on July 28, 1877. (438, 526)

Lewis, Cass County. Lewis was established on February 6, 1854, as the county seat. The name was inspired by the county name. Cass County was named for Lewis Cass, a U.S. senator who had helped sponsor treaties with the

Indians that had opened the area for settlement. Lewis was incorporated on May 14, 1874. (257, 318, 438)

Liberty Center, Warren County. A post office was established at the site on March 7, 1865, and called Liberty Centre. The name was changed to Liberty Center on December 8, 1893. The name appears to reflect community sentiment regarding the Civil War. The town is not incorporated. (246, 315)

Libertyville, Jefferson County. The settlement was originally known as the Colony, or the Little Colony. On July 4, 1842, the settlers renamed their village Libertyville. Clearly the name reflects a sense of patriotism. There is information that the town was officially established in 1845. The town's citizens thought that the community had been incorporated in 1924, but when they discovered that it was not, Libertyville was incorporated in 1974. (163, 277, 358)

Lidderdale, Carroll County. Lidderdale was created when the Chicago Great Western Railroad ran track through the county in the late 1860s. The town was named for Lord Lidderdale, an Englishman who was a stockholder in the railroad. It was incorporated on November 27, 1905. (74, 373)

Lime Springs, Howard County. The first Lime Springs was settled by Oscar Chesebro and Joseph Knowlton in 1854. When the railroad put track through the area in 1868, it missed the old town by about three-quarters of a mile. A new town called Lime Springs Station was established near the track and near the old town. The post office in the new town was called the Glen Roy Post Office to distinguish it from the post office in the old town. It can be assumed that the name at the original site was a literal one for a spring or springs there. Lime Springs was incorporated on April 17, 1876. (8, 438)

Linby, Jefferson County. Linby was established as a depot at a railroad intersection in 1902, but there appears to be no record as to why it was so named. Perhaps it was a transfer name from England. Linby, Nottingham, is famous for two things, the invention of pancakes and the valor of its women. When the Danes invaded the town, the local men ran away. The women in the village killed the invaders. Perhaps Linby, Iowa, was named to describe the character of the women living there. The town is not incorporated. (360, 463)

Lincoln, Tama County. The Spencers started a post office at the site of the present-day Lincoln. They could not call it Spencer since there already was one in Iowa. Mr. Spencer then wanted to call it Augusta, for his wife, but there was a town in Iowa with that name as well. Augusta Spencer then proposed that it be called Bellin, for a town in Scotland. When the name was submitted to the Post Office Department, there was a problem in reading the name. The postal department assumed that due to the number of German settlers in the area, the name was Berlin and registered it as such. During World War I, when anti-German sentiment was high, the town's name was changed to the name of the township in which it was located. Since Lincoln Township was established in 1861, it seems possible that it was named for President Abraham Lincoln. The town was established in 1883 and was incorporated in 1913. (71, 292)

Linden, Dallas County. Linden was named for the linden trees found in the area. It was established in 1878 and was incorporated on January 12, 1893. (237, 438)

Lineville, Wayne County. Lineville was named because of its proximity to the state line. The first house was built there in 1851 by Alexander Faulkner. Faulkner sold general merchandise on the Iowa side of the house and liquor on the Missouri side. The town was incorporated on November 6, 1871. (46, 438)

Linn Grove, Buena Vista County. Linn Grove was founded in 1855 and was incorporated on March 4, 1912. The town was named for a grove of linden trees at the site when it was surveyed in 1855. (218, 364, 438)

Lisbon, Linn County. Lisbon was established by John Kurtz, John Eby, and Michael Hoover in May 1851. Kurtz named the town for Lisbon, Portugal. Lisbon was incorporated on February 10, 1875. (282, 438, 528)

Liscomb, Marshall County. Liscomb was planned and founded by J. W. Tripp in 1869. The town was named for H. P. Liscomb, a railroad official. It was incorporated on March 23, 1874. (285, 438)

Little Cedar, Mitchell County. Little Cedar was originally named Wheeler when it was established in 1891. In 1896 the name was changed to avoid confusion with another town named Wheeler. Little Cedar referred to the number of cedar trees in the area. The town is not incorporated. (286)

Little Rock, Lyon County. The town was established by the Cedar Rapids and Iowa Falls Town Lot Company on November 4, 1884. It was named for the nearby Little Rock River. Little Rock was incorporated on November 26, 1894. (346, 438, 464)

Little Sioux, Harrison County. Little Sioux was founded on October 1, 1855, and was named because it is situated by the Little Sioux River. Little Sioux was incorporated on November 26, 1883. (312, 438)

Littleport, Clayton County. Littleport was established in 1857 by Dennis Quigley, who had lived at the site since 1846. The location had been used as a council location by the Indians in the region. Quigley is credited with naming the town as a "little port" on the Volga River. Littleport was incorporated on November 21, 1907. (163, 261, 438)

Littleton, Buchanan County. Littleton was first settled by Thomas Little in 1853. The town was established in 1856. Littleton is not incorporated. (61)

Livermore, Humboldt County. The town was originally going to be named Washburne, as that was the name applied to the planned town in 1879. The name Washburne was to honor Cadwalader Washburn, who was influential in establishing the railroad in the area. The name was probably changed to avoid confusion with a Washburn that was being established in Black Hawk County. The town of Livermore was formally established on January 24, 1880, by G. W. Bassett, A. McBane, and W. M. Grant. There is no firm proof as to why that name was selected, though some in the community believe that it was named for a railroad employee. Since Livermore, Maine, was the birthplace of Washburn, it seems more likely that the name was probably a transfer from that site. Livermore was incorporated on March 11, 1882. (130, 275, 438)

Lockridge, Jefferson County. The site was first settled when W. G. Coop established a trading post there in 1836. Coop then founded the town of Lockridge in 1837, and the Lockridge Post Office developed in 1840. The town was formally established in 1874. Lockridge was named for the ridges over the Lick and Wolf creeks, which intersect and appear to lock. Lockridge was incorporated on June 17, 1913. (21, 163, 204, 318, 438, 513)

Logan, county seat, Harrison County. The town was established by Henry Reel on July 19, 1867. Logan was named in honor of Civil War general John A. Logan. It was incorporated on April 22, 1876. (312, 438)

Lohrville, Calhoun County. In 1881 the Western Town Lot Company established the town on land owned by Jacob A.

and Mary E. Lohr, from whom the town takes its name. Lohrville was incorporated on December 14, 1882. (438, 532)

Lone Rock, Kossuth County. The Western Town Lot Company established the town in 1899. It was named for a rock found when the town was being surveyed. Lone Rock was incorporated on August 5, 1915. (438, 528)

Lone Tree, Johnson County. Lone Tree was established by John Jayne in 1872. It was named after a large white elm that grew there and was the only tree for many miles. Lone Tree was incorporated on May 20, 1890. (331, 438)

Long Grove, Scott County. Long Grove was settled in 1838 and was named for the large grove of timber that was nearby. It was incorporated on August 1, 1912. (438, 509)

Lorimor, Union County. Lorimor was named for the man who donated the land for the town, J. S. Lorimor. The town was established in 1877 and was incorporated on December 16, 1892. (163, 318, 438)

Lost Nation, Clinton County. There are several accounts about the possible origins of the name Lost Nation. One version, not widely credited, is that a tribe of Indians starved and froze to death in the area in earlier times. A more popular option is that a man named Balm was looking for some relatives living in the area, and when he was asked where he was going replied that he was looking for the "lost nation." H. V. Cook is said to have come to the area to buy stock from Balm, after Balm had settled there. Since it took Cook a day and a half to find Balm's cabin, he is reputed to have called it the "lost nation." Another possibility is that a group of hunters noted a little settlement, and one of them commented about the little nation. Another member of the party replied that given the location, it was more likely a lost nation. The Sabula, Ackley and Dakota Railroad established a station at this point in 1871 and named it Lost Nation because the surrounding countryside had been called that for some time. The town surrounding the station was founded on July 11, 1872, by a Mr. and Mrs. Long. Lost Nation voted to incorporate on June 9, 1903. (438, 591)

Lourdes, Howard County. Lourdes was first known as Crane Creek and was in existence as early as 1858. The town was renamed by Francis Guyette, a native of France, who named the town for the famous shrine in his homeland. Lourdes is not incorporated. (209)

Loveland, Pottawattamie County. A. J. Bell and E. Loveland built a mill on the Boyer River, where the town of Loveland was established in 1865–1866. It was named for E. Loveland. The town is not incorporated. (191, 528)

Lovilia, Monroe County. The town was founded in 1853 and named Bremen. When it was learned that there was another Bremen in Iowa, the town was renamed for the daughter of a Mr. Dickerson, Lovillia. It was incorporated on April 21, 1933. (417, 438)

Low Moor, Clinton County. Low Moor was founded April 30, 1858, by Milo Smith, W. H. Mudgett, and Jackson H. Tong, the owners of the site. The town was named for the mill stamp on the rails used to construct the rail line through the area. The steel rails were from the Low Moor Foundry. Low Moor was incorporated on February 10, 1897. (438, 528, 591)

Lowden, Cedar County. Lowden was founded in 1857. The name for the town was derived from Loudenville, Ohio. Lowden was named by Thomas Shearer, who had moved from the town in Ohio. It was incorporated on March 12, 1869. (248, 438, 528)

Lowell, Henry County. Lowell was also known as Smith Mills and McCarverstown during its history. In 1840 M. McCarver established the town as McCarverstown. In 1842 a Dr. Archibald petitioned the state legislature to change the name to Lowell after the town of Lowell, Massachusetts, in his native state. The petition was granted in 1843. Hiram Smith and James Caudill opened a mill there in 1843, and for a while the site was also identified as Smith Mills, though the name Lowell is the one that endured. The town is not incorporated. (245)

Luana, Clayton County. Luana was established in December 1867 by William Scott. He named the town after his wife, Luana. The community was incorporated on May 29, 1911. (261, 438)

Lucas, Lucas County. The town was named for the county, and the county was named for Robert Lucas, the first territorial governor of Iowa. Lucas was founded in 1868 and was incorporated on March 18, 1887. (318, 438, 525)

Luther, Boone County. Luther was established in January 1893. The town was probably named for an area businessman named Luther Clark, though there is another story that the town was named for Martin Luther. Luther was incorporated on December 29, 1903. (51, 163, 246, 438)

Luton, Woodbury County. Luton was established on May 1, 1889, on land owned by the Strange family. The town was named after Luton, England, a London suburb. Luton is not incorporated. (294)

Lu Verne, Humboldt and Kossuth counties. The town was founded by the Western Town Lot Company in 1881 and was first called Whitman, for an officer of the Chicago and North Western Railroad. The town's name was eventually changed to Lu Verne, for Luverne, Minnesota, which had been named for the daughter of the town's founder. Lu Verne was incorporated on July 6, 1887. (438, 528)

Luxemburg, Dubuque County. Luxemburg was founded in June 1846. At one time the town was known as Flea Hill. It seems probable that the town was named for Luxembourg in Europe. Luxemburg was incorporated on January 2, 1912. (163, 318, 395, 438)

Luzerne, Benton County. Luzerne was established on April 17, 1868, on property owned by Isaac B. and Hannah R. Howe. Isaac Howe named the town for Lucerne, Switzerland. Luzerne was incorporated on October 24, 1895. (280, 438, 528)

Lyman, Cass County. Lyman was founded in 1880 and named after Congressman Joseph Lyman. The town is not incorporated. (422)

Lynnville, Jasper County. Lynnville was founded by John and Mary Arnold on July 23, 1856. It appears that the town draws its name from the township that it is in, Lynn Grove. The town was incorporated on August 9, 1875. (163, 438, 573)

Lytton, Calhoun and Sac counties. Lytton was founded on October 3, 1899, and was incorporated on July 21, 1911. The town was named in honor of Lord Lytton, a British author and statesman. The section of the town in Calhoun County was planned on April 29, 1901, by A. T. Martin. (235, 438, 532)

M m ++++++++++++++++++++

Macedonia, Pottawattamie County. Macedonia was established in 1880 and named Clayton City in honor of a railroad official. The name was later changed to Macedonia, the name of an old Mormon camping site nearby. The Mormons probably named their camp for the biblical references to Macedonia. The town was incorporated on June 21, 1892. (191, 438)

Macksburg, Madison County. Macksburg was founded in 1876 and named for a Dr. Mack, one of the town's founders.

Macksburg was incorporated on December 24, 1876. (163, 375, 438)

Madrid, Boone County. Madrid was established four times: the first time by Thomas Sparks on February 25, 1852; the second time by S. C. Wood on December 9, 1853; the third time by S. Underhill on July 16, 1855; and the final time by L. Regan on September 14, 1857. The first two times the town was planned out it was called Swede Point. A Mr. Gaston, executor for a Mrs. Dalander's estate, was responsible for the change to Madrid. Dalander had owned the property at the town site. There was a dispute between Dalander's sons and Gaston. Out of resentment toward them, he changed the name to Madrid. Apparently, Gaston had in his employ a Spaniard who often spoke fondly of Madrid. Gaston held the employee, his country, and his references to his country's capital in low esteem. He renamed the town Madrid to insult the Dalander family, who were of Swedish descent. Madrid was incorporated on June 9, 1883. (210, 438)

Magnolia, Harrison County. Magnolia was planned as the county seat on July 5, 1854, and the town was founded on February 23, 1855. It was named by the state legislature for the magnolia tree. Magnolia was incorporated on November 30, 1909. (312, 438, 563)

Maharishi Vedic City, Jefferson County. Maharishi Vedic City was established and was incorporated in 2001. "'Maharishi" is for the founder of Maharishi International University in nearby Fairfield. "Vedic" comes from the Sanskrit word for knowledge, *veda*. (327, 377)

Malcolm, Poweshiek County. Malcolm was founded in 1872 and reportedly named for a railroad surveyor. The community was incorporated on April 23, 1872. (163, 438, 474)

Mallard, Palo Alto County. Mallard was named by the president of the Des Moines and Fort Dodge Railroad, Charles E.

Whitehead. An avid hunter, he named the town for the duck that he had hunted in the area. Whitehead also named the towns of Curlew and Plover. Mallard was established in 1882 and was incorporated on June 25, 1895. (398, 438)

Maloy, Ringgold County. The town was first named Delphi, though it was popularly known as Foxtown because of a merchant's building that had a painting of a red fox on it. Maloy was named for one of the original settlers in the area, David Maloy. It was founded in 1887 and was incorporated on June 18, 1901. (163, 379, 438, 497)

Malvern, Mills County. Malvern was settled because of its proximity to the Burlington and Missouri River Railroad in 1869. The town was originally called Milton, in honor of Milton Summers, an early settler in the area. When the town petitioned for a post office, the Post Office Department replied that there already was a post office named Milton in Iowa. The settlers decided to call the town Milton Junction, but the name was similar enough that there still was confusion. A Dr. Brothers suggested the name of Malvern in honor of his hometown of Malvern, Ohio. The community was incorporated on February 24, 1872. (409, 438)

Manchester, county seat, Delaware County. The town was founded as Burrington in 1854 and was named for one of the early settlers, Levings Burrington. When the community applied for a post office, the office was accepted on the condition that the name be changed, since Burrington could be confused with Burlington. One story about the origin of the name is that it was suggested by a Judge Dyer. The judge was from England and wanted to name the town for one of the cities in his homeland. The other story is that the name was a derivation of the name of one of the founders, William Chesterman. The likelihood is that it was named for Manchester, England, since if it were named for the founder it probably would have been called Chesterman. Manchester was incorporated on March 19, 1864. (163, 404, 438)

Manilla, Crawford County. Manilla was established in 1886. The town's name was decided by a tug of war between proponents of the name Paupville, for the prior owner of the land, Les Paup, and Manila, a name suggested by a Mr. Blackburn, a hardware store owner, who sold a twine called Manila Binder Twine. The contest, carried out with a rope furnished by Blackburn, ended in a victory for the backers of Manila. Somehow an additional l was added to the name. Manilla was incorporated on October 3, 1887. (284, 438)

Manly, Worth County. Manly was first called Manly Junction when it was founded in the summer of 1877. Manly was named for a contractor with the railroad. The town was incorporated on November 19, 1898. (138, 436, 438)

Manning, Carroll County. The land selected for the town was chosen by O. H. Manning, an agent for the Western Town Lot Company. Manning was created in 1881 and named for O. H. Manning. It was incorporated on February 17, 1882. (42, 438)

Manson, Calhoun County. Manson was founded on November 11, 1872, by the Sioux City and Iowa Falls Town Lot and Land Company, although a settlement at the site had developed in 1870. The town was first named Vincent, but the name was changed to Manson to honor a man living in Waterloo. Manson was incorporated on May 5, 1877. (438, 532, 562)

Maple Hill, Emmett County. Maple Hill was founded on August 23, 1899. The town was named for a grove of maple trees in the area. Maple Hill is not incorporated. (28, 381)

Maple River Junction, Carroll County. Maple River Junction was founded in 1872. The town was named for the maple trees that lined the banks of the Raccoon River, which runs north of the town. Maple River Junction is not incorporated. (74)

Mapleton, Monona County. Mapleton was organized in the fall of 1856 and named by the first settler, William Wilsey, for the maple trees growing along the Maple River. Mapleton was incorporated on May 10, 1878. (287, 318, 438)

Maquoketa, county seat, Jackson County. The town was founded by J. E. Goodenow in 1838 as Springfield. Goodenow named the town for Springfield, Massachusetts. The name was changed to Maquoketa in 1856 to reflect its proximity to the Maquoketa River. The name Maquoketa is of Indian derivation and appears to mean "there are bears." The community was incorporated on January 27, 1857. (276, 438, 528, 561)

Marathon, Buena Vista County. Marathon was founded in 1881 and named for the village of Marathon in Greece. It was incorporated on October 31, 1892. (438, 455, 528)

Marble Rock, Floyd County. The village was founded in October 1856. The name Marble Rock came from a limestone formation that had the appearance of marble. Marble Rock was incorporated on February 8, 1881. (438, 456)

Marcus, Cherokee County. Marcus was named for one of John Blair's sons. Blair controlled the Iowa Falls and Sioux City Railroad during its construction days. The town was founded by the Iowa Falls and Sioux City Railroad Land and Town Lot Company on November 27, 1871. Marcus was incorporated on June 15, 1882. (401, 438)

Marengo, county seat, Iowa County. A commission selected the town site as the county seat on August 13, 1845. Marengo was founded by E. C. Lyon on May 24, 1847, and named for the plains of Marengo in Italy. It was incorporated on July 4, 1859. (163, 164, 438)

Marion, Linn County. Marion was founded as the county seat in 1839 and named in honor of General Francis Marion, one of the heroes of the Revolutionary War. Marion was incorporated on August 10, 1865. (282, 438)

Marne, Cass County. The Marne Town Company bought 160 acres of land and established the town in 1875. Some of the men who owned shares in the company were from northern Germany and named their corporation, and the town, for the German city of Marne. The community was incorporated on June 10, 1892. (30, 257, 438)

Marquette, Clayton County. Marquette was first named North McGregor when it was established on July 21, 1858. The name was changed to honor the French explorer Father Jacques Marquette in 1915. It was incorporated on June 2, 1874. (131, 318, 423, 438)

Marshalltown, county seat, Marshall County. The town was established on August 15, 1853, by the Iowa Town Lot and Land Company. The town was named Marshall by H. Anson and John Childs for Marshall, Michigan, the town they were from. When it was discovered there already was a Marshall in Iowa, the name was changed to its current form. Marshalltown was incorporated on March 5, 1923. (285, 438, 528)

Martelle, Jones County. Martelle was a station on the Chicago, Milwaukee and St. Paul Railroad. The village was established in November 1872 and reportedly named for someone affiliated with the railroad. The town was incorporated on April 28, 1899. (142, 163, 438)

Martensdale, Warren County. Martensdale was established in 1913 and was named for John Martens, who participated in the founding of the town. It was incorporated on October 29, 1920. (507)

Martinsburg, Keokuk County. Martinsburg was founded in November 1855 and was named after Daniel and Sarah Martin, who had settled there. The town was incorporated on December 30, 1887. (279, 438)

Marysville, Marion County. Marysville was founded on March 4, 1851. The town was created at the instigation of Joseph Brobst. He named the town Marysville because of the number of women in the Brobst family named Mary. Marysville was incorporated on July 31, 1875. (438, 594)

Mason City, county seat, Cerro Gordo County. The site of the present-day Mason City was established as a farm when John B. Long settled there in 1851. Long named his home and farm Masonic Grove in honor of the Freemasons. The first settlement, established by Long with some partners, was known as Shibboleth. Long bought out his partners in 1854 and renamed the town for his son, Mason. The town was finally established as Mason City in 1855. Mason City was incorporated on December 21, 1869. (21, 438, 528)

Masonville, Delaware County. Masonville was established by the Iowa Land Company on July 22, 1858, on land owned by Francis Daniels. It was named for R. B. Mason, the president of the company. The community was incorporated on June 28, 1901. (438, 504)

Massena, Cass County. Massena was established by the Chicago and Burlington Railroad in 1883–1884. It was named for a town in New York and was incorporated on January 18, 1887. (318, 350, 438)

Massillon, Cedar County. Massillon was first known as Denson's Ferry. The location was named after Joseph Denson, who first settled there and established the ferry. The town was founded in 1854 and named for Massillon, Ohio, from which some of the settlers came. Massillon is not incorporated. (258, 335)

Matlock, Sioux County. Matlock was founded by the Western Town Lot Company on February 6, 1888. The town was originally called Morris, but there was already a town named Maurice in the county, so the name was changed to Matlock.

Matlock was suggested by Robert Allen, an area landowner who came from Matlock, England. The community was incorporated on July 5, 1897. (433, 438)

Maurice, Sioux County. Maurice was established by the Western Town Lot Company in 1882. It was named for Count Maurice of Nassau, the son of William of Orange, a Dutch hero. Maurice was incorporated on May 23, 1891. (438, 528)

Maxwell, Story County. Maxwell was established in 1881 on the Chicago, Milwaukee and St. Paul Railroad and named after one of the founders, J. W. Maxwell. It was incorporated on December 17, 1883. (16, 163, 438)

May City, Osceola County. May City was founded as Lexington in 1869. The town had been named by Frederick Mayer. When issues with the name arose, the town was renamed for Mayer's daughter, Margaret. How May was derived from her name is not explained. May City is not incorporated. (548)

Maynard, Fayette County. Maynard was named in honor of an early settler, Henry Maynard. It was founded in 1873 and was incorporated on June 9, 1887. (189, 438)

Maysville, Scott County. James May founded the town of Maysville in 1856. It was named in his honor. The community was incorporated on June 21, 1909. (291, 438)

McCallsburg, Story County. McCallsburg was first established in 1868 and named after T. C. McCall. The post office in the community was named Latrobe until it was changed to McCallsburg in 1883. McCallsburg was incorporated on February 25, 1901. (429, 438)

McCausland, Scott County. The town was named for the McCausland brothers who donated the land for the rail station in 1882. McCausland was incorporated on May 28, 1909. (399, 509)

McClelland, Pottawattamie County. When the Chicago Great Western Railroad was built through the area in 1903, the town of McClelland was founded. McClelland was named for W. H. McClelland, who owned the land where the town was located. McClelland was incorporated on December 14, 1904. (143, 191, 438)

McGregor, Clayton County. McGregor was established on July 24, 1850, on land owned by James McGregor and Duncan McGregor. Alexander McGregor established a ferry at the site, and the place became known as McGregor's Landing. The town voted to incorporate on March 7, 1859. (261, 438)

McIntire, Mitchell County. McIntire was named for John McIntire, who donated land to the railroad for the town in 1889. The town was incorporated on July 9, 1894. (286, 438)

Mechanicsville, Cedar County. In 1855 John Onstot and Daniel A. Comstock founded Mechanicsville. Onstot named the town for the number of craftsmen living in the community. Mechanicsville was incorporated on November 25, 1867. (258, 438)

Mediapolis, Des Moines County. Mediapolis was founded by W. H. Cartwright and W. W. King in 1869 as a stop on the Burlington, Cedar Rapids and Minnesota Railroad. The town was named because it was midway between Burlington and Wapello. It was incorporated on June 14, 1875. (24, 163, 438)

Melbourne, Marshall County. Melbourne was founded on February 23, 1882, by the Milwaukee Land Company. The town was to be named Wenselville, for James Wensel, but he demurred. Melbourne was named for a railroad employee. It was incorporated on October 29, 1895. (163, 366, 438)

Melcher-Dallas, Marion County. Melcher-Dallas is a community formed from two separate towns that abutted one another. Dallas was formally established in September 1857.

The town was originally called Little Ohio when settlement started in 1845, but the post office, which had been established in 1855, was called Dallas, reportedly for George Dallas, a prominent politician. The town's name was changed to conform to the name of the post office. When the railroad laid track through the area in 1910, it ran the tracks just south of Dallas because of the terrain. Melcher was established in the spring of 1912 as a station on that railroad and located next to Dallas. Melcher was named after a Massachusetts railroad man, Frank Otis Melcher, who was killed in a railroad accident shortly before the town was created. Melcher-Dallas was incorporated on April 24, 1913. (163, 243, 438, 594)

Melrose, Monroe County. Melrose was founded in 1866 and named for Melrose, Massachusetts. The community was incorporated on March 20, 1882. (246, 438)

Melvin, Osceola County. Melvin was founded in 1900 as a station on the Rock Island Railroad. Melvin replaced another town called Old Melvin, which had been established in 1897 but was some distance from the railroad track. The community was named in honor of an early settler, Ed Melvin. The town was incorporated in 1901. (460, 548)

Menlo, Guthrie County. B. F. Allen founded Menlo on July 8, 1869. The town was first known as "The Switch," then Guthrie Switch, then Guthrie, before being known as Menlo. The town was possibly named for Menlo, Ireland. The community was incorporated on February 2, 1881. (271, 438)

Meriden, Cherokee County. Meriden was first established as Hazard by John Blair on December 22, 1870. The residents did not care for Blair and petitioned both the federal government and the Illinois Central Railroad, the railroad in control of the rail line at the time, to change the name to Meriden. No evidence remains as to why that name was selected, but there is speculation that it was for Meriden, Connecticut. The community was incorporated on December 24, 1881. (87, 401, 438)

Merrill, Plymouth County. Merrill was established on February 27, 1872, by the Sioux City and Iowa Falls Town Lot and Land Company and named for Governor Samuel Merrill. It was incorporated on April 24, 1894. (163, 294, 438)

Meservey, Cerro Gordo County. The town was established on April 1, 1887, as Kausville, for the town site owners. The name was soon changed to Meservey in honor of S. T. Meservey, who was involved in railroad development in the area. Meservey was incorporated on August 25, 1893. (84, 163, 438)

Meyer, Mitchell County. Meyer was named after John Joseph Meyer, the oldest living resident at the time the town was established. The area was first settled in 1872. The town is not incorporated. (286)

Middle Amana, Iowa County. Middle Amana, established in 1862, was named for its location in the Amana Colonies. The name for the colonies was brought to Iowa by members of the Amana Society. The name is drawn from the Bible and means "to believe faithfully." Middle Amana is not incorporated. (19, 163)

Middletown, Des Moines County. The town was founded by Josiah Smith in 1839 as Lewis Point. The name of the town was changed at the suggestion of John Sharp, who had lived in a town in Pennsylvania named Middletown. It was incorporated on May 11, 1914. (24, 318, 438)

Miles, Jackson County. The town was established by F. W. Miles on October 10, 1872. The town site had been called Shoo Fly. Mr. Miles apparently wanted to call the town Merrill, but since there was already a Merrill in Iowa, the name became Miles, for him. Miles was incorporated on June 4, 1893. (276, 438)

Milford, Montgomery County. Milford was officially established on June 29, 1858, by Thomas Donaho. The town apparently was named for a mill at the site. Milford was incorporated on January 12, 1892. (403, 438)

Miller, Hancock County. Miller was named for one of the property owners, R. C. Miller. It was founded in October 1895. The town is not incorporated. (242)

Millersburg, Iowa County. Millersburg was founded by Reuben Miller in 1852 and named for him. It was incorporated on January 16, 1911. (164, 438)

Millerton, Wayne County. Millerton was founded in December 1912 and named for H. C. Miller. The town was incorporated on April 26, 1915. (438, 572)

Millville, Clayton County. The town was established in July 1856 by Isaac Preston and named for the township in which it is located. Millville was incorporated on April 27, 1967. (261, 438)

Milo, Warren County. Milo was established as a rail station in 1879. There is a story that the town was named with letters from the names of S. H. Mallory and another person. There appears to be no concrete record as to why Mallory selected the name Milo. Milo was incorporated on November 4, 1880. (410, 438, 507)

Milton, Van Buren County. Milton was established in 1851 and was incorporated on June 20, 1878. The town was named for the poet John Milton. (318, 336, 438)

Minburn, Dallas County. J. B. Hill and D. F. Rogers established the town of Minburn in 1869. They wanted to name the town Norwood, but Nat Baker, a railroad representative, convinced them that it should be called Minburn. The Scotch term for "stream" is *burn*, and *min* means "small," so the town was named for the Raccoon River, which Baker viewed as a *min burn*. Minburn was incorporated on October 6, 1880. (105, 318, 438)

Minden, Pottawattamie County. Minden was established in 1875 when Casper Foster of Davenport, Iowa, purchased 10,000 acres from the Rock Island Railroad. Foster insisted that a town be established along the track and be named Minden, for Minden, Germany. There is some evidence that settlement at the site had started as early as 1868. The community was incorporated on October 6, 1880. (143, 191, 438)

Mineola, Mills County. The town was established and named Lewis City in 1879 on land purchased from a Mr. Lanz by the Western Town Lot Company. In 1880 the residents changed the name to Mineola, because of the small population of the town. The town is not incorporated. (409)

Mingo, Jasper County. Mingo was founded on May 27, 1884, and was incorporated on February 13, 1903. Mingo was named for a town in Ohio and is a term associated with the Iroquois, either as the Delaware term for the Iroquois meaning "stealthy and treacherous" or as the Iroquois word for men. It could also be associated with the Mingos written about in James Fenimore Cooper's novels. (438, 561, 573)

Missouri Valley, Harrison County. The town was planned by John Blair on January 28, 1867. The site was known as McIntosh's Point and then New St. Johns before it was established as Missouri Valley Junction. The name was a literal one for the town's location and function for the railroad. Eventually "Junction" was dropped from the name. Missouri Valley voted to incorporate on October 30, 1871. (312, 318, 438)

Mitchell, Mitchell County. Settlement started in 1854 at several adjacent sites: East Mitchell, West Town, and the development that bridged the two. Mitchell was named for the county and served for a time as the county seat. The county was named for the Irish hero John Mitchell. The town was incorporated on June 27, 1879. (163, 286, 438)

Mitchellville, Polk County. Thomas Mitchell established the town in May 1867 and named it after himself. Mitchellville was incorporated on September 30, 1875. (106, 289, 438)

Modale, Harrison County. The town was founded by Alonzo and Hanna Beebe on March 2, 1874. They had originally named the site Missouri Dale. When they established a post office, they sent the name in as an abbreviation, Mo. Dale, and it was registered in Washington, D.C., as Modale. The community was incorporated on April 22, 1882. (312, 438)

Moingona, Boone County. Moingona was founded on July 6, 1866, and a railway station was established there. The name is derived from an Indian tribe that had lived in Iowa in the 1600s and had a village at the site. The Indians had moved east to become part of the Illinois Confederacy. The word means "loon." The town is not incorporated. (210, 561)

Mona, Mitchell County. Mona was originally called Hustad and was founded in 1869. The name was later changed to Mona at the request of William Caine, whose sweetheart, Ramona Johnson, died before she was able to join him in the settlement. The town is not incorporated. (286)

Mondamin, Harrison County. Mondamin was established by John Blair on September 10, 1868. *Mondamin* is an Indian word for corn, and since the town was located in a corn-growing region, the word was selected as the town's name. Mondamin was incorporated on December 23, 1881. (312, 438)

Moneta, O'Brien County. Moneta was established by Charles Colby on May 10, 1901. The town was named using the ancient name for the island of Anglesey. The town is not incorporated. (460, 528)

Monmouth, Jackson County. Monmouth was founded in 1855 by W. F. Douglas. An adjoining town, Coloma, was established in 1856 by Dr. L. T. Hubbard. The towns abutted one another, and when the railroad came through the area, they were consolidated as Monmouth. Monmouth was probably named for the Revolutionary War battle site. The second possibility is that it was named for Monmouth, Illinois, since one of the county officials had previously lived there. It was incorporated on July 12, 1894. (163, 323, 438, 528)

Monona, Clayton County. Monona was founded in July 1851. Local legend holds that the town was named after a young Indian woman who leaped to her death from a promontory into the Mississippi River when she was separated from her true love. Supposedly, the townspeople later discovered that her name was Winona, not Monona. However, Monona was a character in a play written by Lewis Deffebach in 1821 called *Oolaita, or the Indian Heroine*. Monona was the scheming older man who attempted to force the young woman to marry him. She leaped into the nearby lake to escape the union. Since Monona is not an Indian name, that play would be the most likely source for the name. The settlers probably chose it for the way it sounded rather than for what it represented. Local legend took over from there. The town was incorporated on May 11, 1897. (163, 261, 438, 561)

Monroe, Jasper County. The town site was first established by Adam Toole in 1851 and called Toole's Point. The settlement was renamed the following year for President James Monroe. Monroe was officially founded by Daniel Hiskey and his wife on December 18, 1856, and was first incorporated in 1868. (318, 573)

Montezuma, county seat, Poweshiek County. The town was established in 1848 as the county seat. Montezuma was the name of an Aztec ruler in Mexico and reflects the influence of the war with Mexico. That war was concluding the year the town was founded. Montezuma was incorporated on February 21, 1868. (438, 561, 578)

Montgomery, Dickinson County. Montgomery was named for the property owner, John Montgomery. The post office, which would probably parallel settlement, was established at the site in 1896. The post office was closed in 1982. The town is not incorporated. (163, 458)

Monticello, Jones County. Monticello was founded in September 1853 and named for Thomas Jefferson's home. It was incorporated on September 24, 1889. (142, 163, 438)

Montour, Tama County. Montour had originally been called Orford, for Orford, New Hampshire, when it was settled in 1863. When the name was changed to Montour in the early 1870s, the name was also a transfer name from the East, either for Montour Falls in New York or for Montour County in Pennsylvania. Both of those place-names originated to honor members of the Montour family. The Montours were a French-Indian family who were very helpful to the early Euro-American settlers in the East. The town was incorporated in 1870. (163, 419, 458, 528, 561)

Montpelier, Muscatine County. The original Montpelier, several miles from the current town, was established by Benjamin Nye in 1834 and named for his former home, Montpelier, Vermont. The current town was established on May 9, 1881. Montpelier is not incorporated. (318, 428, 484)

Montrose, Lee County. The location was originally the site of an Indian settlement called Cut Nose village. In 1832 Captain James White developed an outpost at the site. He then sold his property to the U.S. government in 1834 as a military post. The fort was named Ft. Des Moines. When the fort was abandoned in 1837, David Kilbourne founded a town at the site. He called it Mount of Roses, referring to the profusion of wild roses growing in the area. The ownership of the site was apparently in dispute, as there was a lawsuit against Kilbourne, which he lost. The town was surveyed again, and title to the site was distributed to the victors in the suit. The name Montrose evolved from the name Kilbourne had given the town. It was incorporated in 1857. (281, 420)

Moorhead, Monona County. Moorhead was named after its founder, J. B. Moorhead. In 1889 he had arranged to move the buildings in an existing town located nearby to the site. Moorhead was incorporated on October 6, 1902. (287, 438, 444)

Moorland, Webster County. Moorland was established by S. M. Pollock. The town is reported to have been named descriptively, since it was located near marshes. Another possibility is that it was a transfer name, since there are other towns named Moorland in states east of Iowa. The post office was established in 1883, which should coincide with the establishment of the town. Moorland was incorporated in October 1902. (163, 438, 458, 475)

Moravia, Appanoose County. Moravia was established on July 15, 1851. It was settled by members of the Moravian Society. The community was incorporated on September 26, 1881. (26, 438)

Morley, Jones County. Morley dates from 1873, when the town was established as a railroad depot. The town was originally called Viroqua. The name Viroqua was similar to the name of another town, so the name was changed to Morley in 1886, apparently in honor of a railroad official. Morley was incorporated on January 26, 1925. (142, 438, 439)

Morning Sun, Louisa County. Morning Sun was founded by Cicero Hamilton on September 13, 1851. The town's name was the result of an all-night hunt for missing livestock by Hamilton and Henry Blake. As they were returning to the town site in the morning light, they decided on Morning Sun as the name for the new town. Morning Sun was incorporated on June 3, 1867. (163, 438, 526)

Morrison, Grundy County. Morrison was established by the Morrison Town Lot Company in 1877. The founder of the company was Jeff Morrison, and both the company and the town carried his name. Morrison was incorporated on April 24, 1884. (220, 438)

Morse, Johnson County. Morse was founded by A. W. Morse, A. M. Morse, E. K. Morse, Mary A. Morse, and Orrin and Sarah Andrews in March 1871. The town is not incorporated. (332)

Moscow, Muscatine County. Moscow was established in 1836 by a Mr. Webster and a Mr. Drury. The men had moved to the area from Indiana. It appears that the town's name was a transfer from Moscow, Ohio. Some of the settlers in the new town were from that site in Ohio. The town is not incorporated. (492, 559)

Moulton, Appanoose County. Moulton was named for engineer Jonathon B. Moulton, who established the town in 1867. Moulton was originally called Elizabethtown. It was incorporated on February 25, 1869. (26, 318, 438)

Mt. Auburn, Benton County. Mt. Auburn was founded by the property owners, Milton S. and Sarah A. Hall and Thomas D. and Mary A. Lewis, on June 19, 1871. The area had been called Big Hill by the Indians and was first called Mount by the settlers. It appears that the town was named for Mt. Auburn, Illinois. The community was incorporated on November 19, 1906. (163, 280, 438)

Mt. Ayr, county seat, Ringgold County. Mt. Ayr was established by William McCormick in June 1855. It was named by John Sheller, who co-owned the property with the county, to indicate the elevation of the town site and after Ayre, Scotland. The town was incorporated on June 8, 1875. (44, 163, 438)

Mt. Carmel, Carroll County. Mt. Carmel was named for Our Lady of Mt. Carmel. Lambert Kniest, with others, selected the town site on July 16, 1868, the day of the feast of Our Lady of Mt. Carmel. The town is not incorporated. (74)

Mt. Etna, Adams County. Mt. Etna was established by Isaiah Fees on October 14, 1856. It was named by Robert Mansfield, probably for Mt. Etna, Pennsylvania. The town is not incorporated. (250)

Mt. Joy, Scott County. The Mt. Joy Post Office was established in 1856 and ceased operation in 1900. In 1861 the Mt. Joy Methodist Episcopal Church was built. The record of why this name was used appears to have become obscure through time, though Mt. Joy is a name in use in other parts of the country. The town is not incorporated. (169)

Mt. Pleasant, county seat, Henry County. Mt. Pleasant was established in July 1839 on property owned by Presley Saunders. Saunders had called the site Mt. Pleasant, probably because it was on a "beautiful high prairie." Mt. Pleasant was first incorporated on January 25, 1842, and was last incorporated on July 15, 1856. (21, 245, 273, 318, 438)

Mt. Sterling, Van Buren County. Mt. Sterling was founded in 1839 by Horace Woods and George Woods when they built and operated both a corn cracker and a sawmill in the area. The town was not initially named by the brothers. The number of dogs owned by the Woods families and the dogs that their customers brought with them when they were grinding corn or getting lumber caused the town to be called Dogtown. The name was later changed to Mt. Sterling to reflect its elevation and desirability as a town site. Mt. Sterling was incorporated on October 29, 1907. (163, 336, 438)

Mt. Union, Henry County. A schoolhouse was built near the site of Mt. Union in 1872. The schoolhouse was used as a Sunday school by the settlers in the area. The settlers with various religious affiliations decided that they would join together so there would be a sufficient number to sustain a class. Because of that, the Sunday school was called the Union Sunday School. The town was established on William Kneen's property at the highest point in the county, with the first building constructed in 1876. The town's name reflects the elevation and the cooperation of the various religious denominations. Mt. Union was incorporated on August 20, 1904. (241, 438)

Mt. Vernon, Linn County. Mt. Vernon was established in 1847 by A. J. Willetts and named for George Washington's home in Virginia. It was incorporated on July 7, 1869. (282, 438, 528)

Moville, Woodbury County. According to the county histories, the town drew its name from Moville, Ireland. John McDermett established a post office in 1868 and called it Moville in honor of the town in Ireland from which he came. With the advent of the railroad in the area, a town site was established nearby by the Western Town Lot Company on April 23, 1887, and the name of the post office was used for the town. Another story is that the name was drawn from the town's proximity to the Missouri River, the abbreviation "Mo." and the suffix "ville," for village. Moville was incorporated on August 13, 1889. (294, 304, 438, 528)

Murray, Clarke County. Murray was founded in 1868 as Oakland. Since there was already an Oakland in Iowa, the town was renamed for a railroad employee named Murray. Murray was incorporated in 1880. (43, 79)

Muscatine, county seat, Muscatine County. Colonel George Davenport established a trading post on the site of Muscatine in 1833. Prior to being formally founded as a town, the site was called Sandstone or Grindstone Bluffs for the sandstone formations in the bluffs along the river. In 1835, when James Casey staked a claim and started selling wood to the passing steamboats, the location became known as Casey's Woodpile or Casey's Landing. When John Vanatta and Captain William Casey founded the town in 1836, they thought about calling it Newburg but ended up calling it Bloomington. This was probably because Vanatta was from Bloomington, Indiana. Some years later the name was changed to avoid confusion with Bloomington, Illinois. The community was named for the county. There is some controversy about where the word Muscatine came from. Suel Foster contacted Anton Le Claire in the 1850s, and Le Claire told him that the island from which the county and the town drew their names was named for the Mascoutin Indians, who had lived on the island for a while. Virgil Vogel writes that the name means "prairie" or "flat place" in the Fox language. There is some evidence to indicate the term is also related to fire. Actually, Le Claire also told another inquirer that the island was named for the Fox word for fire. Perhaps he was just having some fun with the questioners. In any event, his inconsistent responses to the questions about the origin of the name have helped fuel the controversy to this day. It seems most likely that Vogel's explanation for the name is correct. Muscatine was incorporated on February 1, 1851. (288, 318, 438, 492)

Mystic, Appanoose County. Mystic was established on May 28, 1887, on property owned by James Elgin. The most plausible explanation for the name is that Dennis Vandyke, a civil engineer with the railroad and the man who named the town, was from Mystic, Connecticut. Mystic, Connecticut, was named for the Mystic River. The river derived its name from the Mohican and Natick name for the stream, Missituk. Mystic was incorporated on October 29, 1889. (438, 561)

N n ++++++++++++++++++++

Napier, Boone County. Napier was named for Robert Cornelius Napier, a British explorer and general. It was founded in June 1904. The town is not incorporated. (51, 185)

Nashua, Chickasaw County. Nashua was established in 1855 and first called Bridgeport, then Woodbridge. The name was finally changed to Nashua at the suggestion of E. P. Greeley and C. Greeley, for Nashua, New Hampshire. Nashua is an Algonquin word meaning "midway" or "between." The town was incorporated on January 29, 1857. (8, 438, 561)

Nashville, Jackson County. Named after a man named Nash, Nashville was founded by D. S. Teeple on June 15, 1872. The town is also known as Pumpkin Center since Pumpkin Run Creek passes through the town. The town is not incorporated. (323)

National, Clayton County. National was established as a town by Norman Hamilton in 1858. Before the settlement had been formally established, it was known as Farmersburg. When a neighboring community took the name Farmersburg, the town changed its name to National. The name possibly reflects an interest by the citizens in the state of the Union at that point in time. The town is not incorporated. (434)

Nemaha, Sac County. Nemaha was established on October 2, 1899. The name was drawn from an Indian dialect meaning either "muddy water" or "water of cultivation." It was incorporated on January 27, 1915. (235, 438, 561)

Neola, Pottawattamie County. Neola was established when the Chicago, Rock Island and Pacific Railroad constructed a rail line in the area in 1869. The word is reportedly of Indian origin, meaning "a place of lookout." It was incorporated on March 7, 1882. (191, 246, 438)

Nevada, county seat, Story County. Nevada was named by the county commissioners for the Sierra Nevada. It was established in August 1853. The community was incorporated on October 4, 1869. (16, 438, 528)

Nevinville, Adams County. The town was established in 1856 by followers of a New England minister named Nevin. The town was originally known as Nevin. Nevinville is not incorporated. (250)

New Albin, Allamakee County. The town was established as a station on the Clinton, Dubuque and Minnesota railway in 1872. The town was named for Albin Rhomberg, the son of one of the founders. Rhomberg stumbled and fell into a bonfire with his pockets full of gunpowder on July 4, 1872, and died as a result of the accident. "New" was apparently added to the name to prevent confusion with an existing town called Albion. New Albin was incorporated on May 20, 1895. (13, 163, 430, 438)

New Boston, Lee County. New Boston apparently was named for Boston, Massachusetts. A post office was established there in 1855 that operated until 1954, so the settlement was clearly established around 1855. The town is not incorporated. (163, 458)

New Hampton, county seat, Chickasaw County. New Hampton was established in 1855 as Chickasaw Center. It was named New Hampton at the suggestion of Osgood

Gowan, for his hometown in New England. New Hampton was incorporated on April 26, 1873. (8, 438)

New Hartford, Butler County. New Hartford had its start when Titus Ensign and S. B. Ensign built a mill there in 1855. The settlement was named by Titus Ensign after New Hartford, Connecticut. New Hartford was incorporated on December 7, 1883. (254, 438)

New Haven, Mitchell County. The most popular story about the origin of New Haven is that it was originally known as Hell's Town because of the behaviors exhibited in the community's taverns. After the saloons were closed, the residents started calling the town New Heaven, which was then changed formally to New Haven. A less interesting but more plausible explanation would be that it was a transfer name. The site had a post office established as New Haven in 1878, though settlement appears to have started in the mid 1850s. The post office was in operation until early in the twentieth century. The town is not incorporated. (163, 286)

New Liberty, Scott County. New Liberty was founded in 1886 and was incorporated on July 26, 1909. The town replaced an older settlement named Liberty that had been a stage stop. Because Liberty was not on the rail line, a new town was created named New Liberty. The name Liberty reflected the patriotic feeling in the area before the Civil War when the first village was formed. (246, 438, 509)

New London, Henry County. New London was founded by Abraham C. Dover. The town was first called Dover, for its founder. Johnathon King bought the town site from Dover and renamed the town New London. The name was inspired by London, England. It was incorporated on October 22, 1860. (163, 273, 438)

New Market, Taylor County. The town of Newmarket was established on April 3, 1882. A town called Dayton had been located a short distance away from the current town. The town was relocated and renamed when a stockyard was constructed next to a railroad track at the current town site. The name reflects that it was new and a place of commerce. New Market was incorporated on December 9, 1882. (163, 293, 318, 438)

New Providence, Hardin County. New Providence was founded in January 1856 by Daniel Dillon, Eleazer Andrews, Eli Jessup, and John Andrews in Providence Township. Many of the people who settled in the area were Quakers. The names of the township and town reflect their founders' faith and belief in Providence. New Providence was incorporated on January 30, 1893. (414, 438, 500)

New Sharon, Mahaska County. New Sharon was founded on July 22, 1856, by William Zimmerman, J. C. Culbertson, Morgan Reno, and John Michner. The town was named Sharon, after the Plains of Sharon described in the Bible. There was already a town named Sharon in the area, so the post office was named New Sharon, and eventually the town's name was changed to follow suit. New Sharon was incorporated in 1871. (339)

New Vienna, Dubuque County. New Vienna was founded by Fred Rohenkohl, H. Tauke, John Fangmann, and H. Wiechmann in 1844, and apparently named for Vienna, Austria. It was incorporated on July 17, 1895. (163, 266, 438)

New Virginia, Warren County. The town was named New Virginia because many of the settlers in the area were from Virginia, including the section of the state that would later separate and become West Virginia. New Virginia was settled in 1855–1856 but was not formally established until 1859. New Virginia was incorporated on April 27, 1901. (305, 438, 507)

Newburg, Jasper County. The town was founded on September 30, 1878. The origin of the name is a mystery, though it is possibly just a practical name for a new town. Another possibility is that it was a transfer name. There are Newburgs in Indiana, Ohio, and New York all predating Newburg, Iowa. It could also possibly be a transfer name from England or Scotland. The town is not incorporated. (573)

Newell, Buena Vista County. Newell was established as a station for the Dubuque and Sioux City Railroad in June 1870 and named for an official with the Illinois Central Railroad. It was incorporated on September 30, 1876. (163, 438, 455)

Newhall, Benton County. Newhall was established as a station for the Chicago, Milwaukee and St. Paul Railroad in 1881 on property that had been owned by Thomas McGranahan and Samuel McGranahan. The town was named for a railroad official who donated land for a park. It was incorporated on June 3, 1912. (431, 432, 438)

Newkirk, Sioux County. Newkirk had its start when the Reformed Church of North Orange was organized at the site on October 2, 1882. The name was changed to the Newkirk Reformed Church and reflects the origins of the Dutch settlers in the area. Newkirk means "new church," since *kerk* is Dutch for church. A store was located at the site in 1884, and the Newkirk Post Office was established at the store in 1886. The town is not incorporated. (433, 442)

Newton, county seat, Jasper County. Newton was called Newton City when it was platted on July 7, 1846, as the county seat. The community was named for a Revolutionary War soldier, a Sergeant Newton, who had served under General Francis Marion along with a Sergeant Jasper, for whom the county was named. The town was incorporated on January 6, 1857. (318, 438, 573)

Nichols, Muscatine County. Nichols was named by Benjamin Nichols for his father, Samuel, who gave the land for the railroad right-of-way and a depot. The town was established on June 22, 1870. The town site had been known as Elephant Swamp. Nichols was incorporated on March 15, 1884. (438, 492)

Nodaway, Adams County. Nodaway was originally called East Nodaway, after the river that runs past the town. In the 1870s the town was known as Rachelle. After only a year the townspeople changed the name to Nodaway. Nodaway is an Ojibwa term for their enemies, the Iroquois to the east and the Sioux to the west of their territory. The word can be interpreted as "our enemies" but literally means "snake" or "adder." Apparently, the riverbanks were infested with rattlesnakes, and that probably had something to do with the naming of the river and consequently the town. The town was incorporated on May 28, 1900. (250, 438, 561)

Nora Springs, Floyd County. The original village at the location of Nora Springs was named Woodstock. Woodstock was founded on May 23, 1857, by John West, C. M. Allen, Edson Gaylord, and the surveyor, A. R. Prescott. The name was changed to Nora Springs when a Mr. Greeley promised to build a store, buy and improve the mill at the site, and purchase twenty acres if the town would be named Elnora, in honor of a young woman in Vermont in whom he had an interest. Edson Gaylord was not thrilled with the name and suggested an alternative, "Springs." The men finally agreed on a compromise, Nora Springs. Greeley then ventured back to Vermont but was rejected by the young woman whom he admired. He sold his interests in the town and moved to Nashua, Iowa, never to return to Nora Springs. The community was incorporated on September 17, 1874. (438, 456)

North Buena Vista, Clayton County. North Buena Vista was laid out in 1851. The name is of Spanish origin, meaning "beautiful view," reflecting the view from the town. The "North" part of the name apparently reflects the town's location along the Mississippi River. North Buena Vista was incorporated on October 25, 1907. (224, 261, 438)

North English, Iowa County. North English was originally called Nevada and informally known as Soaptown. The town was named for the nearby North English River. North English was founded by Thomas Watters and Jacob Yeager on June 5, 1855. It was incorporated on March 13, 1891. (163, 164, 438)

North Liberty, Johnson County. A quarry had been operating at the North Liberty site since 1842. North Liberty was founded by Francis Bowman in 1857 and named by Martha Bowman. Given the date that the town was established, the name probably reflects an attitude toward social issues of the time. Other names that had been applied to the area were Squash Bend, Big Bottom, and North Bend. North Liberty was incorporated on November 10, 1913. (330, 438)

North Washington, Chickasaw County. The town was originally called Washington. "North" was added when Washington was rejected by the postal department as a name since there were other Washingtons in the area. North Washington was established and was incorporated on April 16, 1904. (163, 438, 472)

Northboro, Page County. Northborough was founded in September 1881. Northborough was changed to Northboro in 1893. There is speculation that the town was named for Northborough, Massachusetts. Northboro was incorporated on October 14, 1902. (163, 359, 438)

Northwood, county seat, Worth County. The first settler in the area was Gulbrand O. Mellem, who came in the summer of 1853 and built a cabin on the future site of Northwood. The town was first named Gulbrand in his honor. The name the town now carries came from two clusters of trees called north woods and south woods, named because of their physical relation to the town site. The first post office was located near the north grove, and therefore the office was called Northwood. The town drew its name from the post office. Northwood was incorporated on June 7, 1875. (138, 163, 438)

Norwalk, Warren County. The town was first called Pyra but was renamed for Norwalk, Ohio. Norwalk is based on a Mohegan Indian word or term. The town was incorporated on June 15, 1901. (438, 507)

Norway, Benton County. Norway received its name because Osborn Tuttle, Norwegian by birth, donated five acres to the Chicago and North Western Company on the condition that the new town should bear the name of his native country. The town was established in 1864. A few years later the town was renamed Florence for a time, although the station name remained Norway. Norway was incorporated on December 20, 1894. (280, 438)

Numa, Appanoose County. Numa replaced a town called Bellaire or Bell Air, named after a town in Ohio. When the Chicago, Rock Island and Pacific Railroad went through in 1876, Numa was established as a station. Bellaire was about a mile from the railway. The people living in Bellaire relocated to Numa, and the town of Bellaire vanished. There are several stories about the naming of Numa. One is that Numa was named in honor of an Indian girl, Nooma, whom the settlers knew. After the girl became ill and died, the settlers changed the town name. The other story about the naming of the town is that the name was suggested by a local minister, E. E. Harry, as an abbreviated version of

Idumaeans, a name drawn from the Bible. Other possibilities for the name are Numa, the second king of Rome, or *pneuma*, the Greek term for spirit. (26, 163, 438)

O o ++++++++++++++++++++++

Oakdale, Johnson County. While this location is recognized by the Iowa Department of Transportation and identified in the same manner as a town, it is not a town. The site was established as a tuberculosis sanitarium in 1908. It became part of the University of Iowa in 1965, and the sanitarium was closed in 1981. The location is currently a research center for the university. The sanitarium was named for the giant oak trees on the site. (330)

Oakland, Pottawattamie County. Oakland was first known as Big Grove. The first house was built there in 1856. When the railroad came into the area and the town grew, the name was changed to Oakland, reflecting the quantity of oak trees in the area. It was incorporated on March 14, 1882. (191, 318, 438)

Oakland Acres, Jasper County. Oakland Acres was created as a golf course and community by Cliff Thompson and Cloyd Thompson in 1961. They named the location Oakland Acres because of the large number of oak trees at the site. It was incorporated on February 24, 1975. (438, 541)

Oakville, Louisa County. Charles W. Edwards and Joseph H. Creighton chose the name Oakville for the site as they were standing under a bur oak tree. Oakville was formally established by Abe Parsons and Harry T. Parsons on December 11, 1891, as a depot on a newly installed railroad. Oakville replaced a town named Palo Alto, which had the misfortune of being a quarter of a mile south of the rail line. Oakville was incorporated on October 27, 1902. (368, 438, 526)

Ocheyedan, Osceola County. Ocheyedan was founded when the Burlington, Cedar Rapids and Northern Railroad crossed Osceola County in 1884. "Ocheye" was taken from the Dakota language and means "where they cry." Since the Dakotas would seek out hills or rises on which to express their grief, the word is also associated with elevated sites. The "dan" in the town's name defined the location as small or little. Ocheyedan was incorporated on February 20, 1891. (438, 462, 561)

Odebolt, Sac County. Odebolt was established by the Blair Town Lot and Land Company on August 22, 1877, and was named for a nearby creek that, in turn, had been named for a French trapper named Odebeau who had lived in the area in the 1850s. The community was incorporated on June 17, 1878. (235, 438, 528)

Oelwein, Fayette County. Oelwein was first called Hazelton but was renamed for the property owner, Frederick Oelwein. The town was established in 1873 and was incorporated on November 29, 1887. (163, 189, 438)

Ogden, Boone County. Ogden is a product of the Chicago and North Western Railroad. The town was established by John Blair on June 6, 1866. A dispute arose between the railroad and E. C. Litchfield as to the title of part of the land on which the town was laid out. Litchfield was victorious in the legal contest that followed. His agent, a Mr. Brown, resurveyed the town and recorded the location on May 6, 1870. The town was named in honor of W. B. Ogden, a distinguished railroad man. Ogden was incorporated on April 29, 1878. (210, 438)

Okoboji, Dickinson County. The town started as a post office on the shore of East Okoboji Lake in 1855. The word

"Okoboji" is from the Sioux language. The meaning is disputed among various experts. Possible meanings include: "place of rest," "rushes," "field of swamp grass," "blue waters," "planting in the spaces," "to cause to float downstream," and "spreading out to the south." Okoboji was incorporated on July 28, 1922. (318, 438, 561)

Olds, Henry County. Olds was established in 1885 on property owned by a Mr. Olds. He had donated the land on the condition that the town would be named for him. It was incorporated on December 12, 1900. (163, 245, 438)

Olin, Jones County. The early settlement at the location was called Elk Ford. The post office located there in 1841 was named Walnut Fork. When a town was founded at the site in March 1842, it was called Rome. The name was changed to Olin in honor of D. A. Olin, general superintendent of the Chicago, Milwaukee and St. Paul Railroad, in July 1872. Olin residents filed a petition for incorporation on November 13, 1879. (142, 438)

Ollie, Keokuk County. Ollie was first called Fairview when it was founded around 1840. When a depot was located there for the railroad in 1881, the name was changed to honor Ollie Fye, the daughter of a prominent family living there. Ollie was incorporated on March 1, 1892. (279, 438)

Onawa, county seat, Monona County. Onawa was established by the Monona Land Company in the summer of 1857, though it was not formally recorded until October 1858. The county seat was moved from Ashton to Onawa by a vote of the citizens of the county in 1858. There were several attempts to move the county seat from Onawa. The town prevailed against attempts to move the county seat to Belvidere, Arcola, and Mapleton. Ashton, Arcola, and Belvidere are now gone as viable towns. Onawa was incorporated on March 22, 1859. (287, 438)

Oneida, Delaware County. Oneida was established on October 8, 1896, for the Oneida Building and Improvement Company and Elisabeth Hoag Barr. The name was drawn from New York, where numerous places were named for the Oneida Indians, one of the Six Nations of the Iroquois. Oneida is not incorporated. (404, 561)

Onslow, Jones County. Onlsow was founded in 1871. W. T. Shaw, who owned the town site, named the town for a former governor of Maine. It was incorporated on June 20, 1888. (438, 528, 596)

Oran, Fayette County. The town of Oran replaced another community, Winkler, which had the misfortune to be about a mile away from the railroad track that was laid through the area. Oran was established as a station for the Chicago Great Western Railroad in 1906. The name came from the township that it was in, Oran Township. The town is not incorporated. (163, 189)

Orange City, county seat, Sioux County. Orange City was founded by Henry Hospers in 1870. The town was named to honor William of Orange, a hero in Dutch history. Orange City was incorporated in 1884. (38, 433)

Orchard, Mitchell County. Orchard was founded by Moses Orchard in 1869 when the Illinois Central Railroad went through the town. The community was incorporated on July 10, 1913. (286, 438)

Orient, Adair County. Orient was founded in 1879 and named for the township in which it was located. Orient Township was probably given the name because Orient means to the east, and the township is east of the county seat, Somerset. Orient was incorporated on February 23, 1884. (249, 438, 443)

Orleans, Dickinson County. Orleans developed around the Hotel Orleans, which was constructed in 1883. The town was named for the hotel. There are two explanations for the name of the hotel. It was either named after New Orleans or for Orleans in France. The community was incorporated on July 3, 1895. (438, 524)

Osage, county seat, Mitchell County. Osage would have been called Cora, after the daughter of a Dr. Moore, who planned the town in 1854, but the town site was not properly recorded. Osage was named in honor of capitalist Orrin Sage of Massachusetts. The town was officially established in 1856 and was incorporated in 1871. (286, 445)

Osceola, county seat, Clarke County. Osceola was selected by commissioners appointed by the state legislature in 1851. The name was suggested by Dickinson Webster in honor of Osceola, the leader of a group of Seminole Indians in Florida. There are sites in many states named for him. In fact, there are more sites and towns named for him than any other American Indian. Osceola was incorporated on December 24, 1866, and later was reincorporated in 1886. (43, 561)

Oskaloosa, county seat, Mahaska County. Oskaloosa was created on January 24, 1835, by an act of the territorial legislature. The town was selected on May 11, 1844, by Jesse Williams, Ebenezer Perkins, and Thomas Henderson as the county seat. The most believable story about the naming of Oskaloosa is that the name was originally going to be Mahaska, but one of the people involved objected. The name of Ouscaloosa was proposed. The settlers believed that she was a Creek princess who was a wife of Osceola. The name was accepted, but a clerk misspelled the name when it was filed, and the town was registered as Oskaloosa. Beyond this core information, there are several conflicting stories about the origin of the name Ouscaloosa. There appears to be no credible evidence that anyone of that name was married to Osceola, though the name is very likely a derivation of a word in the Muskhogean language, which the Seminoles spoke. The meaning is possibly "black mother," which fits into a story about an unnamed wife of Osceola who was seized as a suspected runaway slave by authorities at Ft. King, Florida, in 1835. This action renewed the Seminole Wars. There are several fanciful stories about the naming of Oskaloosa. One is that Oskaloosa was the wife of Mahaska, but she was not. Another story posted by a reporter with a big imagination in the *Oskaloosa Weekly Herald* in 1896 was about a son of Mahaska's named Oska and Lucy Jones, the daughter of one of the early settlers who was captured by the Iowas. Oska and Lucy fell in love and ran away at some personal peril. Oskaloosa was incorporated in 1853. (124, 339, 447, 561)

Ossian, Winneshiek County. Ossian was founded by John Ossian Porter on April 30, 1853, and named for the founder. It was incorporated on February 7, 1876. (33, 448)

Osterdock, Clayton County. Osterdock was established in December 1872 on property owned by the Bowman family. The site was originally called Osterdock Ferry for Dominic and Mary Keble Osterdock, who operated the Osterdock Ferry on the Turkey River. The name was later shortened to Osterdock. The town was incorporated on April 16, 1904. (224, 261, 438)

Otho, Webster County. The town started as the Otho Post Office, located on a stagecoach route. When the Minneapolis and St. Louis Railroad built a line through the area, Otho was established as a depot. The town was named after the township, and the township was named for Otho I, founder of the Holy Roman Empire and an early king of Germany. It was incorporated on June 3, 1954. (17, 438, 475)

Otley, Marion County. Otley was established on August 14–15, 1867. It was located at the site of a depot for the Des Moines Valley Railroad. A Mr. Otley, a civil engineer for the railroad, had located the station. The town was named in his honor. Otley is not incorporated. (594)

Oto, Woodbury County. Oto was established on February 25, 1879, by Samuel Day and O. S. Day. The town was named for a Sioux tribe and their chief by Samuel Day. Oto was incorporated on July 10, 1888. (294, 438)

Otranto, Mitchell County. Otranto was established by Mary Bartlett in 1877. The settlement was known as Bartlett's Grove. When the railroad came through, the town became known as Otranto Station, named after the township. The township was named for the prince in a story by Horace Walpole, *The Castle of Otranto*. The town is not incorporated. (163, 286)

Ottosen, Humboldt County. Ottosen was named for C. Ottosen, who began buying grain at the site starting in August 1895. The town was established in May 1896 and was incorporated on July 16, 1909. (275, 438)

Ottumwa, county seat, Wapello County. Ottumwa was the name the Indians used for the location. When a town was developed at the site, the name was carried over. The most commonly accepted meaning for the term was "rapids" or "swift water" in the Fox language. Ottumwa was briefly called Louisville before reverting to the name the Indians applied. The town was founded by some land speculators in May 1843. It was incorporated on February 2, 1888. (298, 438, 561)

Owasa, Hardin County. Owasa was founded on March 28, 1884, by J. H. and Mary Smith. The name was probably inspired by the Ojibwa term for bluebird, *owaissa*. *Owaissa* was referred to in Longfellow's *The Song of Hiawatha*. Another possible reason proposed is that the name was drawn from the Sac word for bear, *owasse*. The town was incorporated on March 18, 1920. (163, 414, 438, 561)

Oxford, Johnson County. Oxford was named after a town in New York at the suggestion of Mrs. W. H. Cotter, who had lived in the New York community. The petition for the establishment of the town was drawn with a blank space for the name. W. H. Cotter, who was responsible for submitting the petition, had it at his house. His wife suggested filling in the blank with the name Oxford, the name of the township in which she lived when she was a child. Several other names were suggested. They were written on slips of paper, and a drawing occurred to choose a name. Fred, the Cotters' three-year-old son, drew the name Oxford. The blank was filled in, and Oxford was named. The town was founded in 1868 by P. C. Wilcox. It was informally known as "The Tank" because of the presence of a water tank for the railroad. Oxford was incorporated on April 8, 1881. (331, 438)

Oxford Junction, Jones County. Oxford Junction was founded as a railroad station in August 1872. The town was named for a nearby mill site and the intersection of two railroads. Oxford Junction was incorporated on January 15, 1884. (142, 163, 438)

Oxford Mills, Jones County. Oxford Mills was established in May 1861. The town was named for the mill that was located there. Since the mill was in Oxford Township, the name reflected that. The "Oxford" in the name reflects the influence of the English roots of at least some of the founders. The town is not incorporated. (142, 246)

Oyens, Plymouth County. The town was founded by the Sioux City and Iowa Falls Town Lot and Land Company on October 22, 1886. There is anecdotal information that the name was inspired by a railroad employee named Owen or Owens. The community was incorporated on January 29, 1909. (107, 294, 438)

P p ┼┼┼┼┼┼┼┼┼┼┼┼┼┼┼┼┼┼┼┼

Pacific Junction, Mills County. In 1871 land owned by D. N. Smith was surveyed, and the town of Pacific Junction was built at the intersection of the Council Bluffs and St. Joseph Railroad and the Chicago, Burlington and Quincy Railroad. The name was taken from Pacific City, a nearby town that had been a staging area for people heading west, and the railroad intersection at the new town site. Pacific Junction was incorporated on January 11, 1882. (318, 409, 438)

Packwood, Jefferson County. Packwood was established in 1883 and named for "Uncle" Sam Packwood. The community was incorporated on May 7, 1894. (438, 486)

Palmer, Pocahontas County. The proposed town was initially named Hanson in honor of the man who owned the land where the town was located. In late 1899 postal officials requested that the town planners change the name to eliminate confusion with Manson, a nearby town. When the town was formally established in 1900, it was named for Iowa's railroad commissioner at that time. Palmer was incorporated on June 21, 1901. (67, 438)

Palmyra, Warren County. Palmyra was founded by John Farley and J. F. Moorman in 1847. It was probably named for the city constructed by Solomon and mentioned in the Bible. The town is not incorporated. (166, 315, 507)

Palo, Linn County. Palo was formally established on June 10, 1854. It was named for the battle of Palo Alto, which had been fought in 1846. The community was incorporated on April 25, 1905. (163, 282, 438)

Panama, Shelby County. Before Panama was founded, the area was known as Crandall Settlement. The town was established by the Milwaukee Land Company on April 12, 1882. While there is no evidence as to the origin of the name, it is thought that it might be part of an Indian phrase meaning "an abundance of fish." Panama was incorporated on May 17, 1886. (438, 453, 587)

Panora, Guthrie County. Panora was the first town established in the county and was the original county seat. It was founded by James Laverty on November 18, 1851. The name is a contraction of "panorama," reflecting the settlers' enthusiasm for the view. Panora was incorporated on July 6, 1872. (271, 318, 438)

Panorama Park, Scott County. Panorama Park was established by residents determined to get some of the benefits of incorporation, to obtain funding to fix the town's main road, and to avoid annexation by Bettendorf. Prior to that time, it had been an unincorporated area near Bettendorf, where settlement had started in 1858. Panorama Park was incorporated on July 7, 1953. While there is no park in Panorama Park, the name clearly reflects the view of the Mississippi from the site. (438, 511)

Paris, Linn County. Paris was established by Amos Bond and Daniel McCrellis on April 14, 1855. The town apparently was named for Paris, France. Paris is not incorporated. (282, 583)

Paris (Bunch), Davis County. Paris was founded on December 18, 1891, on property owned by Jackson Paris. Consequently, the town was named for him. When Paris applied for a post office, the townspeople were informed that there already was a Paris Post Office in Linn County. The residents decided to change the name of the town to Bunch in honor of a local doctor. The railroad refused to recognize the name change since it would require changing all of its printed schedules and timetables, so the depot remained Paris. Although the Davis County legal plats call the location Paris, the post office is Bunch, and most of the residents, at least in 1969, called the town Bunch. Ironically, the town has neither a post office nor an active train depot anymore. The town has been known for some time as Paris (Bunch). Paris (Bunch) is not incorporated. (151, 345)

Park View, Scott County. Park View was named for the view of Scott County Park from the site. The town was established by Dick Millage in the late 1960s. The town is not incorporated. (511)

Parkersburg, Butler County. Parkersburg was established in 1865 and named for P. P. Parker, a settler in the area. It was incorporated on December 7, 1874. (254, 438)

Parnell, Iowa County. From its beginning in 1884, Parnell was a functioning town. The railroad had missed the town of Lytle City by about three miles, so the citizens in that town moved everything, including the buildings, to a location along the railroad track. The new town was named for Charles Stewart Parnell, an Irish statesman. Parnell was incorporated on March 24, 1891. (438, 454)

Paton, Greene County. Paton was named for a Mr. Paton, a New Yorker who invested in the land in the area. It was founded in June 1875 and was incorporated on February 20, 1884. (216, 438, 531)

Patterson, Madison County. Patterson was founded in March 1872 by Andrew Pattison, who named the town after himself. When the town site was recorded, the name was misspelled, hence the name Patterson. The town was incorporated on December 7, 1877. (375, 438)

Paullina, O'Brien County. Paullina was established by the Western Town Lot Company on January 20, 1882. The town was named for the Paullina brothers who were early settlers and landowners in the area. It was incorporated on October 30, 1883. (438, 460, 528)

Pekin, Jefferson and Keokuk counties. Pekin was first known as Ioka Station when it was established along a railroad track south of the town of Ioka. The railroad did not pass through or by Ioka, so the new town carried the name Ioka Station when it was established in 1882. The name Pekin is probably a transfer name, since there were Pekins in Illinois, Indiana, and Ohio. The town is not incorporated. (35, 461)

Pella, Marion County. Pella was established on June 6, 1848, by Hedrick P. Scholte. The town was named from the Hebrew word signifying "a city of refuge." Pella was incorporated on April 10, 1868. (438, 594)

Peoria, Mahaska County. The town was originally called Warrensville. It was founded on May 21, 1853, by Theodric Spain, aided by George Westlake and Sanfred Haines. The town was named for Peoria, Illinois. Peoria is the name of a tribe of Indians who lived near the location of Peoria, Illinois. The town is not incorporated. (339, 561)

Peosta, Dubuque County. Peosta was first called Caledonia before it was renamed for a member of the Fox tribe named Peosta. The settlement was founded in April 1883 by the Brady and Clarke families. There is some controversy about the origin of the name Peosta. Whether there was a man named Peosta, whose wife discovered the lead deposits near where Dubuque would be located, or whether the wife herself was named Peosta is not clear, since both stories have been put forth. In the version of the story where Peosta is the wife, her daughter marries Julien Dubuque. After the Eighteenth Amendment was repealed, a number of the small, unincorporated towns feared they would not be permitted to have a tavern unless they were incorporated. The towns incorporated so that they could ensure the sale of beer in their communities. Peosta was incorporated on June 16, 1933. (344, 438, 561)

Percival, Fremont County. Percival was named for its founder, Robert Percival. He had established a post office at the site in 1868. The town was first known as Gaston. Percival is not incorporated. (226, 361)

Perkins, Sioux County. Perkins was named in honor of George Douglas Perkins, who was for many years the editor of the *Sioux City Journal*. The town was established on property owned by Henry Miller in 1890. Perkins is not incorporated. (433)

Perry, Dallas County. Perry was named for a Colonel Perry of Keokuk. It was founded in 1869 by John Willis and Harvey Willis and was incorporated on June 18, 1875. (263, 438)

Pershing, Marion County. Pershing was founded in 1928. The town was named for the Pershing Coal Company that operated there. The company was named for General John Pershing, who had distinguished himself in World War I. The town is not incorporated. (384, 385)

Persia, Harrison County. Persia was founded by L. C. and Alice Baldwin on June 6, 1882. The town was given that name because a peddler who was passing through told the settlers that the area looked like his old home in Persia. Persia was incorporated on April 30, 1891. (108, 312, 438)

Petersburg, Delaware County. Petersburg was probably named after Sts. Peter and Paul Catholic Church at the town site. The church was established in the same year as the town, 1874. The post office at the site was first called Petersburgh, but the name was changed to Petersburg in 1894. The town is not incorporated. (458, 504)

Peterson, Clay County. A post office was located in the area of the present-day Peterson in 1858. A Mr. Peterson, who had worked to establish the post office, had suggested the name Howard, but the Post Office Department changed the name to honor him, since there was already a Howard Post Office in the region. When the town was founded in 1881 by the Western Town Lot Company, the name was maintained. Peterson was incorporated on November 12, 1886. (260, 438)

Pierson, Woodbury County. Pierson was established by the Blair Town Lot and Land Company on August 3, 1883, and named for Andrew Pierson, an early settler in the area. It was incorporated on November 27, 1891. (294, 438, 528)

Pilot Grove, Lee County. Pilot Grove was established on April 16, 1858, and named for a grove of trees that was a landmark for people traveling through the area. The town is not incorporated. (163, 281)

Pilot Mound, Boone County. Pilot Mound was formally established on September 8, 1881. There had been a Pilot Mound Post Office at the site since November 14, 1865. There was a geologic feature at that location that was called Pilot Mound, so it was a natural choice to call both the post office and the town Pilot Mound. The post office was known as Pilotmound from December 1895 until 1905, when it was renamed Pilot Mound. The community was incorporated on June 23, 1897. (210, 438, 458)

Pioneer, Humboldt County. J. M. Anderson opened a store at the location of the present-day Pioneer in the spring of 1890. It would seem likely that the name was a tribute to the early settlers in the area. Pioneer was incorporated on February 8, 1910. (275, 438)

Pisgah, Harrison County. Pisgah was founded by the Western Land and Town Lot Company and the Boyer Valley Railway on January 20, 1899. The town was named for Mt. Pisgah, a post office that had been in the area. The post office had been named for the Palestinian mountain mentioned in the Bible. Pisgah was incorporated on July 2, 1904. (312, 438, 528)

Plain View, Scott County. Information about the origin of the community of Plain View is somewhat sketchy. There was a post office at the site from 1873 to 1902. The name reflects either a view of the plains from the site or an uninspiring view. It is probably the former. The town is not incorporated. (458, 510)

Plainfield, Bremer County. Plainfield was established on October 16, 1866, by H. S. Hoover, county surveyor. Many of the settlers were from Plainfield, Illinois, and consequently they named their new town Plainfield. It was incorporated on October 17, 1895. (253, 438)

Plano, Appanoose County. Plano was founded on November 21, 1879, by F. J. and Emmeline Steel. Before the name Plano was settled on, the town was known successively as Steele Station, Camden, and Palo. The name Plano was selected in the 1880s, reportedly for Plano, Illinois. Plano was incorporated on October 5, 1916. (26, 318, 438, 537)

Pleasant Hill, Polk County. The area of Pleasant Hill was first settled in 1844. The town was named for the Pleasant Hill School District. The district was probably named Pleasant Hill because of its location. Pleasant Hill was incorporated on May 12, 1956. When the citizens were voting to incorporate as a community, many of them thought the town was to be called Youngstown, but when the petition was filed, Pleasant Hill was listed as the town's name. (109, 163, 438)

Pleasant Plain, Jefferson County. The community was first settled by Quaker farmers in 1836 and was originally given the name Pleasant Prairie before it was changed to Pleasant Plain. It would appear to be a descriptive name. Pleasant Plain was incorporated on April 12, 1900. (57, 438)

Pleasanton, Decatur County. The town was founded by Daniel Bartholow in 1854 as Pleasant Plain. In the late 1860s the Nine Eagles Post Office, operating in the area since 1849, was going to be renamed to match the town. The Post Office Department would not allow the name Pleasant Plain, since that name was in use in Jefferson County. The town and post office may have simply been renamed with a name that was similar to the original descriptive name. Another possibility is that since the name was changed in the late 1860s, the town might have been named for General Alfred Pleasanton. As a young soldier Pleasanton had served in the area, had served in the war with Mexico, and was well known to many Iowans for his service in the Civil War. Pleasanton was incorporated in February 1884. (44, 438, 458)

Pleasantville, Marion County. Pleasantville was established in 1849 by Wesley Jordan and was named for the beauty of the location. It was incorporated on June 11, 1872. (438, 594)

Plover, Pocahontas County. Plover was one of several towns named for game birds by Charles E. Whitehead, president of the Des Moines and Fort Dodge Railroad. He also named the towns of Curlew and Mallard. Plover was founded in 1882 and was incorporated on October 18, 1900. (163, 438, 465)

Plymouth, Cerro Gordo County. Plymouth was established on December 23, 1870, on property owned by Thomas Tenney, his son, and Charles Gracie. It was the second attempt by the Tenneys to establish a town named Plymouth. Their original town site was platted in 1858 on another site that they owned. The town was probably named for Plymouth, England. It was incorporated on October 18, 1900. (246, 270, 438)

Pocahontas, county seat, Pocahontas County. Pocahontas was established in 1870 and was named the county seat on October 12, 1875. The town was named for the county, and the county was named for the daughter of Chief Powhatan of Virginia. Pocahontas was incorporated on May 16, 1892. (192, 438)

Polk City, Polk County. Polk City was established in May 1850 by George Bebee at the site of an Indian village called Wauconsa. Both the town and the county that it is in were named for President James K. Polk. Polk City was incorporated on March 13, 1875. (289, 438, 528)

Pomeroy, Calhoun County. Pomeroy was established by Frederick Hess in 1870 on land owned by John Blair and named after a Senator Pomeroy of New Hampshire. The community was incorporated on April 22, 1880. (438, 469, 532)

Popejoy, Franklin County. Popejoy was established as Carlton, but the name was soon changed to Popejoy, for John Popejoy, an area resident and landowner. The Popejoy Post Office was established in 1888, which would be an indication that settlement had started. Popejoy was incorporated on July 24, 1908. (163, 438, 458)

Portland, Cerro Gordo County. Portland was established as a station on the Chicago, Milwaukee and St. Paul Railroad in 1878 by A. S. Felt. The town was named Portland after the township that it was in. The township's name is probably a transfer name, although there is no clear evidence to support that. Portland is not incorporated. (270, 337)

Portsmouth, Shelby County. The town site of Portsmouth was established by the Milwaukee Land Company on August 8, 1882. The origin of the town's name appears to be a mystery, although it is clear that the original inspiration for the name had to have been Portsmouth, England. Portsmouth was incorporated in 1883. (233, 587)

Postville, Allamakee County. In 1848 Augustus C. Dodge, then senator from Iowa, recommended the establishment of a post office at the "half-way house" on the Military Road. It was to be called Postville, with Joel Post as postmaster. The town was established in June 1853 and was incorporated on March 30, 1905. (9, 230, 438)

Prairie City, Jasper County. Settlement at the site started in 1851 when William Means built a house there. The location was called Elliot, probably for James Elliot, who settled there shortly after Means. It was named Prairie City when the town was officially established on June 7, 1856, by James Elliott and his wife. The town was named to describe its location on the prairie. Prairie City was incorporated on August 7, 1874. (438, 573)

Prairieburg, Linn County. Prairieburg was established on July 30, 1867. Henry Ward gave the town a practical and descriptive name, as it was located on the prairie. Prairieburg was incorporated on March 30, 1905. (282, 438)

Prescott, Adams County. The settlement that became known as Prescott started along a newly laid track of the Burlington Northern Railroad in 1868. The town was first called Motley, then Glendale. Finally, the name Prescott was settled on in 1869 to honor a man who was deeply involved in the development of the rail line through the area. Prescott was officially established on June 6, 1870, and was incorporated on November 26, 1890. (250, 438)

Preston, Jackson County. Preston was established in 1870 and named for a Colonel Preston, who was affiliated with the railroad that ran through the area. Preston was incorporated on November 11, 1890. (276, 438)

Primghar, county seat, O'Brien County. Primghar was established by W. C. Green and James Roberts on November 8, 1872. The name of the town came from the initials of the eight men who were instrumental in developing the town.

In fact, there is a short poem that memorializes the men and their names:

> Pumphrey, the treasurer, drives the first nail;
> Roberts, the donor, is quick on his trail;
> Inman dips slyly his first letter in;
> McCormack adds M, which make the full Prim;
> Green thinking of groceries, gives them the G;
> Hayes drops them an H, without asking a fee;
> Albright, the joker, with his jokes all at par;
> Rerick brings up the rear and crowns all "Primghar."

Primghar was incorporated on February 15, 1888. (438, 460)

Princeton, Scott County. The town site of the present-day Princeton was first settled in 1836. When Princeton was incorporated on January 29, 1857, it absorbed two adjacent settlements, Pinnacle Point and Elizabeth City. The town was named for Princeton, New Jersey, because of that city's importance in the Revolutionary War. (246, 438, 509)

Prole, Warren County. Prole was founded in 1884 and was named for Albert Westren Prole, a businessman in the community. The town is not incorporated. (315)

Promise City, Wayne County. Promise City was established by Burris Moore and Richard Given in the spring of 1881 at the site of a Mormon camp. It was first called the Town of Promise at Tommie Howland's suggestion. The name was changed at a later date to Promise City. Both names reflect the optimism of the residents in their new town. Promise City was incorporated on August 23, 1901. (318, 438, 572)

Protivin, Howard County. A Czech community had started to form in the area of Protivin around 1855, but the town really was established when the people in the area decided to build a church there in 1878. The town was named for the prior home of Marie Jira Chyle by her husband. Protivin was incorporated on August 1, 1894. (163, 438, 480)

Pulaski, Davis County. Pulaski was named by Columbus Hains, the first postmaster at that location, after Count Casimir Pulaski, a Polish officer who fought in the American Revolution. The post office was established in 1850, and the town followed on October 12, 1856. Pulaski was incorporated on May 3, 1893. (151, 264, 438)

Q q ++++++++++++++++++++

Quarry, Marshall County. Quarry was planned in 1868 by the LeGrand Quarry Company and named for that operation. The town is not incorporated. (285)

Quasqueton, Buchanan County. The location of the town was at the intersection of a number of Indian trails at a fording point on the Wapsipinicon River. The site was known by its Fox name, Quasquetuck, which means "swift running water." The town was established in 1847. Quasqueton was incorporated on July 1, 1902. (61, 438)

Quimby, Cherokee County. Quimby was founded on October 3, 1887, on property owned by George Sellers and A. J. Clark. It was named for F. W. Quimby, an officer of the Illinois Central Railroad. Quimby was incorporated on June 7, 1906. (401, 438)

R r ++++++++++++++++++++

Radcliffe, Hardin County. Radcliffe was established in 1880 by the Toledo and Northwestern Railroad. The town was named by a Mr. Bliss, land agent for the company, and was drawn from the title of a novel, *The Heir of Radcliffe*. Radcliffe was incorporated on July 8, 1891. (272, 438, 528)

Rake, Winnebago County. Rake was founded on August 9, 1900, by Arent Rake on property owned by Thomas H. and Mary Brown. The town was named for its founder and was incorporated on January 20, 1908. (303, 438, 482)

Ralston, Carroll County. For years the site of Ralston was known as Slater Siding. When a railroad station was built there in 1891, the name was changed to Ralston. The town was named for an officer in the American Express Company. The community was incorporated on October 31, 1903. (74, 438)

Randalia, Fayette County. Randalia was established when the railroad built a depot at the site in 1873. Andrew Randall was the surveying engineer for the railroad that developed the town. Andrew Randall and his brothers, Alonzo, Pitney, and Josie, were credited with founding the town, hence the name Randalia. It was incorporated on April 30, 1896. (163, 189, 438)

Randall, Hamilton County. Randall, established in 1878, was named for a well-known politician, Samuel Randall. It was incorporated in 1940. (163, 228, 485)

Randolph, Fremont County. Randolph was founded in 1877. Volney Bass, one of the property owners, had suggested two possible names for the town, Lambert and Randolph. Randolph was selected. Reportedly, Randolph was the name of a former slave whom Bass knew. The community was incorporated on July 6, 1881. (226, 438, 545)

Rathbun, Appanoose County. Rathbun was named for an official of the Star Coal Company, Charles H. Rathbun. The town was founded by the coal company in May 1892 and was incorporated either in 1893 or 1894. (26)

Raymond, Black Hawk County. A post office named Mullarky's Grove was established at the location on March 15, 1858. The post office was renamed Raymond on February 27, 1862. The town was founded on June 14, 1867. There is no documentation on why the name Raymond was selected. It has been speculated that the town might have been named for Jarvis Henry Raymond, a well-known journalist and politician from New York. Raymond was incorporated on June 31, 1956. (178, 438, 478)

Readlyn, Bremer County. A representative of the Chicago Great Western Railroad named Read bought the land from the Ohlendorf family for a railroad station in 1903. The name of the town was derived from Read's name and the role that he played in getting track laid through the area, Read's line. The name was established as Readlyn. The community was incorporated on February 1, 1905. (389, 438)

Reasnor, Jasper County. Reasnor was founded in August 1877 by Samuel and Mary Reasoner. The name was given because of the number of people named Reasoner in the area. The town was first called Reasoner, but the post office and the rail depot were always called Reasnor. Reasnor was incorporated in May 1912. (110, 458, 573)

Red Oak, county seat, Montgomery County. Red Oak was founded in 1869 and named for the nearby Red Oak Creek. The creek was named because of the number of oak trees growing along its banks. The community was incorporated in 1876. (403)

Redding, Ringgold County. The town was founded in 1880 as a stop along a branch of the Chicago, Burlington and Quincy Railroad. The name for the town was taken from the Redding Post Office, which had been established in 1855 at a site about two miles from the current town. The reason for the naming of the post office appears to be lost.

The town was incorporated on April 10, 1882. (44, 438, 488)

Redfield, Dallas County. Redfield was founded as New Ireland by Patrick Thomas Cavenaugh and Michael Cavenaugh in 1852–1853. The Cavanaughs then sold the entire town site to Colonel James Redfield and a Mr. Moore. The town's name was changed to Redfield to honor the colonel. Redfield was incorporated on March 21, 1881. (263, 438)

Reinbeck, Grundy County. Reinbeck was established by a Mr. Methfennel on April 30, 1877. The town was named for Reinburg, Germany. Reinbeck was incorporated in 1878. (220, 489)

Rembrandt, Buena Vista County. Rembrandt was established in 1900, the year the Minneapolis and St. Louis Railroad was built through the area. The town was first called Orsland, for the man who owned the property. The post office was responsible for the name change honoring the Dutch painter Rembrandt. The town was incorporated in 1901. (163, 455)

Remsen, Plymouth County. Remsen was founded on August 28, 1876, by the Sioux City and Iowa Falls Town Lot and Land Company. It was named for William Remsen Smith, an area landowner, and was incorporated in 1889. (294)

Renwick, Humboldt County. Renwick was founded by the Western Town Lot Company on January 24, 1882. The name carries no meaning. The original owners of the land, two individuals named Smith and Frank, created it. Renwick was incorporated on October 17, 1891. (275, 438, 528)

Rhodes, Marshall County. Rhodes was called Edenville when it was founded on August 29, 1856, by Conway Rhodes. The name was changed to Rhodes in 1928 to honor the town's founder. The town was incorporated on March 16, 1883. (402)

Riceville, Howard and Mitchell counties. Riceville was founded by the three Rice brothers in 1855. It was incorporated in 1892. (246, 490)

Richland, Keokuk County. Richland was named because of the quality of the soil at the site, although one early settler had proposed the name Frogtown after a heavy rain had left much water standing at the location. The area has been settled since 1838. The town was founded in 1841 and was incorporated on December 31, 1868. (279, 438, 491)

Richmond, Washington County. Richmond was founded in November 1840 by Thomas Dawson. He was from Virginia and named the town for Richmond, Virginia. The town is not incorporated. (299, 569)

Rickardsville, Dubuque County. There was a post office established at the site in 1857 named Jefferson. The settlement's name was changed in 1868 to honor Salmon Rickard, a settler who had donated land for a school. Rickardsville was incorporated on November 17, 1964. (344, 438, 458)

Ricketts, Crawford County. Ricketts was established by the Western Town Lot Company in 1899 and named for a pioneer in the area. The community was incorporated on March 19, 1902. (438, 493, 528)

Ridgeway, Winneshiek County. Ridgeway was founded when J. L. Flowers built a grain warehouse at the town site in July 1867. Several more businesses were soon established, and a post office was located there in the same year. The name was probably inspired by the physical location of the town. It was incorporated on March 15, 1894. (33, 163, 438)

Rinard, Calhoun County. Rinard was founded by the Iowa Townsite Company on June 21, 1904. The town was named after a railroad employee. The citizens voted to incorporate on October 27, 1914. (163, 532)

Ringsted, Emmett County. Ringsted was founded on April 6, 1899. The town was named after Ringsted, Denmark. Ringsted was incorporated on March 29, 1900. (184, 438)

Rippey, Greene County. Rippey was established as a station along the Des Moines Valley Railroad track in June 1870. The town was first called New Rippey. Incorporated in 1896, the town was named after a fading village in the area that was the original Rippey. The original Rippey was named for Captain C. M. Rippey. (246, 531)

River Junction, Johnson County. River Junction was the site of a ferry across the Iowa River and also a depot on the Burlington, Cedar Rapids and Northern Railroad. The post office at the site had previously been called "77." River Junction was named because it was near both the Iowa River and a railroad junction. John and Louisa Porter established River Junction in 1873, at about the same location as Sepanemo, a town founded in 1837. River Junction is not incorporated. (330, 332)

Riverdale, Scott County. The location of Riverdale had been an unincorporated area near Bettendorf, where settlement had started in 1858. The area that became Riverdale was primarily rural until Alcoa established an aluminum rolling mill there in 1948. Bettendorf was interested in annexing the land because of the potential for growth and tax revenue. The people who lived in the area decided that they needed to incorporate to avoid being swallowed up by Bettendorf. The residents incorporated their community as Riverdale on December 27, 1950, although there was litigation between Bettendorf and Riverdale until 1953, when the Iowa Supreme Court upheld Riverdale's incorporation. The town is probably named for its proximity to the Mississippi River. (149, 438)

Riverside, Washington County. Riverside was established in December 1872. The town's name was probably drawn from its location by the English River. A Dr. Mott had proposed the name. Riverside was incorporated on March 22, 1882. (163, 299, 438)

Riverton, Fremont County. Riverton was founded in 1870. The town was possibly named for its location along the East Nishnabotna River. Riverton was incorporated on June 22, 1876. (226, 438)

Robins, Linn County. Robins was named for its founder and owner of the town site, John Robins. He founded the town in 1888. Robins was incorporated on May 3, 1910. (78, 318, 438)

Rochester, Cedar County. Rochester was established at a ferry site in August 1856 by William Gordon. Rochester was named for Rochester, New York. The town is not incorporated. (258)

Rock Falls, Cerro Gordo County. Rock Falls was founded by Elijah Wiltfong in 1858. The town was named after the post office that had been located in the area in 1855. The post office was called Shell Rock Falls, for the falls on the nearby river. When the railroad came through, it called the depot at the town Rock Falls to distinguish it from another railroad station called Shell Rock. Rock Falls was incorporated on July 17, 1882. (270, 438)

Rock Rapids, county seat, Lyon County. The town site was discovered in 1869 when D. C. Whitehead, Matthias Sweeny, and Delos Townsley were exploring the Rock River valley and noted the location as particularly suited for development. The town was established on February 28, 1874, on property owned by a Mr. and Mrs. Cheney, a Mr. and Mrs. Whitehead, a Mr. and Mrs. Bradley, and a Mr. and Mrs.

Howard. Rock Rapids was named for the rapids in the Rock River at that location. The community was incorporated on April 8, 1885. (438, 464, 528)

Rock Valley, Sioux County. The town was established on December 16, 1879. It appears that Abram Warren, who owned the property where the town was founded, suggested the name to note the town's location in the valley of the Rock River. Rock Valley was incorporated on November 26, 1886. (433, 438)

Rockford, Floyd County. The town was founded in 1856 by George Wyatt and three investors from Rockford, Illinois, whom he had recruited. The town was named for Rockford, Illinois. It was incorporated on March 19, 1878. (438, 456)

Rockwell, Cerro Gordo County. Rockwell was named for the owner of the land where the town was located, George B. Rockwell. The town was platted by Mr. Rockwell and the Iowa Valley Construction Company in 1870. It was incorporated on July 9, 1881. (270, 438)

Rockwell City, county seat, Calhoun County. Rockwell City was established in 1876 and named for its founder, John Rockwell. The community was incorporated on May 2, 1882. (255, 438, 501)

Rodman, Palo Alto County. Rodman was named after a Mr. Rodman, who gave the railroad a half interest in his property on the condition that it create a town on his land and call it Rodman. Since the rail line was constructed through this area in 1881, the town's origin is most likely close to this time. Rodman was incorporated on June 17, 1899. (398, 438)

Rodney, Monona County. Rodney was established by the Milwaukee Land Company as a station for the Chicago, Milwaukee and St. Paul Railroad on June 6, 1887. The town was named for Rodney Rice, the first passenger to step off the train in the town. A whimsical story about the naming of the town is that as a man dismounted from a railcar, he hit his knee on an iron rod and cursed about the rod hitting his knee, and that inspired the town's name. The town was incorporated on February 2, 1892. (163, 287, 438, 444)

Roland, Story County. Roland was founded in October 1881. The name was drawn from Norwegian history and was suggested by John Everson, one of a number of Norwegian settlers in the area. The town was incorporated on December 29, 1891. (16, 438)

Rolfe, Pocahontas County. Rolfe was founded in September 1881 by the Northwestern Land Company. Rolfe replaced Old Rolfe, which at one time had been important in the area's history but had faded away. That town was the first Pocahontas county seat. It was first called Highland or Highland City, then Milton, and finally Rolfe at the suggestion of Charles Converse, an area landowner. His suggestion was to honor John Rolfe, who married Pocahontas. The town was incorporated on January 4, 1884. (111, 192)

Rome, Henry County. James Phelps had a trading post at the site of the present-day Rome in 1834–1836. A man named Thompson made the first claim to land in the area across the river from the location. Elijah Turner planned the town in 1837. There is no information on the reason for the name, but Rome, New York, or Rome, Indiana, would be strong possibilities. The town was finally established in October 1840 by Joseph Jeffers and was incorporated on January 1, 1869. (163, 241, 438)

Rose Hill, Mahaska County. Rose Hill was originally called Ornbaum. The town was founded on August 23, 1873, by the Ornbaum Town Company. When the railroad established a depot there in 1875, it refused to call the depot Ornbaum and in fact called it Rose Hill. The Post Office Department changed the name of the post office to Rose Hill. The community members, recognizing the dissonance, voted to incorporate as Rose Hill on August 22, 1876. The town was probably named for an abandoned town named Rosehill, which had gotten the name from the wild roses in the area. (339)

Roselle, Carroll County. Roselle is actually named Hillsdale. The town was established in 1881 as Hillsdale and has not been officially changed. The town had been using the name Roselle even before it was officially established. Roselle is a woman's name in German culture, reflecting the roots of the settlers in the area. The town is not incorporated. (74)

Roseville, Floyd County. A post office was established at the site in 1903. The request for an office was sent in with the name Rose. Whether it was for the name of the post office founder's wife or descriptive of the wild roses growing in the area is the subject of some debate. In any event, the postal department accepted the post office but added "ville" to the name. The town is not incorporated. (147, 458)

Ross, Audubon County. Ross was founded in 1882 by the Western Town Lot Company. The town was named for a local farmer named Ross. The town is not incorporated. (528)

Rossie, Clay County. Rossie was established as a station for the Chicago, Rock Island and Pacific Railroad in 1900. The town apparently was named Rossie to honor Rosie Davidson, the wife of one of the men associated with the railroad. Rossie was incorporated on August 30, 1922. (260, 438)

Rossville, Allamakee County. In 1849 a commission appointed by the Iowa General Assembly staked out the location, known as the Old Sinke, as the site at which to locate the county seat. That did not happen. William F. Ross was the first settler there in 1850. A post office was established and called Rossville in 1852 for Ross. Rossville was originally known as Maud. The Milwaukee Railroad called it Rossville Station. The town is not incorporated. (230)

Rowan, Wright County. Rowan was named after the Rowen family who had settled in the area. When the settlers sought to establish a post office, the name was not accepted because of the similarity to Bowen, another post office in the state. The spelling was changed to Rowan by the postal department. Rowan was established by the Cedar Rapids, Iowa Falls and Northwestern Town Lot Company on August 25, 1884. It was incorporated on December 21, 1901. (47, 438)

Rowley, Buchanan County. Rowley was established when the Burlington, Cedar Rapids and Northern Railroad laid track in the area in the fall of 1873. It was named in honor of D. W. C. Rowley, who was secretary of the railroad when the line reached the town. Rowley was incorporated on April 20, 1920. (85, 438)

Royal, Clay County. Royal was developed as a station on a rail line in 1900. It was named by Eliza Nelson, the first postmistress. She was told to keep the name simple, as in one word, and she selected Royal for reasons that appear to be lost. The town was incorporated on August 30, 1910. (260, 438, 502)

Rubio, Washington County. Rubio was established as a station on the Milwaukee Railroad in 1900. The station was named Rubio in honor of Pascual Ortiz-Rubio, a Mexican engineer and statesman. Ortiz-Rubio went on to prominence in later years, including becoming president of Mexico. The town is not incorporated. (479, 569)

Rudd, Floyd County. Rudd was founded in 1869 by James Swartwood, who initially called the town Danville, though the site had been referred to as Bennet's Ford since the mid 1850s. The name was changed because a man named Rudd promised $1,000 for a church if the town was named after him. The name was changed, but he did not honor his promise. The town was incorporated on February 7, 1900. (318, 438, 456)

Runnells, Polk County. Runnells was established in 1881 and named after one of the founders. It was incorporated on May 21, 1903. (163, 413, 438)

Russell, Lucas County. Russell was founded by H. S. Russell on October 8, 1867, and was incorporated on April 25, 1887. (283, 438)

Ruthven, Palo Alto County. Ruthven was established in 1878 on property owned by Robert Ruthven and Alex Ruthven. They gave half of the land to the railroad in return for locating the town at their site. Ruthven was incorporated on March 12, 1885. (398, 438)

Rutland, Humboldt County. Rutland was established in 1869 by H. G. Bicknell and named for Rutland, Vermont. Rutland was incorporated on July 6, 1907. (275, 438, 528)

Ryan, Delaware County. Ryan was established on August 28, 1888, by J. A. Thomas, Arthur Flint, and Andrew Anderson and named for Father Patrick Ryan, a priest at the local church. Ryan was incorporated on May 6, 1901. (318, 404, 438)

S s ++++++++++++++++++++

Sabula, Jackson County. Sabula's name came from the Latin term for sandy soil, *sabulum*. It is the only town in Iowa located on an island. The town was established in 1837. Sabula had been called Carrolport and then Charleston before it finally became Sabula in 1846. Carrolport was dropped because a local man named Carroll was rather universally disliked, and the townspeople did not want it to be thought that he was the inspiration for the town's name. They really wanted a change when a package was delivered to the village of "Carrion Point," and shortly after that the town became Charleston. Unfortunately, there was confusion with other towns with similar names, and so the name Sabulum was suggested by William Hubbell. A Mrs. Woods suggested that Sabula sounded better, and that name was adopted. Sabula was incorporated in 1864. (175, 276, 318)

Sac City, county seat, Sac County. Sac City was founded on July 3, 1855. The owners of the town site were Judge Eugene Criss, W. S. Wagoner, Henry A. Evans, and Joseph Gammon. Sac City was named for the Sac Indians. Both the township and county that Sac City is in are also named Sac. The word is derived from combining *osaw*, or "yellow," and *aki*, or "earth." It was incorporated on December 22, 1874. (235, 438, 561)

Sageville, Dubuque County. Sageville was established by Chester Sage and Brayton Bushee around 1834 when they built a mill at the site. Clearly the town was named for Chester Sage. After the Eighteenth Amendment was repealed, a number of the small, unincorporated towns feared they would not be permitted to have a tavern unless they were incorporated. The towns incorporated so that they could ensure the sale of beer in their communities. Sageville was incorporated on June 2, 1933. (266, 344, 438)

St. Ansgar, Mitchell County. St. Ansgar was named and platted by the Reverend Claus Clauson in 1854. He named it St. Ansgar in honor of the patron saint who brought Christianity into the Scandinavian countries in the ninth century. St. Ansgar was incorporated on February 9, 1876. (286, 438)

St. Anthony, Marshall County. St. Anthony was founded by Anthony R. Pierce, J. Q. Saint, and A. J. Mabie on February

22, 1882. The name was drawn from the names of two of the founders. The town was incorporated on November 6, 1897. (163, 357, 512)

St. Benedict, Kossuth County. St. Benedict was named for the church established at the location in 1877 by Father Eberhard Gahr, a member of the Benedictine Order. The town is not incorporated. (11)

St. Catherine, Dubuque County. St. Catherine is an unincorporated village south of Dubuque. The town was first named for Judge John King and settled in 1836. St. Catherine's Catholic Church, established in 1851, was located near the settlement of King. The current church, built in 1887, was named after St. Catherine of Alexandra. This was a compromise because the Irish and German settlers each wanted a different saint as the namesake for the church. (171)

St. Charles, Madison County. St. Charles was founded in 1851 by George Hartman and Jesse C. Young, who owned the property where the town was established. St. Charles was named for St. Charles, Missouri. The town was incorporated on May 15, 1876. (163, 376, 438)

St. Donatus, Jackson County. St. Donatus was founded as Tete des Morts in March 1839. The name was changed to St. Donatus in 1855 both to honor that saint and to get rid of the grisly name that the town had carried. The town was incorporated on June 8, 1964. (276, 438)

St. Joseph, Kossuth County. St. Joseph had been called Hale's Post Office or Hale, for Oscar Hale who owned property in the area. A house was first built at the site in 1865. The church from which the town later took its name was established in 1871. The town is not incorporated. (280)

St. Lucas, Fayette County. St. Lucas developed around, and was named for, St. Luke's Catholic Church, which was established in 1855. The town was incorporated on March 6, 1900. (269, 438)

St. Marys, Warren County. St. Marys was founded and named by George Durschell in 1870. There was a St. Mary's Church at the site, so the town was probably named for it. The town was incorporated on April 5, 1923. (438, 507)

St. Olaf, Clayton County. St. Olaf was established in February 1874 by Thomas Thompson, the owner of the property where the town was located. St. Olaf was named for the Norwegian king who became a saint. The town was incorporated on May 31, 1900. (246, 261, 438)

St. Paul, Lee County. St. Paul was established on April 30, 1866, and named for the saint. It was incorporated on April 1, 1895. (163, 281, 438)

Salem, Henry County. Salem was planned in 1836 by Aaron Street Jr. and Peter Boyer and was formally established on March 30, 1839. The community was the first Quaker settlement west of the Mississippi and became an important station on the Underground Railroad. Salem, the Hebrew word for peace, was a popular name in the Street family. This community was one of four towns around the country that the Streets named Salem. The town was incorporated on January 24, 1855. (245, 273, 318, 438)

Salix, Woodbury County. Salix was established by the Missouri Land Company on July 29, 1875, and named for the many willows growing nearby. Salix is the botanical name for willow. The community was incorporated on April 19, 1893. (294, 438, 528)

Sanborn, O'Brien County. Sanborn was platted by Johnathon Stocum and John Lawler on December 18, 1878. The town was named after a railroad official, George Sanborn. Sanborn was incorporated on March 15, 1880. (438, 460)

Sand Springs, Delaware County. Sand Springs was founded on property owned by T. H. Bowen and L. H. Langworthy in January 1858. The original name was Sand Spring. It is probable that the name was descriptive of the location. The town is not incorporated. (404)

Sandyville, Warren County. Sandyville was founded in 1851 by Jeremiah W. Sandy and named for Prairie Joe Sandy and Timber Joe Sandy, who were early settlers. It was incorporated in 1905. (315)

Saratoga, Howard County. Charles Salmon established the village of Saratoga in 1854. Saratoga was named for Saratoga Springs, New York. The town is not incorporated. (8, 318)

Saylorville, Polk County. The original Saylorville was established by John B. Saylor in 1850. Both the town and the township were named for him. A new town, established by Saylor in 1855, replaced the old town and was called Saylorsville. The name was changed to Saylorville in 1895. The town is not incorporated. (289, 458)

Scarville, Winnebago County. Scarville was established on October 11, 1899, and named for Ole Scar, an area landowner. The town was incorporated on April 11, 1904. (303, 318, 438)

Schaller, Sac County. Schaller was named in honor of an area businessman and veteran of the Civil War, Phillip Schaller. He was also the owner of the land where the town was located. The town was founded on October 4, 1882, by the Blair Town Lot and Land Company. It was incorporated on May 25, 1883. (235, 438, 528)

Schleswig, Crawford County. Schleswig was founded in 1899 and named for a province in Germany. The community was incorporated on February 15, 1900. (407, 438)

Schley, Howard County. Schley was founded in 1899. The town was named for a noted naval officer whose career spanned the time from the Civil War through the Spanish-American War, Winfield Scott Schley. Schley is not incorporated. (309, 506)

Scotch Grove, Jones County. The location of Scotch Grove was known as Applegate's Crossing when the town and a depot were established there in 1872 by James Applegate and Charles Applegate. They renamed the town for the large number of Scotch settlers in the area. The town is not incorporated. (142, 163)

Scranton, Greene County. Scranton was platted in the summer of 1869 along the route of the Chicago and North Western Railroad. The town was named in honor of industrialist George Whitefield Scranton, from Scranton, Pennsylvania. Scranton was incorporated on May 18, 1880. (438, 531)

Searsboro, Poweshiek County. Searsboro was a station on the Iowa Central Railroad. Since the railroad was completed through Poweshiek County in 1869, Searsboro had to be established at about that time. Searsboro was named for a Mr. Sears, who surveyed the town. It was incorporated on August 3, 1876. (21, 163, 438)

Selma, Van Buren County. Selma was established around 1851. The town was first known as Independent, though its popular nickname was Stumptown, for George Stump, who ran a store and was the first postmaster. The town's name was later changed to Hickory and then finally to Selma. Selma was possibly named for Selma, Alabama. The first house built in the area was put up in 1835, before settlers could legally be there. The town is not incorporated. (163, 336, 438)

Seney, Plymouth County. Seney was established by the St. Paul and Sioux City Railroad on December 7, 1872, and named for George L. Seney, one of the railroad company's directors. The town is not incorporated. (294, 528)

Sergeant Bluff, Woodbury County. Sergeant Bluff was founded by several men, including T. Elwood Clark, Samuel Watts, and Moses Shinn, on July 14, 1857. The town was named in honor of Sergeant Charles Floyd, who died on the Lewis and Clark expedition. Sergeant Bluff was incorporated on May 2, 1904. (294, 438)

Sewal, Wayne County. Sewal was established in 1887 beside track laid by the Milwaukee Railroad. Sewal is both a surname, Judge Samuel Sewall of the Salem witch trials in the late 1600s is an example, and also a given name, as in, for example, Sewal Foster, a surveyor who worked in Iowa. In any event, there is no concrete information on the basis for the name. The town is not incorporated. (572)

Sexton, Kossuth County. Sexton was established on December 6, 1889. There are a number of explanations for the name of the town. The commonly accepted version is that it was named for a railroad employee. The town is not incorporated. (14, 352)

Seymour, Wayne County. Seymour started when a railroad track was established near the site in 1870. The town's founders were J. C. Fox, William Wade, Hiram Evans, and H. S. Rogers. The town was called Seymour because the chief engineer for the Rock Island Railroad was a Mr. Seymour; the governor of New York at the time the town was founded was named Seymour; and one of the founders, a Mr. Fox, admired Seymour, Indiana. The town was incorporated on February 28, 1874. (46, 438)

Shambaugh, Page County. Shambaugh was a Mennonite community founded by James Shambaugh in 1878. It was incorporated on April 21, 1903. (318, 438)

Shannon City, Union County. The first choice of a name for the community was Shannon. The story goes that one of the railroad employees was said to have commented that the area looked just his old home in the "Shannon Valley." It is believed that he was from the Shannon River valley in Ireland. The post office objected because of the similarity of the name Shannon to other towns in the area. Loomis was proposed to honor a Dr. Loomis, but he demurred the honor and suggested that "City" be added to Shannon. Shannon City was incorporated on December 26, 1892. (163, 438, 495)

Sharpsburg, Taylor County. Sharpsburg was founded on January 2, 1884, as a stop on the Chicago, Burlington and Quincy Railroad. There is a story that the town was named for a family named Sharp, although there appears to be no written confirmation of that information. The Sharpsburgh Post Office was established in 1886, and the name was changed to Sharpsburg in 1892. Sharpsburg was incorporated on April 25, 1905. (112, 438, 458)

Sheffield, Franklin County. Sheffield was named for a Mr. Sheffield of Dubuque, who had been the original owner of the town site. The town was established on March 2, 1874, and was incorporated on April 8, 1876. (270, 438)

Shelby, Shelby County. Shelby was platted by Benjamin F. Allen and Thusie Allen on December 29, 1870, and named for the county. The county was named for Isaac Shelby, a general in the Revolutionary War. Shelby was incorporated on October 11, 1877. (438, 587)

Sheldahl, Boone, Polk, and Story counties. Sheldahl was established by J. S. Polk in October 1874. Sheldahl was named by Rev. D. Kjaldahl, for himself. The spelling was changed to facilitate pronunciation. There is another story that it was named for a Story County resident named Osmund Sheldahl. It was incorporated on January 18, 1882. (163, 165, 438, 528)

Sheldon, O'Brien County. Sheldon was founded by the Sioux City and St. Paul Railroad on January 3, 1873, and named after Israel Sheldon, a resident of New York who owned stock in the railroad. The town was incorporated on April 24, 1876. (438, 460)

Shell Rock, Butler County. Shell Rock was founded by George and Elizabeth Adair in March 1855 and named for the Shell Rock River. Shell Rock was incorporated on June 1, 1875. (254, 438)

Shellsburg, Benton County. Shellsburg was established in June 1854. John Sells, one of the early settlers of the township, wanted the town to be named after himself, but the proprietors preferred another name. Still wanting to oblige Sells, they decided to compromise by naming the town Shellsburg. Another story indicates that the town was named for Schellsburg, Pennsylvania. Shellsburg was incorporated on February 19, 1874. (163, 246, 438)

Shenandoah, Page County. Shenandoah was established in 1870 by the Burlington and Missouri River Railroad. It was named for the perceived similarity between the Nishnabotna River valley, where it is located, and the Shenandoah River valley in Virginia. Many of the settlers in the area were Civil War veterans who had fought in Virginia. Shenandoah was incorporated on June 20, 1871. (21, 318, 438)

Sherrill, Dubuque County. Sherrill was named for Adam Sherrill and Isaac Sherrill, two brothers who were among the earliest settlers and landowners in Dubuque County. The Sherrill United Methodist Church was erected in 1844, and the Sherrill Post Office was established on July 30, 1858. After the Eighteenth Amendment was repealed, a number of the small, unincorporated towns feared they would not be permitted to have a tavern unless they were incorporated. The towns incorporated so that they could ensure the sale of beer in their communities. Sherrill was incorporated on June 29, 1933. (171, 344, 438)

Shueyville, Johnson County. Shueyville was named for W. H. Shuey and B. L. Shuey, who settled near there in 1854, and was incorporated on March 8, 1968. (330, 438)

Sibley, county seat, Osceola County. The town was established in 1872 by the Sioux City and St. Paul Railroad and first called Cleghorn. Sibley was named for General Henry H. Sibley, who had defended the area during his service as a military officer. General Sibley was also the first governor of Minnesota. The community was incorporated on April 5, 1876. (438, 528, 548)

Sidney, county seat, Fremont County. Sidney was organized in June 1851 as the county seat. The town was originally called Dayton, but the name was changed to Sidney at the request of Milton Richards. He wanted it named after Sidney, Ohio, where he had once lived. Sidney was incorporated on June 7, 1870. (361, 438)

Sigourney, county seat, Keokuk County. Sigourney was established on October 1, 1844. The town was named by Dr. George H. Stone, who was an admirer of Lydia Huntley Sigourney, a popular writer of the era. Sigourney was incorporated on October 4, 1858. (279, 438)

Silver City, Mills County. In 1879 Henry H. Huffaker furnished the land for the town, and his wife suggested Silver City as its name since the town site was located near Silver Creek. Silver City was incorporated on June 23, 1883. (409, 438)

Sioux Center, Sioux County. The first Sioux Centre was established in the 1870s about a mile southeast of the current community and named because of its physical location in the county. The county was named for the Dakota Indians. The term "Sioux" is the latter part of an Ojibwa-French pejorative applied to the Dakotas, meaning "snakes." A town was established at that site in 1881. The current Sioux Center was founded as North Sioux Center in 1889 and was incorporated on October 1, 1891. (163, 433, 438, 561)

Sioux City, county seat, Woodbury County. Sioux City was founded by Dr. John Cook on May 5, 1855. The town was named for the Big Sioux River, which joins the Missouri River at the town's location. The river was named for the Dakota Indians. The term "Sioux" is the latter part of an Ojibwa-French pejorative applied to the Dakotas, meaning "snakes." Sioux City was incorporated on January 16, 1857. (294, 438, 561)

Sioux Rapids, Buena Vista County. Sioux Rapids was established by the Western Town Lot Company in 1881 and named for the rapids on the nearby Big Sioux River. The river was named for the Dakota Indians. The term "Sioux" is the latter part of an Ojibwa-French pejorative applied to the Dakotas, meaning "snakes." Sioux Rapids was incorporated on April 6, 1882. (438, 528, 561)

Slater, Story County. There was an Iowa law created in 1883 that required that a depot had to be located where two or more rail tracks crossed. That year the Milwaukee Railroad and the Northwestern Railroad constructed Sheldahl crossing, where their tracks intersected. Some of the people settling there were unhappy with the layout of the new town and moved their buildings to the Slater crossing between 1887 and 1889. Slater was named for Michael Slater, who had owned the property where the town was located. The community was incorporated on May 5, 1890. (429, 438, 528)

Sloan, Woodbury County. Sloan was named in honor of Samuel Sloan, who had been president of the Delaware, Lackawanna and Western Railroad. Sloan was founded on July 9, 1870, and was incorporated on October 16, 1883. (304, 438)

Smithland, Woodbury County. Smithland was originally called White Settlement to honor William White, an early settler. Since O. B. Smith had donated the most land to the community, the settlers decided to rename the place in his honor. Smithland was incorporated on October 16, 1883. (304, 438)

Soldier, Monona County. Soldier was established by the Western Town Lot Company in 1899 and named for the nearby Soldier River. The river was named for an anonymous U.S. soldier buried close to the river. A post office had been in operation at the site since 1871. Soldier was incorporated on April 1, 1901. (287, 438, 528)

Solon, Johnson County. Solon was founded by John West in 1842. West abandoned the project in 1847. The town was platted again in 1850 by H. H. Kerr and P. B. Anders. The town was named for Anders's deceased son. Solon was incorporated on April 28, 1877. (163, 278, 438)

Somers, Calhoun County. Somers was founded in April 1900. Another town named Muddy was abandoned when the railroad missed the town by the literal mile. The citizens moved to the new location, which was named after an area physician, Dr. J. W. Somers. The town voted to incorporate on March 17, 1902. (163, 438, 522, 532)

South Amana, Iowa County. South Amana was founded in 1856 as one of the Amana Colonies. The name for the colonies was brought to Iowa by members of the Amana Society. The name is drawn from the Bible and means "to believe faithfully." South Amana is a geographic description of its location in relation to the initial colony of Amana. The town is not incorporated. (19, 163)

South English, Keokuk County. South English was named for the South English River. The town was founded in 1855 and was incorporated on July 13, 1892. (279, 438)

Spencer, county seat, Clay County. Spencer was named for George Spencer, who had lived in Iowa and had also served as a U.S. senator from Alabama. The town was founded in 1871 and was incorporated on March 9, 1880. (260, 438)

Sperry, Des Moines County. Sperry was established in 1869 by John Sperry on land that he owned. The town is not incorporated. (24, 65)

Spillville, Winneshiek County. Spillville was founded on April 14, 1860, by Joseph Spielman. The town was named for Spielman, but only the first syllable in his name was used, and the spelling was changed. Spillville was incorporated on December 5, 1894. (33, 163, 438)

Spirit Lake, county seat, Dickinson County. While the site had been settled since the 1850s, Spirit Lake was not formally established until 1870. The town was named for the nearby lake. The lake was named after an interpretation of the Dakota name Mini-wakan, or "spirit water," by which the Dakotas had called the lake. Spirit Lake was incorporated on October 14, 1878. (438, 521, 561)

Spragueville, Jackson County. Spragueville was named for Laurence Sprague, an early settler in the area. The town was established in 1867 by a Mr. Alexander and was incorporated on May 18, 1912. (276, 438)

Spring Hill, Warren County. Spring Hill was founded in 1872 by a Dr. Bevington on property owned by William Ashworth. The town was named for its location on a hill and near a spring. Spring Hill was incorporated on November 22, 1881. (315, 438)

Springbrook, Jackson County. The first Spring Brook, or Old Spring Brook, was founded by settlers from Pennsylvania in 1841. The town was named for the abundance of springs in the area. There was a post office established there in 1846, along with a school, a church, and a cemetery. New Spring

Brook was created in the 1850s when a strongly Catholic town was founded by immigrants from Luxemburg. The post office, renamed Springbrook, was moved to the new town in 1895, and the old town died off. The remaining residents moved two miles to the west to the new town. Springbrook was incorporated on March 2, 1897. (318, 438)

Springdale, Cedar County. The settlement in this vicinity was made chiefly by Quakers. In 1849 John H. Painter established a home site, though he did not move to the area until 1850. In 1850 the second pioneer, Ann Coppic, built a frame house. She later married Joseph Raley. Springdale was most probably named for one of the Springdales established in Ohio or Pennsylvania. The town is not incorporated. (258)

Springville, Linn County. Springville was organized by Moses White, Moses Wynans, J. P. Hoffman, and Joseph Butler on March 22, 1856, and named for the number of springs in the area. Springville was incorporated on January 27, 1914. (113, 282, 438)

Stacyville, Mitchell County. Stacyville was named after H. I. Stacy, who owned the land where the town was located. The town was founded on August 23, 1856, by Fitch B. Stacy and his wife. Postal records show that the town's name was spelled Staceyville for a while, but it was officially changed to Stacyville and the new name registered with the postal department on November 5, 1883. Stacyville was incorporated on March 30, 1900. (286, 438)

Stanhope, Hamilton County. Stanhope was established in 1883 by the Western Town Lot Company. It was named for the author Lady Hester Stanhope and was incorporated on December 14, 1897. (438, 528)

Stanley, Buchanan County. Stanley was founded by the property owner, S. C. Irvine, in 1866. The town was called Stanley after Captain G. M. Stanley, a relative of the Soules family who originally owned the land where the town was built. Stanley was incorporated on May 23, 1914. (85, 438)

Stanton, Montgomery County. Stanton was founded on October 24, 1870, by the Burlington and Missouri River Railroad. The Swedish immigrants who settled the town wanted to call it Holmstad. The railroad resisted the change, and Stanton was retained as the town's name. There appear to be three possible inspirations for the name. It could have been for Lincoln's secretary of war, Edwin Stanton; for Elizabeth Cady Stanton, a well-known women's rights advocate; or for the poet Frank Stanton. Exactly why the name was selected is lost, but one of the three names suggested is probably the source. Stanton was incorporated on March 12, 1883. (403, 438, 527)

Stanwood, Cedar County. Stanwood was created by the Chicago and North Western Railroad in 1869 and named for an official with that railroad. It was incorporated in the fall of 1886. (114, 258, 528)

State Center, Marshall County. State Center was established in 1863 and first called Centre Station. The name was changed to State Center to reflect the geographical location of the town in the state. It was incorporated on August 26, 1867. (285, 438)

Steamboat Rock, Hardin County. Steamboat Rock was founded in May 1855 and first called Lithopolis, meaning "Rock City" in Greek, but in 1870 the name was changed. Steamboat Rock was named because of a distinctive landmark on a river bluff nearby. A large rock jutted out of the bluff and gave the appearance of an anchored steamboat. A tree on the rock was struck by lightning in 1858, and the resemblance was lost because the wheelhouse of the image fell off from the shock. Steamboat Rock was incorporated on October 7, 1875. (272, 438, 579)

Stockport, Van Buren County. Stockport was established around 1888, with a post office commencing operation on February 27, 1888. The first store was erected at the site in 1887. The town was named by James Beswick, who paid $25 for the right, in honor of his home in England. Stockport was incorporated on January 9, 1903. (297, 336, 438, 458)

Stockton, Muscatine County. Stockton was called Farnham, Fulton, and Prairie Mills before Stockton was settled on. The name appears to be a descriptive one, as the community was noted for the quality of the cattle and hogs raised in the area, and it was a shipping point for livestock. There is a possibility that the name is a transfer name, for a town in Illinois. The town was established on September 14, 1855, by A. C. Fulton, J. M. Burrows, N. Fejervary, J. M. Witherywase, and R. M. Prettyman. Stockton was incorporated on February 11, 1902. (163, 438, 492)

Stone City, Jones County. The reason for the village was the nearby stone quarry. The post office, established there in September 1873, is an indicator of the date the town was founded. Stone City was named for the local quarries. The town is not incorporated. (142, 318)

Storm Lake, county seat, Buena Vista County. Storm Lake was settled in 1869 with the coming of the railroad to the area. The town was named for the nearby lake. The lake was originally called Boyer Lake when it was thought that it was the origin of the Boyer River. When it was discovered that the Boyer River had another source, the name was abandoned. Storm Lake was supposed to have been named by an old trapper in 1855 after a particularly violent storm had blown his tent down. The community was incorporated on February 28, 1873. (163, 438, 455)

Story City, Story County. Fairview, which later became part of Story City, was established in 1855. Story City, an adjacent community, was established in 1878 and named for the county. Story County was named for a U.S. Supreme Court justice, Joseph Story. Fairview was absorbed by Story City when that town was incorporated on December 12, 1881. (438, 534)

Stout, Grundy County. Stout was established on June 18, 1872, on property owned by A. V. Stout, hence the name. It was incorporated on June 25, 1909. (438, 528, 597)

Stratford, Hamilton County. Stratford was established by the Western Town Lot Company in 1880. It was reported to have been named for Stratford, Pennsylvania. Another story about the naming of the town is that Colonel John Whittaker suggested naming the town for Stratford, England. Stratford was incorporated on September 27, 1883. (228, 438, 528)

Strawberry Point, Clayton County. Strawberry Point was founded by W. H. Stearns and D. M. Stearns in 1853 and first called Franklin. Since there was already a Franklin Post Office in Iowa, the post office at the site retained its previous name, Strawberry Point. The post office had been named because of the quantity of wild strawberries that grew there. The town was incorporated on December 19, 1887. (246, 261, 438)

Struble, Plymouth County. Struble was established on December 4, 1889, by the Northern Land Company and named for Congressman Isaac Struble. It was incorporated on August 17, 1895. (163, 294, 438)

Stuart, Guthrie County. Stuart was founded by Charles Stuart, Joseph Kenworthy, B. F. Allen, and John F. Tracy on September 29, 1870. The town was named for Charles Stuart. It was incorporated on February 6, 1877. (271, 438)

Sully, Jasper County. Sully was established by Robert Ryan on August 3, 1882. The town was named for an area resident,

Alfred Sully. It was incorporated on February 23, 1901. (115, 438, 573)

Sulphur Springs, Buena Vista County. Sulphur Springs was established as a town in 1871 and named for the sulfurous springs southwest of the town. The town is not incorporated. (64)

Sumner, Bremer County. Sumner was established in 1870. It was named for a noted Massachusetts senator, Charles Sumner. The community was incorporated on June 1, 1894. (163, 423, 438)

Sunbury, Cedar County. Sunbury was established as a railroad station in 1891 and probably named for a town in Pennsylvania. The town is not incorporated. (77, 163)

Superior, Dickinson County. A depot was established at the site when a railroad company laid track through the area in 1882. The town was named for the township that it was in. Superior was incorporated on December 11, 1895. (438, 521)

Sutherland, O'Brien County. Sutherland was founded by the Western Town Lot Company in March 1882. The town was named for the Duke of Sutherland. His name was used either because he was visiting a railroad official at the time the town was being planned or because some of his neighbors from England settled in the new town. Sutherland was incorporated on October 29, 1883. (438, 460, 528)

Swaledale, Cerro Gordo County. Swaledale was established on March 29, 1887. The name appears to be a manufactured one selected for its sound. Swaledale was incorporated on March 31, 1892. (84, 163, 438)

Swan, Marion County. Swan was established in the fall of 1879 and named for the township in which it is located. The community was incorporated on June 26, 1884. (438, 594)

Swea City, Kossuth County. Swea City had its start when Swedish immigrants arrived at the location in 1870. The town was first called Reynolds, but the name was changed officially to Swea City in 1893. Swea is drawn from the Swedish word "Svea," an affectionate term for Sweden. The town was formally established by R. M. Richmond and was incorporated on May 7, 1895. (318, 438)

Swedesburg, Henry County. Swedesburg was first called Freeport when settlers came in 1864. The town really developed when a church was built there in 1866. After the preacher built a parsonage, others started to build in the area. The town's name was changed in 1870 to reflect the number of settlers of Swedish origin in the area. At first Swedesburg was spelled Swedesburgh. The residents of the community link the founding of the church and parsonage as the founding date for the town. The town is not incorporated. (241, 273)

Swisher, Johnson County. Swisher was established in 1904 and named for an area farmer, Benjamin Swisher. It was incorporated on July 25, 1933. (330, 438, 535)

T t ╫╫╫╫╫╫╫╫╫╫╫╫╫╫╫╫╫╫

Tabor, Fremont County. Tabor was founded in 1852 by settlers originally from Oberlin, Ohio. These pioneers wanted to establish a college similar to Oberlin College. They also were fervently antislavery and established Tabor as a stop on the Underground Railroad. A mountain in Palestine was the inspiration for the name of the town. Tabor was incorporated on October 5, 1868. (163, 438, 545)

Taintor, Mahaska County. Taintor was founded when the Iowa Central Railroad ran a track through the area in 1882.

Charles Miller was given the honor of naming the town, and he named it for a friend of his, a Bostonian named Giles Taintor. The town is not incorporated. (339)

Tama, Tama County. Tama was first called Iuka after a Civil War battle site in Mississippi. The town was founded by J. H. Hollen in 1862. The Post Office Department changed the name of the post office from Iuka to Tama City in 1866 in honor of the county. The county was named for a well-known Fox chief. The town voted to incorporate as Tama City on July 29, 1869. It was last incorporated on March 16, 1887, as Tama. (71, 438, 561)

Teeds Grove, Clinton County. A Mr. Teed settled in a grove of oak timber in 1836. In 1837 government surveyors came through and told him that he had settled on a section reserved for a school. He left the area in disgust. As time passed a settlement developed there and was named for Teed. The town is not incorporated. (591)

Templeton, Carroll County. The town was founded in 1882 and named for a brakeman or conductor on the Chicago, Milwaukee and St. Paul Railroad. Templeton was incorporated on September 28, 1883. (74, 438)

Tennant, Shelby County. Tennant was founded in 1902 and named for a railroad official. It was incorporated in 1915. (233, 587)

Terril, Dickinson County. Terril was founded in 1895 and first called Trilby. Since there was a post office with a similar name already established in Iowa, the name Terril was suggested as an alternative. Terrill was the name of the man who had owned the land where the town was located. The community was incorporated on December 30, 1899. (163, 438, 521)

Thayer, Union County. Thayer was established in 1868, or at least the first house at the town site was erected that year.

Thayer was named after a Judge Thayer, who assisted in developing the town. It was incorporated on May 21, 1894. (45, 438, 540)

Thompson, Winnebago County. Thompson was named for an officer with the Chicago and Iowa Western Land and Town Lot Company, J. F. Thompson, who established the town on March 24, 1892. It was incorporated on February 24, 1894. (303, 438)

Thor, Humboldt County. Thor was established by the Western Town Lot Company in 1881. The town was named for the Scandinavian god of crops. It was incorporated on April 23, 1900. (275, 438, 528)

Thornburg, Keokuk County. Thornburg was founded as a station on the Burlington, Cedar Rapids and Northern Railroad in 1879. The name was suggested by the civil engineer who mapped out the town site. He named it Thornburgh in honor of his friend Major Thomas T. Thornburgh, who had been killed in the Meeker Indian Massacre. When the post office was established, the name was registered as Thornburg. The town was incorporated on September 25, 1883. (279, 438)

Thornton, Cerro Gordo County. Thornton was established on October 3, 1887. The town was named for the mother of J. T. Knapp, an area landowner. Her maiden name was Thornton. Thornton was incorporated on August 22, 1892. (84, 337, 438)

Thurman, Fremont County. Thurman was first known as Fremont City, then as Plum Hollow, and then finally as Thurman. The town was established in 1856 by Abraham Fletcher and named for Allen G. Thurman, a well-known politician. Thurman was incorporated on February 10, 1879. (226, 438, 545)

Tiffin, Johnson County. Tiffin was first called Copi when it was established in December 1867. The town was renamed by

Rolla Johnson, the former owner of the land where the town was located. He named the town for Tiffin, Ohio. Tiffin was incorporated on December 27, 1906. (278, 332, 438)

Tingley, Ringgold County. Tingley was founded in 1881 along the Humeston and Shenandoah Railroad. Tingley was named either for Tingley Cornwall, a local settler, or for the railroad surveyor who had laid out the town, Major Richard Tingley. Tingley was incorporated on June 17, 1884. (44, 163, 438)

Tipton, county seat, Cedar County. Tipton was established by a commission appointed to locate a county seat for Cedar County in March 1840. Two of the three commissioners thought that the location where Tipton is now located was an appropriate one. The third commissioner, Henry W. Higgins, was not as sure. When the other two commissioners allowed Higgins to select the name for the new town, he agreed not to contest the location. Higgins named the new town for an old friend of his, a General Tipton of Indiana. Tipton was incorporated on January 27, 1857. (258, 438)

Titonka, Kossuth County. Titonka was founded on October 2, 1898. It was first known as Ripley, until there was some confusion with another town with a similar name. A Captain Ingham suggested the new name to commemorate a buffalo hunt that he had participated in many years earlier. *Titonka* or *tetonka* is a Sioux word meaning "big house." It is also reputed to have been the name of a Sioux Indian involved in the Spirit Lake Massacre. Titonka was incorporated on February 1, 1900. (438, 544, 561)

Toddville, Linn County. Toddville was named for Jacob Todd, who owned a mill that was established at the site in 1850. He apparently wanted to name the town for his wife, Jane, but there was already a Janesville. The town is not incorporated. (163, 282)

Toeterville, Mitchell County. Toeterville was named in honor of Henry Toeter, a prominent farmer in the area. The town was established in January 1894 by Toeter and his wife. The town is not incorporated. (286)

Toledo, county seat, Tama County. J. M. Ferguson and R. B. Ogden were the commissioners appointed to locate the county seat. They established the town in 1853. The town was named for Toledo, Ohio. Another story is that it was named for an earlier post office that had been named Toledo by J. H. Hollen after a book he had been reading, *Knight of Toledo in Spain*. The problem with this story is that the town was established in the same year as the post office, so there was no existing Toledo Post Office. The town was incorporated on January 1, 1866. (71, 221, 292, 528)

Toolesboro, Louisa County. Toolesboro was laid out by William L. Toole. The town was established on July 23, 1837, and was reentered for record on May 7, 1840. It was first called Black Hawk. The town is not incorporated. (526)

Toronto, Clinton County. Toronto was established by George W. Thorn on July 5, 1853. Thorn named the town after Toronto, Ontario, where he had once lived. It was incorporated on July 26, 1909. (438, 591)

Tracy, Marion County. Tracy was established by Alexander Tracy, the proprietor of the town, on November 11, 1875. The town is not incorporated. (594)

Traer, Tama County. Traer was founded in 1873. The primary story about the naming of the town is that it was named for a Judge Traer. Another story is that it was named for a man who owned a tavern at the town site and reportedly established the town. The town was incorporated on January 18, 1875. (163, 438, 528, 580)

Trenton, Henry County. Michael Crane made the claim where Trenton stands in 1836. He established a village and called it

Lancaster, after Lancaster, Pennsylvania. He sold the town site, and the new owners named it Trenton at the suggestion of James G. Green, after the capital of New Jersey. The town is not incorporated. (273)

Treynor, Pottawattamie County. Treynor was founded in 1893 and named for the postmaster at Council Bluffs, a Mr. Treynor. It was incorporated in 1905. (143)

Tripoli, Bremer County. Tripoli was named by H. J. Wynhoff in honor of a prior town of the same name in Frederika Township. The first Tripoli had been established in 1856, but when the railroad later built a rail line some distance from the town, a new Tripoli was established on the rail line about a mile away from the first town. The town was named after the site of the battle of Tripoli. Tripoli was incorporated on October 16, 1894. (163, 253, 321, 438)

Troy, Davis County. Troy was founded by John W. Ellis on February 15, 1848. The town was named by J. I. Earhart after Troy, Ohio, where he was from. The town is not incorporated. (264)

Troy Mills, Linn County. A mill was established at the site in 1853. The town was founded by T. R. Ward in 1870. While there is no definitive proof, there is speculation that the town was named for one of the mill owners. The town is not incorporated. (41, 282)

Truesdale, Buena Vista County. Truesdale was established as a station on the Minneapolis and St. Louis Railroad. The Truesdale Post Office was established in 1900 with a store following in 1901. The town was named for W. H. Truesdale, a man associated with the railroad. Truesdale was incorporated on May 15, 1917. (318, 438, 455, 458)

Truro, Madison County. Truro was founded as Ego in August 1881, when James and Jane Holmes Hull donated land for the project. The townspeople wanted to change the name, and in 1884, when a railroad engineer suggested Truro, for Truro, Massachusetts, where he was from, they changed it. The name apparently is derived from the term "tri-row," meaning "three measures of land." Truro was incorporated on February 24, 1902. (376, 438)

Turin, Monona County. Turin was founded by the Western Town Lot Company in 1887 as a station on the railroad line in the county. First called Bluff Point, the name was changed to Turin, for Turin, Italy. Turin was incorporated on April 6, 1900. (287, 438, 528)

U u ┼┼┼┼┼┼┼┼┼┼┼┼┼┼┼┼┼┼┼┼┼

Udell, Appanoose County. Udell was founded on December 20, 1895, by James McDonald and C. O. Read. The town was named for a county resident, Dr. Nathan Udell. Udell was incorporated on April 9, 1903. (26, 163, 438)

Ulmer, Sac County. Ulmer was founded by Carrie and W. T. Martin on November 21, 1900. There does not appear to be information on the reason for the name, though Ulmer appears to be a surname of a number of people who had settled in the area. The town is not incorporated. (235)

Underwood, Pottawattamie County. Underwood was established in 1869 and was named for the first Rock Island Railroad engineer to drive a train through the town. Underwood was incorporated on January 28, 1902. (143, 438)

Union, Hardin County. Union was established in 1868 by R. J. Davis. It was possibly named to reflect the sentiments in the North following the Civil War. Union was incorporated on October 26, 1874. (163, 414, 438)

Unionville, Appanoose County. Unionville was established by J. F. Stratton on September 5, 1849. The town was probably named to reflect the settlers' sentiments about the tension between the North and the South prior to the Civil War. Unionville was incorporated on July 1, 1922. (163, 438, 537)

University Heights, Johnson County. University Heights was founded in 1928 and was incorporated on August 13, 1935. University Heights incorporated to avoid absorption by Iowa City, which now completely surrounds the smaller community. University Heights was named for its location near the University of Iowa and atop the bluffs to the west of the Iowa River. (116, 330, 438)

University Park, Mahaska County. University Park was founded in 1909 and was incorporated on April 13, 1909. The name was chosen because the community developed around the college known as Central Holiness University. That college still exists and is now called Vennard College. (117, 438, 447)

Urbana, Benton County. Urbana was established in May 1847 by Joseph Remington as Marysville. The town was also known to early settlers as Hoosier Point. In 1857 the postal department changed the name from Marysville to Urbanna, because of confusion with other towns with similar names to Marysville. The spelling of Urbanna was used until 1880, when one n was dropped, and it became Urbana. The word is a Latin term meaning "from the city." Urbana was incorporated on November 4, 1892. (246, 365, 438)

Urbandale, Polk County. The location was first settled in 1858 and remained an agricultural area right up to the point in time when it was incorporated on May 3, 1917. The town decided to incorporate to establish its own school district. The residents were concerned about the growth of the Johnson School District and were worried that their children would be hauled to Johnson by horse and buggy if they were absorbed into the Johnson system. While there is no established record, it seems reasonable that the town was named for the Interurban Railroad that ran from Des Moines to Boone and passed through the site. (118, 438, 552)

Ute, Monona County. In 1875 a post office was established at the site, with Isaac Cummins as the postmaster. He named the post office Ute in tribute to the Ute Indians, who had saved his family when he had been a younger man. Cummins and his family were moving west when he and his three daughters were stricken with illness, and the family was abandoned by their wagon train. The family was discovered by a group of Indians, who took them to a fort, where Cummins and his daughters recovered. The family then promptly returned to Iowa. Cummins wanted the post office's name to pay tribute to the western Indian tribe responsible for saving them, the Utes. When a rail station was constructed close by on the Chicago, Milwaukee and St. Paul Railroad in 1887, the post office and the name were transferred to the new location. Ute was incorporated on November 4, 1891. (287, 438, 553, 561)

V v ++++++++++++++++++++

Vail, Crawford County. Vail was founded in 1869 and named by John Blair for his relative, C. E. Vail. The town was incorporated on October 1, 1875. (407, 438, 528)

Valeria, Jasper County. Valeria was established as a station for the Chicago Great Western Railroad by N. W. Johnson and his wife on October 24, 1883. It was named for the Johnsons' daughter, Valeria. Valeria Johnson was being courted by a railroad civil engineer, who placed the railroad's track through the Johnsons' property, thus setting up the location for the town. The town's motto is "the town created by a railroad romance." (554, 555, 573)

Van Horne, Benton County. Van Horne was named for William C. Van Horne, a former officer of the Chicago and Alton Railroad. The town was founded and was incorporated in 1883. (40, 438, 558)

Van Meter, Dallas County. Van Meter was founded as Tracy in 1869 on property that had been owned by a man named Wilson. The name was changed to Van Meter in honor of R. J. Van Meter, a respected citizen of the county. The community was incorporated on December 29, 1877. (163, 263, 438)

Van Wert, Decatur County. Van Wert was settled in 1853 as Florence. The town went through several names, Florence, then Prairie City, then Prairieville, and finally, in 1880, Van Wert. Some of the settlers in the community were from Van Wert, Ohio, and they wanted their new home to be named after their old one. Van Wert was incorporated on March 4, 1891. (119, 174, 438)

Varina, Pocahontas County. Varina was founded in 1899 by the Chicago, Milwaukee and St. Paul Railroad. The town's name was suggested by R. E. Flickinger, since Varina, Virginia, was the home of Pocahontas and her husband. Varina was incorporated on March 29, 1901. (192, 438)

Ventura, Cerro Gordo County. The community was established on November 16, 1885. Ventura was first called Thayer's Siding. It is believed the town was to be called Venture, but an error was made when the name was recorded. The town was incorporated on May 28, 1960. (337, 438)

Victor, Iowa County. Victor, founded by Joseph Blackburn on May 5, 1863, was first called Wilson for one of the settlers in the community. The town's name was changed to

Victor in 1865 for a nearby post office. The post office, established in 1854, had been named in honor of Victor, New York. Victor voted to incorporate on November 30, 1868. (382, 438)

Villisca, Montgomery County. Villisca, a name drawn from the Sac and Fox tribes, was mistakenly believed by the founders to mean "pretty place." In fact, the tribes used the term *waliska*, the most likely origin of the town's name, to mean "an evil spirit" or "Satan." The town was first referred to as "The Forks." The current name has gone through several changes in spelling, from Valiska to Vallisca, to the final version, Villisca. The town was established on May 20, 1858, by David M. Smith, for the Burlington Railroad. It remained virtually a "paper town" until the railroad actually laid track there in 1869. Villisca was incorporated on September 3, 1869. (403, 438, 561)

Vincent, Webster County. Vincent was established by Hamilton Browne in 1887 and named in honor of Webb Vincent. It was incorporated on May 27, 1898. (438, 475, 560)

Vining, Tama County. Vining was founded in 1881 by the Chicago, Milwaukee and St. Paul Railroad. The origin of the name appears to be a mystery, although there were people with the surname Vining living in Iowa at the time the town was founded. It was incorporated on May 26, 1913. (71, 438)

Vinton, county seat, Benton County. Vinton was established as the county seat by the county commissioners and was initially named Northport by them in 1846. The town was formally established in 1848. The plat was signed by Samuel M. Lockhart, Loyal F. North, and Thomas Way, and by them named Vinton, in honor of a member of Congress from Ohio. The town was later incorporated as Fremont on November 29, 1849. The name Fremont was changed to

Vinton by an act of the Iowa General Assembly in January 1853. Vinton was incorporated on July 17, 1869. (246, 438)

Viola, Linn County. Viola was established on June 21, 1861, and first called Crow Creek Station, but the postal authorities requested that the town select another name. A Mr. Leonard, who owned the property, named the town for his daughter, Viola. The town is not incorporated. (282)

Volga, Clayton County. Volga, first called Volga City, was founded in November 1851. The town was named for its location on the Volga River. The river was named for the Volga River in Russia. The community was incorporated on October 16, 1895. (163, 261, 438)

Voorhies, Black Hawk County. Voorhies was founded on June 17, 1900, and named for the chief civil engineer who helped establish the railroad in the area. The town is not incorporated. (36, 178, 528)

W w ++++++++++++++++++++

Wadena, Fayette County. Wadena was founded in 1857 and named by Major D. B. Herriman for an Ojibwa Indian chief. The name apparently means "sloping hill" or "small round hill." Wadena was incorporated on July 11, 1895. (438, 561)

Wahpeton, Dickinson County. Wahpeton was named after one of the seven divisions of the Dakota Indians. Wahpeton was founded in 1933 and was incorporated on June 24, 1933. (120, 438, 561)

Walcott, Scott County. Walcott was established in 1854 as a railroad station and named for William Walcott, who had been on the board of directors for the railroad. It was incorporated on July 10, 1894. (438, 509)

Walford, Benton County. Walford was founded as Terry in 1884 when the Chicago, Milwaukee and St. Paul Railroad built a branch line southwest from Marion. The name was changed to Walford on November 11, 1899. Walford was incorporated on April 15, 1954. (438, 558)

Walker, Linn County. Walker was established on July 8, 1873, and named for W. W. Walker, a railroad official. It was incorporated on June 13, 1891. (282, 438)

Wall Lake, Sac County. Wall Lake was founded by the Blair Town Lot and Land Company on August 2, 1877. The town was named for Wall Lake, which is a few miles away. The lake was named for the unusual, but naturally caused, piles of rocks along its shore. The town was incorporated on December 7, 1880. (235, 438, 528)

Wallingford, Emmett County. Wallingford was founded by the Iowa Falls and Northwestern Land and Town Lot Company in July 1882. It was named either for a ford near the town or for Wallingford, England. The town was incorporated on November 4, 1913. (163, 184, 438)

Walnut, Pottawattamie County. Walnut was established by the Allen Company in 1871. The town was named for the number of walnut trees in the area and was incorporated on October 2, 1877. (121, 163, 191, 438)

Wapello, county seat, Louisa County. Wapello was named after the Fox chief of that name. There was originally an Upper Wapello, a Center Wapello, and a Lower Wapello. Central Wapello corresponds with the current town's location, while Lower Wapello was the first location established in 1836–1837. Wapello was incorporated on July 15, 1856. (438, 509, 561)

Washburn, Black Hawk County. Washburn was founded on March 13, 1880. The town supplanted a nearby town called Gilbertville. The railroad did not pass by or through

Gilbertville, so a new town was established on the rail line. Washburn was named for an area farmer, Levi Washburn. The town is not incorporated. (163, 236)

Washington, county seat, Washington County. Washington was established in 1839 by a commission selected to locate a county seat for Washington County. The town was named for the county, which was named for George Washington. Washington was incorporated on June 6, 1864. (163, 299, 438)

Washta, Cherokee County. The name of Washta was first applied to the post office that was located at the site in 1868. It was named by A. J. Whisman. There are two stories linked to the reason for the name. The first is that an Indian visiting Whisman's home saw a gun hanging on the wall and took it down, sighted it, and said, "*Washta*," or "good." The second story related by Whisman is that while out hunting on October 27, 1867, he met three armed Indians who, upon examining his gun, exclaimed, "*Washta*." Virgil Vogel notes that it is unlikely that any armed Sioux would be in that area after the suppression of a Sioux revolt a few years earlier. It would be even less likely that a lone pioneer would voluntarily hand his or her rifle to them. The former explanation seems at least a bit more likely in this case. Washta was established when the railroad came through the area, and the town was incorporated on June 6, 1890. (401, 438)

Waterloo, county seat, Black Hawk County. The site where Waterloo is now located was first called Prairie Rapids. When a post office was located there in 1851, it was named Waterloo. Both stories about the naming of the community involve a Mr. Mullen. In one story, Mullen recommended naming it for the famous battle site in Belgium. The other story is that Mullen was delivering the petition for the post office, and the name for the post office had been left blank, so he was asked to fill it in. He looked through a post office directory and selected Waterloo because he liked the sound of it. Waterloo was incorporated on July 1, 1868. (163, 236, 318, 438)

Waterville, Allamakee County. Waterville was never officially platted. Lots were sold off one at a time and were recorded as lots of irregular size, according to the contour of the land. The town was first called Waterville Mill, probably because of a mill at the site. In 1850 the Ellis Grist Mill was built, and in 1877 the Waukon and Mississippi Railroad came to the town. Waterville was incorporated on June 18, 1912. (13, 163, 438)

Watkins, Benton County. Watkins was established on property owned by Charles G. and Eliza Turner on August 16, 1874. It was named for J. B. Watkins, an official with the Chicago and North Western Railroad. The town is not incorporated. (246, 528)

Waubeek, Linn County. Paddington, a town adjacent to and absorbed by Waubeek, was founded on September 20, 1855. Waubeek was established on October 28, 1859. Early records indicate the town was called Waubeck. The town was named by Samuel Buckston. The name appears to have been drawn from Longfellow's *The Song of Hiawatha*, where the term *wawbeek*, or "the rock," was used. There was also a quarry near the town site, lending further credibility to this explanation. The town is not incorporated. (282, 561)

Waucoma, Fayette County. The Waucoma Post Office was established in 1855, which would correspond with early development of this community. The town's name is of Indian origin, either Sac, Ojibwa, or Fox. Part of the meaning in all three languages is "clean" or "clear." Waucoma was incorporated on June 5, 1883. (438, 458, 561)

Waukee, Dallas County. Waukee was founded by L. A. Grant in 1869, who once owned the property where it is located.

The town was originally called Shirley, but the Northwestern Railroad wanted the town to have an Indian name. There apparently was a belief that the name had some meaning to the local Indians. That was not the case, and in fact it would appear that the name was drawn from a contraction of the name Milwaukee. The community was incorporated on December 23, 1878. (263, 438, 561)

Waukon, county seat, Allamakee County. Waukon was founded on December 3, 1853. John Haney Jr. suggested the name of Waukon Decorah, a prominent chief of the Winnebago tribe. It was incorporated on April 4, 1883. (14, 184, 230, 438)

Waukon Junction, Allamakee County. The name of Waukon Junction came from the railroad station that was established at the location. At first the junction was named Adams, for the president of the Waukon Railroad. When a post office was established there, the name was Waukon Junction, to reflect that it was a railroad junction near the town of Waukon. While the town was never officially founded, homes were built at the site starting around 1877, when the railroad track became operational. The town is not incorporated. (14)

Waverly, county seat, Bremer County. Waverly was established by William P. Harmon in 1854. The town was originally going to be called Harmon. The story goes that one of the speakers at the founding of the town had been reading Sir Walter Scott's novel *Waverly*, and when it was time for him to announce the name, he said, "Waverly," and it has been the town's name ever since. Waverly was incorporated on March 2, 1859. (253, 318, 438)

Wayland, Henry County. The town was first known as Crooked Creek, then Marshall, and finally Wayland. Crooked Creek became a voting precinct on October 5, 1840. The site was established as Marshall in 1851. The town was incorporated on January 5, 1890. (273, 438)

Webb, Clay County. Webb was founded in 1899 by Albert Boyden. It was originally called Glenora, but the name was changed because it was confused with Panora. The town's present name was selected by F. D. White, who named it after his mother. Webb was her maiden name. The town was incorporated on April 9, 1901. (260, 438)

Webster, Keokuk County. Webster was established in April 1854 and was incorporated on April 13, 1909. The reason for the naming of the town is a mystery. Perhaps it was named, as was Webster County, for the great orator Daniel Webster. (122, 279, 438)

Webster City, county seat, Hamilton County. William Brewer and William Frakes founded the town as Newcastle on October 27, 1854. W. C. Wilson purchased the entire location and replanned the town as Webster City in 1855. There are several possible reasons for the name. One is that the town was named for a well-known stage driver. Another is that at the time the town was founded, the area was part of Webster County. It could also be in tribute to Daniel Webster. Webster City was incorporated on September 16, 1874. (163, 228, 438)

Weldon, Decatur County. Weldon was established in 1880 when the Humeston and Shenandoah Railroad extended a rail line, and the town was founded as a station along the line. The property owner, a Mr. Kline, wanted the town to be named after himself, but as there was a town with a similar name, the town was named for the Weldon River, which originates on property then owned by Kline. Weldon was incorporated on October 20, 1902. (44, 438, 582)

Wellman, Washington County. Wellman was founded in September 1879 on property owned by Joseph Wellman. It was incorporated on October 28, 1885. (299, 438, 568)

Wellsburg, Grundy County. Settlers started moving into the area around 1879. Wellsburg was established on February 17, 1894, and named for George Wells, one of its founders. The community was incorporated on March 28, 1896. (220, 438)

Welton, Clinton County. Welton was founded on March 28, 1871, by Nicholas and Polly Walrod. The town was named for Welton Dale in England. It was incorporated on April 25, 1908. (318, 438, 591)

Wesley, Kossuth County. Wesley was established in 1871 and named for Wesley Bennett, the son of one of the people involved in building the railroad section house and depot at the site. Wesley was incorporated on April 13, 1892. (318, 352, 438)

West Amana, Iowa County. The community was founded in 1856 as one of the Amana Colonies. The name for the colonies was brought to Iowa by members of the Amana Society. The name is drawn from the Bible and means "to believe faithfully." West Amana is a geographic description of its location in relation to the initial colony of Amana. The town is not incorporated. (19, 163)

West Bend, Palo Alto County. West Bend was named after the township in which it is located. The township was named for the sharp bend on the west fork of the Des Moines River, where the township was located. The town had its start in 1881 when the railroad laid track through the area. It was originally called Ives by the railroad to honor the president of the railroad, but the citizens of the township changed the name to West Bend. The community was incorporated on February 27, 1884. (398, 438)

West Branch, Cedar County. West Branch was established on May 29, 1869, by John W. Wetherel. It was named for the meetinghouse the Quakers maintained at the site. They referred to it as the West Branch of the Red Cedar meetinghouse at Springdale, and so when the town was established, it was called West Branch. West Branch was incorporated on April 12, 1875. (163, 258, 438)

West Burlington, Des Moines County. West Burlington was founded in 1882. The town was named for its proximity to Burlington. It was incorporated on December 15, 1883. (24, 300, 438)

West Chester, Washington County. West Chester, which was first called Chester, was founded in December 1872. The town was named for a railroad employee, Charles Chester. When the townspeople discovered that there was already a town in Iowa named Chester, "West" was added to the name. West Chester was incorporated on April 17, 1899. (163, 299, 438)

West Des Moines, Polk County. West Des Moines was first called Valley Junction when it was established as a station at a railroad junction in the 1850s. The first building at the site was a school constructed in 1849, which preceded the development of the town. Valley Junction was incorporated on August 16, 1893, and was renamed West Des Moines on January 1, 1938. (289, 301, 438, 584)

West Grove, Davis County. West Grove was founded on November 20, 1853. It was named after West Grove Township. The township was named for Dead Man's Grove, where the remains of a murdered man were found. The town is not incorporated. (264)

West Liberty, Muscatine County. The original West Liberty was established in 1838, a short distance from the current town. The new town was founded in 1856, after the railroad came through the area and missed the location of the original town. The original West Liberty was named for Liberty, Ohio, and since it was west of the Ohio community, "West" was added as part of the name. West Liberty was incorporated on July 1, 1867. (163, 438, 492)

West Okoboji, Dickinson County. The town started when a Mr. Miller, who had a camp on the lake, laid out lots and planned the community. West Okoboji was named for the nearby lake. The name Okoboji is from the Sioux language. The meaning is disputed among various experts; possible meanings include "place of rest," "rushes," "field of swamp grass," "blue waters," "planting in the spaces," "to cause to float downstream," and "spreading out to the south." Since the camps in this area were developed when the Milwaukee Railroad started rail service to the area in the 1880s, it is likely that the camp was established around that time. The town was definitely in existence before 1902, since it is referenced in a history of Dickinson County published that year. West Okoboji was incorporated on December 17, 1924. (396, 438, 521, 561)

West Point, Lee County. West Point was founded by Abraham Hunsicker in 1835. The town was called Cottontown, for a settler who opened a store at the location. In May 1836 the site was purchased by William Patterson, Hawkins Taylor, A. H. Walker, and Green Casey. They renamed the town at the suggestion of the officers of a nearby fort after West Point, New York. The town was incorporated in 1854. (281)

West Union, county seat, Fayette County. West Union was originally known as Knob Prairie when it was established in 1849. The name was changed to West Union at the suggestion of William Wells at the Fourth of July celebration that same year. The name was inspired by a town in Ohio.

West Union was incorporated on December 9, 1879. (189, 269, 438)

Westfield, Plymouth County. The current town of Westfield was founded on August 3, 1877. The original Westfield was established in 1856, but the town had been abandoned when there was concern about hostilities with the Indians. The name Westfield was used since it was the westernmost town in Iowa. Westfield was incorporated on May 27, 1903. (247, 294, 438)

Westgate, Fayette County. Westgate was named after the Westgate family who owned the property where the town was located. The community was founded when a railroad track was established through the area in 1886. Westgate was incorporated on July 6, 1896. (163, 189, 438, 585)

Westphalia, Shelby County. Westphalia was founded by Emil Flusche on June 22, 1874. The town was named for a region in Germany where many of the settlers were from. It was incorporated on November 7, 1919. (438, 587)

Westside, Crawford County. Westside was named because it was the first town established by the railroad past the ridge where the rivers drained west, into the Missouri River. The town was established in 1869 by the Iowa Rail Road Land Company and was incorporated in 1879. (407, 586)

Westwood, Henry County. Westwood was probably named for its location west of the county seat, Mt. Pleasant. Westwood was established in 1959 and was incorporated on December 2, 1982. (397)

Wever, Lee County. Wever was founded as a station on the Chicago, Burlington and Quincy Railroad in 1891. Wever was named for General Clark Wever, who lived in Ft. Madison. The town is not incorporated. (163, 281, 318)

What Cheer, Keokuk County. What Cheer was originally named Petersburgh after Peter Britton, who established the town in 1865. When the town applied for a post office, the postal department rejected the name Petersburgh. Major Joseph Andrews, a local politician, succeeded in getting the town's name changed to What Cheer in 1879. The name probably stems from the old English greeting or expression of happiness brought from England to New England, and then on to Iowa. Reportedly, the term was used by a Scotch miner when he discovered a seam of coal near the town. What Cheer was incorporated on February 27, 1880. (279, 438, 528)

Wheatland, Clinton County. Wheatland was founded and named by John L. Bennett in 1858. He named it Wheatland in honor of President James Buchanan's home, Wheatland. The town was incorporated on July 13, 1869. (591)

Whiting, Monona County. Whiting was established by the Sioux City and Pacific Railroad Company on July 5, 1873. It was named by John Blair after his friend Judge Charles Whiting. Judge Whiting lived nearby. Whiting was incorporated on May 15, 1883. (287, 438, 528)

Whittemore, Kossuth County. Whittemore was founded by W. H. Ingham and Lewis Smith in the fall of 1878. The town was named in honor of Don J. Whittemore, an employee of the Chicago, Milwaukee and St. Paul Railroad. It was incorporated on November 19, 1891. (3, 280, 438)

Whitten, Hardin County. Whitten was founded in the fall of 1880 along the Chicago and North Western Railroad. It was named for C. C. Whitten of Tama, an advocate for the railroad in this part of Iowa. Whitten was incorporated in 1882. (272, 528, 581)

Whittier, Linn County. Whittier was named for the author John Greenleaf Whittier and established by the Bedell family in 1854, though the first business did not develop at the location until 1893. The town is not incorporated. (78, 246)

Wick, Warren County. Wick was established in 1883. It was named for Matthias Wick, who worked with the Chicago, Burlington and Quincy Railroad. The town is not incorporated. (315)

Willey, Carroll County. There is some uncertainty about the date that Willey was established. The settlement had a store by 1875 and a church by 1882. The town was named for a Willey family who settled in the area. Since there were several Willey families, it is not certain with which one the name originated. It was most probably the Thomas Willey family, who had settled in the area by at least the 1860s, since the Josiah Willey family did not arrive until 1882. Ironically, the Thomas Willey family moved away from the area. Willey was incorporated on February 29, 1912. (74, 438, 588)

Williams, Hamilton County. Williams was founded by John Blair in 1869. He named the town for Major William Williams, who had commanded the soldiers sent to aid the settlers after the Spirit Lake Massacre. Williams was incorporated on September 13, 1883. (228, 318, 438)

Williamsburg, Iowa County. Williamsburg was founded by Richard Williams on May 20, 1856, and was named for the founder. The Williamsburg Web site, however, indicates the town was actually started in 1854. The town was incorporated on December 3, 1884. (163, 164, 438)

Williamson, Lucas County. Williamson had been named Gunwald, but in 1922 the name was changed to honor George Williamson Sr., who founded the town in 1914. It was incorporated on June 14, 1922. (283, 438)

Wilton, Muscatine County. Wilton was established on property owned by a Mr. Stone and a Mr. Green in September 1854. A number of names were considered, including the suggestion of a Mr. Butterfield, formerly of Wilton, Maine, for Wilton. The two final choices were Wilton and Glendale.

Glendale was selected, but before the town's name was registered, the founders reconsidered, and the name given the community was Wilton, actually Wilton Junction, since there was a railroad junction there. Wilton was incorporated on February 12, 1878. (438, 492)

Windsor Heights, Polk County. Windsor Heights was named after the Windsor Elementary School. The school was named for the Windsor family who donated the land for it. The first developments established were Elmcrest and Evergreen Heights in 1925. Windsor Heights was incorporated on July 19, 1941. (7, 163, 438)

Winfield, Henry County. Winfield was established on June 12, 1852, by Asbury Porter. It was named for General Winfield Scott. Winfield was incorporated on March 27, 1882. (245, 273, 438)

Winterset, county seat, Madison County. The town was established in 1846. As the commissioners were discussing the choices for the name of the new town, Summerset and Independence were put forth as names. One of the commissioners, who had fortified himself with whiskey because of the chill in the air, suggested that Winterset would be far more appropriate than Summerset, and that name was adopted. Winterset was incorporated on January 16, 1857. (318, 375, 438)

Winthrop, Buchanan County. Winthrop was founded in 1857 by A. P. Foster. The name of Winthrop was suggested by E. S. Norris, who had lived in Winthrop, Maine. It was incorporated on June 7, 1886. (61, 85, 438)

Wiota, Cass County. Wiota was established in 1872 as a depot on the route of the Chicago, Rock Island and Pacific Railroad. The town site was not formally recorded until November 13, 1877. Wiota appears to be derived from either the Sioux language, *wa-ota*, or the Winnebago and Iowa languages, *niota*. *Wa-ota* seems to be related to the passage of time, as the translations vary from "many snows" to "many moons" or "many suns." The term *niota* is the best prospect for the source of the name since it means "much water," and Turkey Creek, near the town, frequently flooded the area. Wiota was incorporated in the spring of 1884. (257, 561)

Woden, Hancock County. Woden was founded on December 20, 1898. The town was going to be called Bingham, for an early settler. When it was discovered that there was already a town in Iowa named Bingham, the name Woden was suggested, since it had been the name of a post office in the area. Woden, or Odin, is a name from Norse mythology. Woden was incorporated on January 7, 1904. (242, 438)

Woodbine, Harrison County. Woodbine was established by John Blair on December 5, 1866. It was named after the Woodbine Post Office that had been in operation about a mile from the new town site. That office had been named by Annie Butler, after her birthplace in England. There is another story that the town was named for the Virginia creeper, or woodbine, that grew in the area. The community was incorporated on November 9, 1877. (312, 438, 528)

Woodburn, Clark County. The town was founded by the railroad company that was laying tracks in the area in 1867. Ottawa, a town nearby, was abandoned, and the people moved to Woodburn to be near the railroad. Therefore the predecessor to Woodburn was Ottawa. The origin of the name Woodburn appears to be a mystery, although Woodburn was a surname known in Iowa at the time. Another possibility is that it could have been a transfer name from the eastern United States or England. Woodburn was incorporated on February 12, 1878. (43, 438)

Woodward, Dallas County. Woodward was established as a depot for the railroad in 1880. The town was initially called

Colton, but because of confusion with another town named Colton, it was renamed Woodward, after the Woodward Gardens in California. Woodward was incorporated on October 13, 1883. (163, 318, 438)

Woolstock, Wright County. Woolstock was established in January 1881 though a post office of that name had existed since 1868. There are two stories about the origin of the name. The first is that Gilbert Perry simply invented the name for the town, and there was no other inspiration for the name. The other story is that the town was named for the large number of sheep raised in the area. Woolstock was incorporated on April 19, 1895. (47, 163, 438, 528)

Worthington, Dubuque County. Worthington was founded in 1857 when a rail line was surveyed between Farley and Cedar Rapids. It was named after the first store owner in the town, Amos Worthington. The community was incorporated on January 10, 1893. (163, 266, 438)

Wright, Mahaska County. Wright was named for the Wright family who were property owners in the area. The town was established in 1884 at a location where two rail lines ran parallel to one another. Wright is not incorporated. (339)

Wyman, Louisa County. Wyman was established in 1880 and named for a railroad surveyor. A post office of the same name had been established in 1879. The town is not incorporated. (368)

Wyoming, Jones County. Wyoming was originally called Marshfield after a Mr. Marsh, who had some influence with a railroad company that was being formed. The post office at the site was called Marshfield, and the first postmaster was installed on October 18, 1854. The town's name was changed by J. A. Bronson, who bought the town site in 1854 and established the town in 1855, although it was not formally established until 1856. Bronson was from Wyoming County,

New York, and he named the new town for his old home. Wyoming was incorporated on October 21, 1873. (123, 142, 438)

Y y ++++++++++++++++++++

Yale, Guthrie County. Yale was founded on October 11, 1882, by Milo Yale, who owned the property. It was incorporated on November 27, 1901. (223, 271)

Yarmouth, Des Moines County. Yarmouth was established in the late 1870s and named for Yarmouth, England. In 1881 the La Vega Post Office that was nearby was closed, and mail service was moved to the "new village" of Yarmouth. The town is not incorporated. (66)

Yetter, Calhoun County. Yetter was founded on July 15, 1899, by E. K. Blanchard on behalf of L. M. Yetter and his wife and was named for them. The town was incorporated on January 11, 1904. (438, 532)

Yorktown, Page County. Yorktown was established by C. E. and Edith Perkins on April 3, 1882. Postal authorities named the post office at the site York, and the town Yorktown. The townspeople rebelled and renamed the town Loy, but after a few months it was renamed Yorktown. The name was inspired by the Revolutionary War battlefield in Virginia. (246, 451)

Z z ++++++++++++++++++++

Zearing, Story County. Zearing was founded in 1881 and first called Ashhurst. A Major Zearing, who was visiting the town shortly after it was founded, said he would build a church in the community if the townspeople would name the town for him. Zearing was incorporated on February 6, 1883. (16, 318, 438)

Zwingle, Dubuque and Jackson counties. Settlement had started in the Zwingle area in the late 1840s. Zwingle, originally named Harmony, was renamed for Ulrich Zwingli, a Swiss Protestant reformer. Zwingle was incorporated on December 17, 1900. (80, 318, 438)

FORMER COUNTIES, TOWNS & POST OFFICES

Just as with Iowa's towns, some county names that existed have slipped away. The following is a list of county names that have disappeared. The information for former counties, towns, and post offices was drawn from the resources listed at the end of this chapter.

Bancroft County is now part of Kossuth County.

Belknap County was originally part of Pottawattamie County; when it was abandoned, it was reabsorbed by Pottawattamie County.

Buncombe County was renamed Lyon County.

Cook County's borders were ambiguous, and it was dissolved in 1837.

Crocker County was absorbed by Kossuth County.

Fox County was renamed Calhoun County.

Grimes County was to be created from a portion of Pottawattamie County, but that was voted down in 1876.

Keokuk County. This county preceded the current Keokuk County and was abolished in 1840.

Kishekosh County was renamed Monroe County.

Risely County was briefly part of Webster County and then established as Hamilton County.

Slaughter County is now Washington County.

Wahkaw County is now Woodbury County.

Yell County was absorbed into Webster County.

The following is a list of town and post office names that are classified as abandoned or are ghost towns; or their names have been altered; or some have simply slipped off the Iowa Department of Transportation (DOT) map; or they were proposed but never developed. Obviously, the sites that have been renamed are in many cases similar to the current names—for example, the change from Grundy Centre to Grundy Center has placed Grundy Centre on this list. Some places are certainly in existence but don't meet the criteria for inclusion on the DOT map, such as Glasgow in Jefferson County. Iowa's changing mobility patterns, from river traffic to stage roads, to railroads, and to the current transit systems, have had an impact on the survival of towns. Many towns have been started, but many have not been able to survive. As the state's agricultural demographics change and fewer people are living in rural environments, there will be fewer and fewer small towns, as people go to more metropolitan centers for their business and recreational needs. While this is an extensive list, I do not claim that it is complete.

Adair County
Adair
Arbor Hill
Arborhill
Avondale
Berea
Canby
Carbondale
Casey
Drakes
Easton
Fisk
Gilead
Groveland
Hebron
Holaday's
Holadays
Howe
Jackson
Leath City
Lemont
Linwood
Manchester
McKinley
Nanito
Prussia
Prussia Centre
Stanzel
Summerset
Swearsburgh
Swedesburgh
Vino
Wah-Ta-Wah

Adams County
Briscoe
Brookville (prior name for
    Brooks)
Canaan City (prior name for
    Brooks)

Carl

Carson

East Nodaway

Eureka

Glendale (prior name for
  Prescott)

Hayes

Hoyt

Icaria

Iveyville

Mercer

Mt. Washington

Queen City

Quincy

Rochelle

Shinn

Simpson (prior name for
  Brooks)

Strand

Summit (prior name for Lenox;
  also in Taylor County)

Williamson

Allamakee County

Adams Junction

Allamakee

Alton

Bergen

Buckland

Bunker Hill

Capoli

Carvers

Center Valley

Centre Valley

Chantry

Clear Creek

Cleveland

Columbus

Connor

Dalby

Egan

Eldergrove

Elon

Fandon

Forest Mills

French Creek

Granger

Grantville

Hardin

Harper's Ferry

Howard Center

Ion

Johnsonsport

Lafayette

Lark

Ludlow

Lybrand

Lycurgus

Lyndale

Makee

Manchester

Mariners Hope

Maud

Mezeka

Milton

Myron

New Galena
Nezeka
North Capoli
Paint Creek Valley
Paint Rock
Paintville
Quandahl
Reeds Ridge
Rex
Smithfield
Stella
Tom Corwin
Union Prairie
Vailsville
Village Creek
Volney
Voss
Waterville Mill
Watson
Webster
Wexford
Widow Post
Willson's Ford
Windsor

Appanoose County
Albany (also in Davis County)
Beetrace
Bellair
Bob Town
Brazil
Caldwell
Caldwell City

Calhoon
Calhoun
Camden
Chaldea
Clarkdale
Coal City
Crete
Darbyville
Dayton
Dean
Dennis
Diamond
Diff
Elizabethtown
Forbush
Griffinsville
Harkes
Hiattsville
Hibbsville
Hilltown
Iconium
Johns Post Office
Johnson Post Office
Johnstown
Kemigala
Kirkwood
Laneville
Lebanon
Leona
Livingston
Mardensville
Memphis
Millard Post Office

Milledgeville
Mt. Gilead
New Hope
New Plains Post Office
Niles Post Office
Orford
Orleans
Orville
Pearl City
Pleasant View
Pleasantville
Ray
Rising Sun
Sedan
Sharon
Sharpton
Shawvills
Soap Creek (also in Davis
  County)
Streepyville
Tranquility
Walnut City
Walsh
Welland
Well's Mills
Williamston

Audubon County
Audubon Centre
Audubon City
Audubon Heights
Ballard
Civil Point

Conkling
Dayton
Fiscus
Grove
Hamlin
Hamlin Grove
Horace
Irwin
Jobes
Kimball Town
Larland
Leroyville
Louisville
Melville
Oakfield
Poplar
Price
Thompson
Viola Center
Viola Centre

Benton County
Benton
Benton Centre
Benton City
Berkley
Beulah
Big Hill
Brooklyn (also in Black Hawk
  County)
Buckeye
Burk
Daggett

Eden
Florence
Fremont
Geneva
Gillespie
Gomersal
Grand Gulf
Guinnville
Gwinville
Hague
Hoosier Point
Irving
Lelia
Likins
Linwood
London
Manatheka
Marysville
Mt.
Northport
Paul
Pickaway
Poker Flat
Potato Hill
Prairie Creek Post Office
Robin
Rogerville
Shellsburgh
Spencer Grove
Summers
Taylor's Grove
Terry
Unity

Van Horn
Williams
Wilmington
Woods

Black Hawk County
Barclay
Benson
Blakeville
Blessing
Boies
Brooklyn (also in Benton
    County)
Calvin
Canfield
Cedar City
Cedar Valley
Crain Creek
Eagle Center
Eagle Centre
East Waterloo
Edwards
Eliza
Elk Run
Emert
Energy
Enterprise
Filkin's Grove
Finch's Ford
Florence City
Frenchtown
Greenfield
Greenville

Gresham

Jubilee

Knox

Laporte City

Lester

Louise

Miller's Creek

Mt. Hope

Mullarkey's Grove

Nantville

Nautrill

Newell's Ford

Ottawa

Prairie Rapids

Stella

Sturgis Falls

Sturgis Rapids

Turkey Foot

Washburn

Winslow

Boone County

Angus

Belle Point

Boone Station

Boonesboro

Boonesborough

Booneville

Bridgeport

Carson's Point

Centerville

Coal Valley

Coaltown

Daily City

Elk Rapids

Fisher's Point

Frasers

Garden

Garden Grove

Garden Prairie

Griffin

Harmon's Switch

High Bridge

Hornbuckles Point

Hull

Incline

Jehu

Jordan

Jordon

Logansport

Mackey

Mackeys Grove

Marcy

Midway

Mineral Ridge

Montana

Paducah

Parkersburg

Prairie Hill

Quincy

Rapids

Renner

Ridgeport

River Side

Riverside

Smith's Point

Somersville

Sweede Point

Unionville

Worth

Yough

Zenorsville

Bremer County

Artesian

Breckenridge

Bremer

Bremer Center

Buck Creek

Dayton

Dickey

Eagle

Grove Hill

Grovehill

Horton

Jackson Point

Jaynesville

Jefferson City

Key

Klinger

Knittel

Knott

Leroy

Martinsburg

Maxfield

Mentor

Minkler

Neutral

Phillipston

Polk

Polk Precinct

Pony

Roxie

Seigel

Sigel

Spring Lake

Sumner

Syracuse

Tripoli

Wapsie

Waverly Junction

Winkler

Buchanan County

Atlanta

Bryantburg

Bryantburgh

Buchanan

Buffalo Grove

Cana

Castleville

Chatham

Coytown

Crowfoot

Erie

Erin

Frink's Grove

Gatesville

Greeley's Grove

Hamerville

Hammerille

Haskinville

Hazelton
Idlewild
Jessup
Kiene
Kier
Littleton
Middlefield
Monti
Mudville
Newtonville
Otterville
Perry Valley
Pine
Shady Grove
Sunny Side
Vista
Ward's Corners

Buena Vista County
Anna
Blaine
Crozier
Elkton
Hanover
Hire's Grove
Hollingsworth
Juniata
Leverett
Manthorp
Mayview
Menoti
Northam
Orland

Orsland
Peach
Plum
Racine
Sargentsville
Sayre
Sweet's Mill
West Scott

Butler County
Algonquin
Beaver Grove
Belgrove
Benezet
Boylan's Grove
Butler Center
Butler Centre
Butler Rapids
Clutterville
Coster
Eleanor
Elmsprings
Georgetown
Hitesville
Island Grove
Leoni
Lowell
Maudville
Monmouth
New Albany
New Albion
New Jerusalem
Oplington

Packard
Parkersburgh
Prosper
Root's Siding
Sinclair
Swanton
Union Ridge
Vilmar
West Point
Willoughby
Wilson Grove

Calhoun County
Brooklyn
Burns
Calhoun
Calhoun Center
Crandall
Eads
Elmgrove
Farnham
Kissemmee
Knoke
Lavinia
Mosley
Muddy
Rands
Richards
Schonberg
Sherwood
Twin Lakes
Vincent
Wightman

Yatesville
Yeatesville
Yetter

Carroll County
Benen
Browning
Carroll City
Carrollton
Coplin's Grove
Divide
Eastside
Elba
Jasper
Kentner
Ketner
Macks
Maple River
Niles Grove
Roselle
Tip Top

Cass County
Cass Centre
Cold Spring or Cold Springs
Dewey
Edna
Galion
Grove City
Gurley
Hedge's Grove
Indiantown
Iranistan

Lorah
Lura
McDill
Newlon's Grove
Pymosa
Reno
Smith
Turkey Grove
Wakefield
Wax
Whitneyville

Cedar County
Antwerp
Apollo
Ayresville
Batespark
Batesport
Brick House
Buchanan
Cameron
Carlisle
Cedar
Cedar River
Cedar Valley
Centerdale
Centredale
Cessford
Denson's Ferry
Elizabethtown
Gower's Ferry
Harwell
Honey Grove

Inland
Lactin
Lime City
Lithgow
Lizard
Massillon
Munn
Onion Grove
Pedee
Pioneer Grove
Plato
Pleasant Hill
Red Oak
Rock Creek
Rock Point
Rosette
Shiloh
Side Hill
Spring Dale
Sugar Creek
Sugar Creek Mills
Union Grove
Wald
Walden
Warsaw
Washington Ferry
Woodbridge
Yankee Grove
York Prairie
Zoar

Cerro Gordo County
Bath

Cartersville
Clear Lake City
Cold Water
Coldwater
Creamery
Freeman
Geneseo
Hanford
Kausville
Lime Creek
Linn
Livonia
Masonic Grove
Masonville
Owen
Owen Centre
Owen's Grove
Rock
Shell Rock Falls
Shiboleth
Terry
Thayer's Siding
Venture
Wheelerwood

Cherokee County
Baum
Blair City (also known as Blaire
    City)
Cherokee
Cherokee Center
Cleghorn
Coulson

De Leon
Diamond
East Hampton
Fielding
Hazard
Maple
New Cherokee
Pilot Rock
Wendell

Chickasaw County
Beaver City
Boyd
Bradford
Bridgeport
Chickasaw Center
Chickisaw or Chickasaw
Dale
Dayton Centre
Deerfield
Devon
Dover
Dresden
Elk Creek
Forest City
Fredericksburgh
Greenwood
Indiantown
Jacksonville
Little Turkey
Mansen
Maplesville
Nansen

North Washington
Pearl Rock
Republic
Saude
Stapleton
Waudena
Williamstown
Woodbridge
Zillo

Clarke County
Balaka
Bartlettville
Bell
Folger
Freehold
Glenn's
Green Bay
Greenbay
Groveland
Hickory Grove
Hickory Point
Hopewell Colony
Jack Creek
Jackson
Jacksonville
Jamison
Jay
La Harp
Lacelle
Laporte
Leslie
Middleport

Milford
Norris
Nortonville
Oakland
Oceola
Osceola City
Ottawa
Prairie Grove
Riley
Shelby
Smyrna
White Breast

Clay County
Annieville
Bridgewater
Clark
Cornell
Cromwell Center
Cromwell Centre
Douglas Centre
Freeman
Gillett
Gillett's Grove
Glenora
Herdland
Ingleville
Platt
Prospect
Summit
Trimello
White's
Willow Creek

Willowcreek

Yankee

Clayton County

Anderson

Beulah

Bismarck

Brookville

Cass

Ceres

Communia

Council Hill

Cox's Creek

East Elkport

Elkport

Enfield

Ewington

Farmersburgh

Flint Hill

Frankford

Franklin

Frenchtown

Froelich Station

Gem

Giard

Graham

Grand Meadow

Hardin

Henderson Prairie

High Grove

Highland

Honey Creek

Jacksonville

Jefferson

Keeleroy

Locust Hill

Lodomillo

McGregor's Landing

Mederville

Mendon

National

New Stand

North McGregor

Osborne

Osborne Station

Osterdock Ferry

Panther Creek

Peck's Ferry

Prairie La Porte

Read

St. Johan

St. Sebald

Sigel

Springfield

Springville

Sylvan

Turkey River

Updegraff

Wabasha

Wagner

Watson

Windsor

Wood

Wood Centre

Yankee Settlement (also in
Delaware County)

Clinton County

Almont
Almont Station
Bliedorn
Bloomfield
Boon Spring
Brookfield
Brookfield Centre
Brown's Station
Buena Vista
Buenavista
Burgess
Cambridge
Chancy
Cherry Wood
Dewitt
Dot
Elk River
Camache
Hauntown
Hermitage
Lyons
Malone
McClure
Mead
New York
O'Brien
Orange
Petersville
Quigley
Ramessa or Ramersa
Riggs
Ringwood

Sanbornton
Saratoge
Smithtown
Spring Rock
Suffolk
Teeds
Teed's Grove
Ten Mile House
Van Horn
Vandenburg
Villanova
Vollamova
Watkyns Glen
Waubesepinecon
Welton

Crawford County

Adena
Adrian
Astor
Bayers Valley
Bell
Belltown
Beloit
Bloomington
Boyer
Boyer River
Buckgrove
Como
Coon Grove
Crawford
Dowville
Ells

Hohenzollern
Johnson
Johnsonville
Johnstonville
Kenwood
Kiron
Lydia
Mason's Grove
Mogan
Otter Creek
Paradise
Swedeboy
Swedeburg

Dallas County
Adell
Alton
Boone
Brough
Chattanooga
Chicago
Chickasaw Station
Colton
Dallas Center
Ephesus
Fairland
Galway
Gardiner
Greenvale
Harvey's Mills
Ingersoll
Kennedy
Langfitt

Linn
McKay
Moran
New Ireland
Nordyke
Ortonville
Osprey
Panther
Panther Creek
Penoach or Penouch
Pierce Point
Shirley
Snyder
Tracy
Uncle Sam
Undine
Van Metre
Waukee Station
Wiscotta
Xenia

Davis County
Adamsville
Ajax
Albany (also in Appanoose
    County)
Ash Grove
Ashgrove
Blackhawk
Brown's Mills
Carbon
Carbon Hill
Chequest

Chequist
Del Norte
Dover
Dunnville
Fox
Fox Landing
Gandytown
Hail
Hall
Harbour
Harpersville
Laddsdale
Lewiston
Lost Rock
Lunsford
Mark
Martinsburg
Martinsville
Monterey
Mt. Cavalry
Napesa
Noblesville
Noseviille
Nottingham
Oak Spring
Oakspring
Pleasant View
Rankin City
Rater
Richmond
Roscoe
Salt Creek

Soap Creek (also in Appanoose County)
Soap Creek Mills
Springville
Stiles
Stilesville
Stringtown
Taylor
Tippo
Uncle Abe
Wanamaker
Weeping Willow
White Elm
Wooleyville

Decatur County
Blockly
Bracewell
Burrell
Cora
Crown
De Kalb
Dekalb
Eldorado
Elk
Fierce
Florence
Franklin
Funk's Mills
Gould
Green Valley
High Point
Highbrier

Highpoint
Hungarian Settlement
Independence
Little River
Long Creek
Milford
Morgan
New Buda
Nine Eagles
Paris
Patriot
Pleasant Plain
Prairie City
Prairieville
Sedgewick
South Independence
Spring Valley
Terre Haute
Turkey Run
Tuskeega
Westerville
Woodland

Delaware County
Abbeyville
Acerville
Almira
Almoral
Almoral Station
Amarill
Bailey's Ford
Barryville
Bay

Broadway (also in Linn County)
Bruff
Burrington
Campton
Coffin's Grove
Cold Water
Cole's Burgh
Colesburgh
Colony
Delaware Centre
Ead's
Ead's Grove
Ehler
Forestville
Giltedge
Golden
Golden Prairie
Green Hill
Grove Creek
Hartwick
Hazel Green
Hoptown
Mangoldville
Millheim
Milo
Mt. Hope
Nottingham
Orrin Glen
Orrinden
Petersburgh
Plum Creek
Plum Spring
Poultney

Robinson
Rockville
Sand Creek
Sand Spring
Silver Creek
Spring Branch
Thorpe
Thorpton
Tower Hill
Uniontown
Viola
Yankee Settlement (also in
    Clayton County)
York

Jacksonville
Kline
La Vega
Latty
Limestone
Linton
Navarre
Northfield
Parrish
Pleasant Grove
Pleasantgrove
South Flint
Van Dyke
Yellow Spring

Des Moines County
Albright's
Amityville
Bluff Dale
Burkhart's Point
Carter's Spring
Centerville
Cora
Danville Center
Dodgeville
Fan
Flint Hills
Franklin Mills
Gibbs
Gibsons Ferry
Hartford
Hawk Eye
Huron

Dickinson County
Austin
Beach
Hayward
Hunters
Inn, The
Lake City
Lakeville
Methodist Camp
Milford
Minnie
Orleans
Spirit Lake
Tribly
Wallace

Dubuque County
Allison

Alma
Arquitt
Aspinwall
Ballyclough
Ballyclough Grove
Bennettville
Buncombe
Caledonia
Center
Center Grove
Centre Grove
Centre Town
Channingville or Channingsville
Cottage Hill
Dacotah
Decotah
Derrinane
Donelan
Dubuque's Mines
Duke
Emna
Evergreen
Factoryville
Falls
Fillmore
Flea Hill
Georgetown
Glassnevin
Glen
Hagerty
Hazel
Hempstead
Higginsport

Hogansville
Jefferson
Julian
Julien
Key West
Keywest
King
Lapage
Lattner
Lattners
Lore
Luxemburgh
Marshfield
McCants
Melleray
Millard
Milleray
Miller's Post Office
Morena
Mosalem
New Vine
Oakland
Ogden
Olympus
O'Neill
Peru
Pin oak
Placid
Plum Creek
Prairie Creek
Rockdale
St. Joseph's Prairie
Salisbury

Sheffield
Sherrill's Mount
Spechts Ferry
Squires Mills
Sylva
Tara
Tivoli
Viola
Washington Mills
Waupeton
Weld's Landing
White Water
Zook Spur

Emmet County
Armstrong's Grove
Brevick
Bubona
Butler Hill
Butter Hill
Emmet
Emmet Grove
Gridley
Halfa
High Lake
Hoprig
Huntington
Iowa Lake
Island Grove
Lakeside
Luzon
Maple Hill
New Bergen

Raleigh
Ringsted
Roslea
Swan Lake City
Twelve Mile Lake
Voss

Fayette County
Albany
Bethel
Brainard
Brush Creek
Corn Hill
Donnan
Douglass
Dover Mills
Eden
El Dorado
Gamble Grove
Hawk Eye
Hazleton
Illyria
Jefferson
Leo
Lightville
Louisville
Lutra
Mill
Mill Grove
Moetown
North Fairfield
Norway
Old Mission

Oran
Orion
Otsego
Penn
Putnam
Richfield
Scott
Scott Centre
Seaton
Stadel Town
Taylorsville
Turnersville
Volga City
Wardena
West Albany
West Auburn
West Field
Westfield
Wilson Grove
Windsor

Floyd County
Aurelia
Beelar's Grove
Carney
Carrville
Charlestown
Colwell
Danville
Ernie
Flood Creek
Floyd Center
Freeman

Gilmantown
Hackberry
Howardville
Niles
Nilesville
Powersville
Ripley
Riverton
Rock Grove City
St. Charles City
Sargent
Scott
Ulster
Watertown
Woodbridge
Woodstock

Franklin County
Benjamin
Boulder
Burdette
Carlton
Chapin
Cold Water
Congress
Cream Hill
Elida or Elide
Faulkner
Ingham
Maysville
Menzie
Oakland Valley
Ollin

Otisville (also in Wright
  County)
Reeve
Shobe's Grove
Union Ridge
Washburn

Fremont County
Austin
Buchanan
Civil Bend
Cora (also listed as Cory)
Dawsonburg
Deer Creek
Eastport
Egypt
Farmer City
Fremont City
Gaston
Hamburgh
High Creek
Highcreek
Knox
Lawrence
Manti
McKissack's Grove
McPaul
Nunda
Osage
Payne
Plum Hollow
Shiloh
Vaughan

Walnut Creek

Greene County
Adaza
Cedar Creek
Eureka
Forbes Station
Green Castle
Greenops
Greys
Hardin
Havanna
Kendrick
New Jefferson
Northville
Paduca
Rippey
Sarney
Scranton City
Scranton Station
Surry

Grundy County
Alice
Andersonville
Arrow
Bois D'Arc
Conrad Grove
Dairyville
Elizabeth
Fern
Fredsville
Greenwood

Greenwood Hill
Grundy Centre
Ivester
Jerusalem
Kingsbury
Lear
Lincoln
Lincoln Centre
Melrose
New Jefferson
Palermo
Taylor Hill
Wadiloup
Wells
Wellsburgh
Zaneta

Guthrie County
Advance
Allen
Allenville
Ava
Bear Grove
Beargrove
Bluff
Brushy Valley
Dale
Dale City
Dalmanutha
Dodge
Erastus
Fairview
Fanslers

Fansler's
Glendon
Gopher Station
Graceville
Guthrie
Guthrie Centre
Guthrie Switch
Harbor Station
Harrison
Herndon
Leadville
Macksville
Mada
Maida
Moffitt
Moffitt's Grove
Monteith
Morrisburgh
Nelson
North Branch
Pennsburg
Ridgeway
Safeside
Sedalia
Switch, The
Tuttle Grove
Van Nest
West Milton
Wilkins
Wilmington
Wilson's

Hamilton County

Blairsburgh
Calahan or Calanan or Callanan
Clybourn Place
Highview
Homer
Hook's Point
Kentucky Grove
Lake Center
Lakin's Grove
Larkin's Grove
Marion
New Castle
Paris
Plow
Poland's Grove
Poplar Grove
Red Cedar
Rose Grove
Rosendale
Russell's Grove
Saratoga
Tremaine
Tunnel

Hancock County

Amsterdam
Bailey
Bailey's Grove
Bingham
Concord
Cuba
Elk Grove
Ellington
Elmo
German
Hancock Center
Harmon
Laconia
Luzon
Magor
Mikesville
Ripley
Stilson
Upper Grove
Wardsville
West Lake
Westlake

Hardin County

Abbott
Berlin
Bunker Hill
Cleves
Cottage
Delanta or Delanti
Denova
Deputy
Duane
Eagle City
Eldora Junction
Ellis
Fontaine
Georgetown
Hardin City
Hazel Green

Hughes
Idaho
La Yerba or La Yuba
Lawn Hill
Lawnhill
Link
Lithopolis
Macy
Midland
New Providence
Pilgrim's Grove
Point Pleasant
Pokeepsie
Poughkeepsie
Quebec
Rathton
Rickord
Robertson
Rocksylvania
Rockwood
Sandersonville
Secor
Sherman
Tipton Grove
Wilke
Xenia

Harrison County
Allen
Beebeetown
Bigler's Grove
Boyer Falls
Buena Vista

Calhoun
California
Cincinnati
Crisp
Echo
Eldorado
Fontainbleau
Fontainblue
Gamet
Harris Grove
Harrison
Howsier
Jeddo City
Martin's Ranch
Martinsville
Melrose
Missouri Valley
Mt. Norris
Needmore
Nephi
New St. Johns
Ojedo
Old St. Johns
Olmsted
Olympus
Orson
Parrish
Raglan
Reeder Mills
Reeder's Mills
River Sioux
Rode
St. John

Seralro
Silver Prairie
Soldier Valley
Unionburgh
Valley View
Whitesboro
Whitesborough
Yazoo
Yorkshire

Stringtown
Swedesburgh
Traxler
Vega
Washington
Wayne
West Mt. Pleasant
Winona
Woodlawn

Henry County
Arthur
Baltimore
Bangall
Beery
Belfast
Boyleston
Cotton Grove
Crooked Creek
Dover
East Grove
Finis
Hillsborough
Jefferson
Lahoyt
Lancaster
Lowell Mill
Marshall
McCabes
McCarverstown
Oakland Mills
Rural
Shockley

Howard County
Acme
Arnoldsville
Bonair
Busti
Cecelia
Crane Creek
Davis Corners
Eatonville
Florenceville
Foreston
Glen Roy
Howard
Howard Center
Howard Centre
Jamestown
Lime Spring (Station)
Limespring
Lowther Station
Maple Leaf
Mapleleaf
New Oregon
Newbury

Oakdale
Osborn
Osborne
Pond Valley
Stergis
Sturgis
Vernon Springs

Humboldt County
Addison
Arnold
Ash
Byron
Dakotah
Eber
Grove
Humboldt
Lotts Creek
McKnight
McKnight Point
Nora
Owlake
Park Grove
Pleasant View
Randolph
Russell Siding
Springvale
Sumner
Sylvan Retreat
Unique
Verbeck
Vernon (also in Kossuth
    County)

Viona
Von
Wacousta
Walbridge Grove
Whitman (also in Kossuth
    County)
Willow Glen

Ida County
Clarendon
Cornelia
Dreessen
Dresser
Ida
Silver Creek
Willow Dale

Iowa County
Alberton
Ambrose
Armah
Boltonville
Boyle
Callan
Carter
Cono
Dayton
Dove
Dover
Downard
Foote
Fox
Fremont

Genoa Bluff
Green Center
Greene Center
Hedge
High
Hinkletown
Ione
Jones
Koszta
Lytle City
Middle
Millersburgh
Moriah
Musquaka
Nevada
Prairie Creek
Rest
Riverdale
Soaptown
Stelapolis
West
West Pilot
West Troy
Williamsburgh
Wilson
York Center
York Centre

Jackson County
Alma
America
Amoy
Belleview

Bridgeport
Carl Port
Carrollport
Centerville
Charleston
Clarkstown
Cobb
Colona
Copper Creek
Cottonville
Crabb
Crabb's Mills
Deventersville
Duggan
Duke
Emeline
Farmer's Creek
Fremont
Garry Owen
Gordons Ferry
Gordon's Ferry
Hickory Grove
Higginsport
Hugo
Iron Hills
Isabel
Lowell
Millrock
Mt. Algor
New Castle
North Maquoketa
Otter Creek
Ozark

Pass
Prairie Springs
Rolley
Saunder's Spur
Silsbe
Smith's Ferry
Spring Brook
Springfield
Spruce Mills
Sterling
Sullivan
Summer Hill
Tete des Mortes
Union Center
Union Centre
Van Buren
Vanburen
Wagonersburg
Waterford
Wickliffe

Jasper County
Adamsonville
Amboy
Baxter
Bush
Carr
Chalybeate Springs
Clyde
Con
Dairy Grove
Dawson
Dixie

Draper
Eliot
Elk Creek
Elliott
Fairmount
Farmersville
Galesburgh
Goddar
Greencastle
Horn
Independence Center
Independence Centre
Jasper City
Kimball
Metz
Minerva
Monroe
Morristown
Murphy
Newburg
Newburgh
Newton
North Skunk River
Oswalt
Palmyra
Parkersburg
Parkersburgh
Pleasant View
Point Pleasant
Prairiebelle
Quincy
Ruchville
Rushville

Seevers
Sugar Creek
Tool's Point
Turner
Vandalia
Vowells
Warren Center
Warren Centre
Williamsville
Wittenburg
Woodville

Jefferson County
Aaronville
Absecum
Acheson
Baker
Beckwith
Belleville
Blue Point
Botavia
Brays
Brookville
Coalport
Collett
Cotton Grove
County Line
County Line Station
Creesville
Deedsville
East Pleasant Plain
Four Corners
Germanville

Glasgow
Glendale
Harmony
Harveys Mills
Jefferson
Krum
Merrimac
Monroe
Mt. Sterling
New Haven
Parsonville
Perlee
Pleasant Grove
Salina
Typee
Vega
Veo
Walnut
Walnut Grove
Whitfield
Woolson
Wooster

Johnson County
Amish
Belle Air
Bon Accord
Carthage
Chase
Copi
Cou Falls
Curtis
Danforth

Dodd

Frank Pierce

Frendale

Graham

Green Castle

Gregg

Hill's Siding

Hueston

Indian Village

Ives

Leona

Mahern

Malvern

Monroe

Morfordsville

Napoleon

Nemora

Newport Centre

Oasis

Palestine

Sepanamo

Seventy Eight

Seventy Seven

Sharon Center

Shoo Fly

Shoofly

South Liberty

Tanktown

Unity

Williamstown

Windham

Jones County

Argand

Big Woods

Blue Cut

Bowen

Bowen's Prairie

Broomfield

Cass

Cass Centre

Castle Grove

Castlegrove

Centre Junction

Clay Mills

Clayford

Condit

Dartmouth

Downersville

Duane

Edinburgh

Elkford

Fairview

Farm Creek

Fuller's Mills

Garfield

Grove Creek

Hale City

Hale Village

Highland Grove

Isabell

Johnson

Johnsontown

Jonesville

Lexington

Madison
Marshfield
Mineral Creek
Newport
Norwich
Pamaho
Pierce
Richland
Rome
Spencerville
Strawberry Hill
Temple Hill
Viroqua
Walnut Fork
Zurich

Keokuk County
Atwood
Aurora
Baden
Baxter
Butler
Chandaller
Chandler
Coal Creek
Cory
Creswell
Divide
Eden or Edom
Edom or Eden
Elizabeth
Elizabethtown
Freedom

Frenchtown
Garibaldi
Hustons
Ioka
Ioka Station
Janetown
Lafayette
Lancaster
Manhattan
Milan
Muscatine
Nassau
Newton
Nugent
Olean
Orville
Pecks
Petersburg
Pleasant Grove
Pleasant Hill
Rosetta
Showman
Slagle
Springfield
Steady Run
Talleyrand
Vulcan
Walbridge
Walden
Warner's Mill
Waugh's Point
West London
Western City

White Pigeon
Wimer's Mills
Witter

Kossuth County
Ashuelot
Buffalo Fork
Buffalofork
Call's Grove
Cresco
Cutler
Darien
Eagle Lake
Eaglelake
Fenton
Fine
Gerled
German Valley
Germania
Greenwood Center
Hale
Hanna
Hatch
Hobart
Hobarton
Irvington
Johnson's Settlement
Kossuth
Kossuth Centre
Lonerock
Lotts Creek
Luverne
Morton Siding

Noebla
Rahm
Ramsay
Reynolds
Seneca
Swea
Vernon (also in Humboldt
    County)
Wesley Station
Whitman (also in Humboldt
    County)

Lee County
Ambrosia
Atlee
Belfast
Benbow
Big Mound
Bricker
Camackville
Camargo
Charleston
Clay's Grove
Cottonwood
Courtright or Courtwright
Cranston
Doantown
Dover
Edwards
Ft. Des Moines
Franklin
Franklin Centre
Franklin Station

Green Bay

Hazen

Hinsdale

Jeffersonville

Jollyville

La Crew

Larson

Madison

Meirotto

Melrose

Monterey

Mooar

Mt. Clara

Mt. Hamill

Nashville

Overton

Pleasant Ridge

Prairie House

Prim Rose

Russellville

Sand Ridge

Sandusky

Sawyer

South Augusta

South Franklin

String Prairie

Summitville

Tuscarora

Van Buren

Viele

Vincennes

Warren

White Lane

Yeargerville

Zarahemla

Linn County

Alice

Babcock

Banner Valley

Boulder

Brandy Brook

Broadway (also in Delaware
County)

Brown

Cedar

Centre Point

Columbus

Cousins

Crabapple

Crow Creek

Dry Creek

Elmont

Flemingville

Ford's Grove

Forfax

Franklin

Hollenback

Hoosier Grove

Ivanhoe

Kenwood Park

Kingston

Kingston City

La Fayette

La Fayette

Lafayette

Lindon
Linn Junction
Louisa
Mayfield
McGonigle
Mondieu
Necot
New Buffalo
New Lindon
Newark
Nugent
Nugent's Grovr
Oak Grove
Otter Creek
Paddington
Palisades
Paralta
Pinhook
Prairieburgh
Prairiesburg
Prospect Hill
Rogers
Rural
St. Julian
St. Marys
Shady Brook
Sisleys Grove
Sisley's Grove
Spring Grove
Sylvia
Torah
Trentham
Valley Farm

Vanderbilt
Waneta
Wapsa
West Prairie
Western
Western College
Westport

Louisa County
Alimeda
Altona
Bard
Big Springs
Black Hawk
Burris
Burris City
Cairo
Cannonburg
Catteese
Clifton
Concord
Cuba City
Elrick
Florence
Forest Hill
Gladwin
Harrison
Hillsboro
Hope Farm
Iowa Town
Lafayette
Long Creek Station
Louisa Centre

Marsh

Mid Prairie

Mt. Sterling

Muscatine

Newport

Oakland

Odessa

Ononwa

Palo Alto

Pittsburg

Port Allen

Port Louisa

Port Washington

Spring Run

Sterling

Tecumseh

Toddtown

Toolesboro

Toolesborough

Twin Oak

Virginia Grove

Walling's Landing

West Port Louisa

Yankee Town

Yellow Banks

Freedom

Freeland

Greenville

Grunwald or Gunwald

Henderson

Irish Grove

La Grange

Last Chance

Linn

Maceville

Mansfield

Milan

Norwood

Oakley

Ola

Olmitz

Polk

Purdy

Tallahoma

Time

Tipperary

Troy

West Alexander

White Breast

Zero

Lucas County

Argo

Belinda

Bucyrus

Cedar Grove

Cleveland

Earle

Lyon County

Ernest

Gibraltar

Granite

Helgerson

Iuka

Iverson

Klondike
Krogness
Lakewood
Lunt's
Park
Pennington
River View
Riverview
Smead
Upland
Warren Grove
Willida

Madison County
Amazon
Barney
Bell's Ridge
Bloomingdale
Brooklyn
Buffalo
Charlottesville
Clanton
Ego
Ellsworth
Fairview
Foster
Gear
Gilpin
Grand View
Hanley
Harrison
Heaton
Independence

Kasson
Lavega
Lefever
Macksburgh
Maple Grove
Maplegrove
McBride
McPherson
Middle River
Montpelier
Narrows
Nem Con
North
North Branch
North River
Ohio
Ord
Pattison
Peru
Pitzer
Pleasant View
Price
Queen's Point
Reed
Richmond
Tileville
Venus
Webster
Wells
Worthington

Mahaska County
Agricola

Auburn
Barnes
Belle Fountain
Bernina
Big Grove
Bluff Creek
Blythe
Brock
Buck Horn
Bucyrus
Buxton
Carbonado
Chandlier
Cherry
Comet
Concert
Cricket
Des Moines City
Enterprise
Eveland
Eveland Grove
Excelsior
Farmersville
Ferry
Fishville
Flint
Gainford
Givin
Granville
Harrison
Hennes
Hopewell
Indianapolis

Lakonta
Laredo
Lostcreek
Mahaska
Mauch Chunk
Mauchchunk
Middletown
Mt. Vernon
Muchachinock
Muchakinoc
Nine Mile
Olivet
Oneska
Ornbaum
Oskaloosa Junction
Oxford
Pekay
Phalanx
Polk
Rex
Rochester
Rose Hill
Scott
Stoneridge
Tioga
Truax
Union Mills
Warren
Warrensville
White Oak
Whiteoak
Widow's Home

Marion County

American City
Amsterdam
Barkersville
Bauer
Bennington
Berry
Bethel
Bethel City
Caloma
Cloud
Cooper Springs
Cordova
Delphi
Divide
Dixonville
Donley
Dunreath
Durham
Durham's Ford
Elm Grove
Ely
Emery
English Settlement
Everist
Fairmont
Fifield
Flagler
Flaglers
Gosport
Hamaker's
Harrison
Harrisonville
Harveyville
Howell
Indiana
Iola
Lake Prairie
Leerdam
Lucas Grove
Melcher
Mennon
Merrill
Morgan Valley
New Castle
New Chicago
New Town
Newark
Newbern
Oak
Ohio
Oradell
Paran City
Percy
Perryville
Pinchey
Pixchey
Poplar Grove
Red Cedar Mills
Reedville
Rizora
Rousseau
Star
Terry's
Weston
Wheeling

Marshall County

Biven's Grove
Bromley
Capron
Cedar Cross Roads
Clemons Grove
Dillon
Edenville
Fredonia
Galvin
Gerard
Gowanda
Green Castle
Green Mountain
Hartland
Illinois Grove
Jebomville
Jeromeville
La Moille
Lafayette
Legrand
Liberty
Luray
Malta
Marietta
Marshall
Maulsby
Minerva
Mormon Hill
Norris
Pickering
Quaker
Reedsville
Rockton
Stanford
State Centre
Timber Creek
Vancleve
Vienna

Mills County

Alpa
Ashleigh
Balfour
Benton
Bethlehem
Boxelder
Cerro Gordo
Clark
Coonville
East Plattsmouth
Egypt
Fayette
Florence
Folsom
Haynie
Henton
Hentonville
Hillsdale
Indian Creek
Ingraham
Jewell
Junction City
Lawrence
Lewis City
Louden

Milton Station
Mt. Olive
Pacific City
Platteville
Potter
Rushville
St. Marys
Sharpsburgh
Solomon
Strahan
Trader's Point
Turner
Wahaghbonsy
Walnut Grove
Ward
White Cloud
Whitecloud

Mitchell County
Bailey
Brownville
Bucknam
Burr Oak
Bush's Mill
Cardiff
Cora
David
Dixie
Doran
Dramen
Dudley
Durea
Fuller

Hustad
Jenkins
Leo
Leoti
Lincoln Center or Lincoln
   Centre
Meroa
Nelson
Newburgh
Newhaven
North Bend
Old Otranto
Olin
Orrville
Otranto
Otranto Station
Rock Creek
Rockcreek
Springer
Staceyville
Stillwater
Wapsie
Wentworth
West Mitchell

Monona County
Albaton
Arcola
Ashton
Badger Lake
Belvidere
Bloomfield
Bluff Point

Bottom

Boyer City

Castana

East Mapleton

Grant Center

Grant Centre

Hall Creek

Hiawatha

Kennebec

King's Ranch

Lossing

Maple Landing

Mapleton

Onawa City

Preparation

Ransom

St. Clair

St. George

Spring Valley

Ticonic

Tieville

Ute

West Fork

Monroe County

Bluff Creek

Bremen

Bridgeport

Brompton

Bucknell

Buxton

Cedar Mines

Chisholm

Clark's Point

Clarksville

Coalfield

Coalton

Consol

Cuba

East Melrose

Elbert

Eldorado

Enon

Fairview

Foster

Fraker

Fredric

Georgetown

Gray's Creek

Halfway Prairie

Haydock

Henn

Hickory Grove

Hilton

Hocking

Holliday

Hummaconna

Hynes

La Grange

Lindville

Lockman

Mantua

Miami

Minerstown

Monroe Centre

Osprey

Pleasant Corners
Princeton
Rexfield
Selection
Smithfield
Thompsonville
Tyrone
Urbanna
Urbanna City
Wanlock
Ward
Weller
White
Whiteburg
Whitesburg

Montgomery County
Alix
Arlington
Biddick
Carr's Point
Climax
Coburgh
Coe's Grove
Flora
Frankfort
Hawthorn
Hawthorne
Holmstad
Milford
Mortgons Mills
Morton Mills
Morton's Mills

Oro
Red Oak Junction
Ross Grove
Rossville
Sciola
Sherman Center
Stennett
Stinson
Tenville
The Forks
Wales
Wallace
Wallin
Wilson

Muscatine County
Adams
Ardon
Bayfield
Bloomington
Bower Landing
Cedar Town
Cedarville
Center Grove
Centre Grove
Fountain
Fulton
Geneva
Glen Dale
Hudson
Iowa
Lacey
Lucas

Melpine
Montpelier
Myrtle
Newburg
Nichol
Nichol Station
Orono
Overman's Ferry
Pike
Pine Mills
Pleasant Prairie
Port Allen
Portland
Powasheek
Prairie Mills
Salem
Springfield
Strawberry Hill
Summit Ridge
Sweetland
Sweetland Centre
Vanderpool
Wilton Junction
Wyoming

O'Brien County
Archer Grove
Crona
Cyreno
Elcho
Erie
Max
O'Brien

Paulina
Philby
Pleissis
Plessis
Ritter
Romano
Shabbona
South
Southerland
Waterman
Woodstock

Osceola County
Cloverdale
Gillman
Gopher
Holman
Lexington
May City
Ocheyedan
Runyan
Rush Lake
St. Gilman

Page County
Amity
Amity College
Bethesda
Bingham
Binns
Centre
Crooks
Daisy

Darwin
Dasie
Davidson's
Davison's
Dayton
Franklin Grove
Harder's Corner
Hawleysville
Hawleyville
Loy
Meade
Morsman
Nodaway
Nodaway Forks
Nodaway Mills
North Grove
North Mills
Northborough
Nyman
Page
Page Centre
Page City
Snow Hill
Tarkio
Tarkio City
Union Grove
Walkerville
Wellsburg
York

Palo Alto County
Black Walnut
Blairgowrie

Cary
Crippen
Depew
Ellenton
Emmetsburgh
Emmitsburgh
Fairville
Fairwell
Fallow
Fern Valley
Forsyth
Great Oak
Ives
Lake View
Lost Island
Old Town
Osgood
Paoli
Poplar Grove
Rush Lake
Sage
Sherlock
Soda Bar
Staketown
West Bend

Plymouth County
Adaville
Broken Kettle
Brookdale
Crathorne
Dalton
Ellendale

Floyd Valley
Furay
Gehlen
Happt Corners
Hinton
Holley
James
Joy
Malton
Mammen
Millnerville
Minnabrook
Mlbourne
Neptune
O'Leary
Plymouth
Plymouth Centre
Plymouth City
Ponona
Portlandville
Potosia
Quorn
Rosbach
Ruble
St. Paul Junction
Struble
Vogt
Yeomans

Pocahontas County
Ben Lomond
Blandon
Blooming Prairie

Buda
Cedarville
Cora
Garlock
Garvey
Hard Times
Highland
Learned
Lilly
Lizard
Lizzard
Lombard
Luella
Marvin
Milton
Old Rolfe
Parvin
Pocahontas
Pocahontas Centre
Powhatan
Powhattan
Rolfe
Rolfe Junction
Rubens
Rusk
Shirley
Spring Flower
Swan Lake
Ware

Polk County
Adelphi
Andrews

Apple Grove
Ashawa
Avon
Avon Station
Ayers Grove
Bloomington
Brooklin
Camp
Campbell
Carbondale
Carleton
Chesterfield
Circleville
Coal Hill
Commerce
Commerce Mills
Cope
Corydon
Cory's Grove
Crocker
Delaware
Dogtown
Dudley
East Des Moines
Elkhart
Enterprise
Everton
Ft. Des Moines
Freel
Gilbert
Greenwood
Hanover
Harvey's Point

Hastie
Hatton
Herrold
Hopkins Grove
Huntsville
Ivy
Jerico
Keen
Keensburg
Kelsey
Kirkwood
Levey
Lincoln
Loring
Lovington
Marquisville
Marybell
McDevitt
McDevitt's Grove
Midway
Mitchell
Montacute
Mt. Auburn
Nobleton
North Des Moines
Norwoodville
Oakwood
Oakwood Station
Oldfield
Ottawa
Palmer
Pelton
Peoria City

Petersburg
Raccoon Forks
Raccoon River
Redhead
Rider
Ridgedale
Rockport
Santiago
Saylorsville
Sevastopol
Springfield
Tibbitt
Towner
Towner Lake
Trent
Tyner
Ulm
Union
University Place
Valley Junction
Wahkonsa
Walnut Creek
West Liberty
Youngstown

Pottawattamie County

Americus
Armour
Ascot
Bentley
Big Grove
Blair
Boomer

Boomer Grove
Botna
Boyer
Bristol
Bullock Grove
Cartersville
Clayton
Cold Spring
Council Bluffs
Council Point
Crescent City
Dermyer
Deseret
Downsville
Dumfries
Ellisdale
Eminence
French
Grable
Harrison
Iola
Islandpark
Kane
Kanesville
Keg Creek
Kegcreek
Kemling
Keown
Lake Manawa
Lima
Living Spring
Losh's Mills
Loveland's Mills

Macedonia

Miller's Hill

Miller's Hollow

Morton

Nanson

Nebraska

Neoga

New Town

Newtown

Nishna

Pacific

Parma

Pigeon

Pottawattamie

Prairie Flower

Quick

Reels

Scottswood

Silver Creek

Snapp

Taylor

Taylor Station

Traders Point

Union

Walnut Creek Station

Waveland

Weston

Wheeler

Wheeler's Grove

Whipple

Willow

Wooster

Poweshiek County

Bear Creek

Blue Point

Brooklyn

Brownsville

Carnforth

Chester Center

Chester Centre

Clearfield

Coells

De Etta

Deep River

Dresden

East Brooklyn

Ewart

Forest Home

Foresthome

Gilead

Glencoe

Greenville

Humbug

Jacob

Jacobs

Lattimer

Manatt

Mill Grove

North Skunk

Oak Grove

Oakgrove

Ottawa City

Searsborough

Sheridan

Sheridan Center

Sherman
Sonora
Stillwell
Sugar Grove
Tilton
Tyro
Verona
West Brooklyn
Western
Westfield

Ringgold County
Blackmore
Bloomington
Borneo
Bozaris
Caledonia
Clipper
Cross
Custer
Delphi
Estella
Eugene
Flushing
Goshen
Ingart Grove
Ingart or Ingarts
Kew
Knowlton
Lee
Lesan
Marena
Marshall

Marshalltown
Mortimer
New Chicago
New Port
Polen
Poyneer
Prairie View
Providence
Quinn's Grove
Redding
Riley
Ringgold
Ringgold City
Shawler
Silver Street
Thomas
Union Hill
Waltham
Watterson
Wirt

Sac County
Cedar Forks
Coon Valley
Elk Run
Fletcher
Grant City
Herring
Leota
Mercer
Mt. Hope
New Munich
Oliver

Pettis
Philo
Schoharie
Southport
Wall Lake Junction
Weed
Wheeler's Ranch

Scott County
Allens Grove
Allen's Grove
Allensgrove
Amity
Argo
Balluff
Barrwood
Berlin
Cadda
Carlson
Churchville
Clarks Ferry
East Davenport
Elizabeth City
Farming Grove
Gambril
Gilbert
Gilberttown
Glendale
Green Tree
Green Tree Tavern
Greentree
Greentree Tavern
Hickory

Husam
Jamestown
Kerr
Le Claire Centre
Linn Grove
Linwood
Middletown
New Buffalo
New Hamburgh
Parkhurst
Pinnacle
Plainview
Pleasant
Pleasant Valley
Point Pleasant
Price
Rockingham
Round Grove
Roundgrove
Spinnetville
Valley City
Walnut Grove
West Buffalo
White Sulphur
Wolcott

Shelby County
Altamont
Botany
Botna
Coon
Defiance
Elkhorn

Iten
Jacksonville
Mallory
Manteno
Marathon
Pomo
Prairie Rose
Rantout
Ravenwood
Redline
Roach
Rochdale
Rock Run
Rorbeck
Samison
Sampson
Shelbyville
Simoda
Somida
Tibbottville

Sioux County
Athol
Bell's Lake
Calliope
Carnes
Corn Valley
Darlington
East Orange
Elmsprings
Farmer
Farmers
Grenville

Highland Park
Hosper
Irene
Kuyper
Maurice
May Bell
McNally
Middleburg
Middleburgh
Nekimi
Newkirk
Orange
Orange City
Orange Grove
Oshkosh
Pattersonville
Ricker
Rock Mills
Royal Ridge
Sheridan
Sioux Centre
Winland

Story County
Agricultural Station
Ashurst
Bloomington
Boardman
Camden
Colbyville
College Farm
Collegeton
Collins Centre

Dayton
Defiance
Elwell
Fairview
Gilbert Station
Goshen
Hubbell
Iowa Center
Iowa Centre
Johnson's Grove
Johnston Grove
Latrobe
New Albany
New Philadelphia
Ontario
Palestine
Peoria City
Point Palestine
Prairie City
Sheffield
Shipley
Smayville
Smithfield
Story
Summit
Sunset
Turtle Creek
Willow Grove

Tama County
Badger Hill
Berlin
Bovina

Bruner
Buckingham
Butlerville
Carroll
Coldville
Collins Grove
Columbia
Connell
Crystal
De Novo
Denniss
Dryden
Ettie
Eureka
Evergreen
Fairhaven
Fifteen Mile
Fifteen Mile Grove
Fisherville
Forks
Fox Point
Geneseo
Gladstone
Heath
Helena
Homan
Hotona
Howard
Indian Town
Irving
Iuka
Janesville
Kars

Kinisaw
Long Point
Midland
Monticello
Moorerville
Oakwood
Ola
Orford
Otter Creek
Potter
Ramona
Redman
Salt Creek
Sana
Spring Creek
Tama City
Tamaville
Unionville
Vineyard
West Irving
West Union
Wolf Creek

Taylor County
Brushy
Buchanan
Conwa
Dan
Enod
Gravity
Grove
Guss
Harmony

Henshaw
Holt
Jenks
Ladoga
Landis
Leonard
Lexington
Litchfield
Lone Office
Memory
Mormontown
Ovid
Platt
Platteville
Rhoads
Sharps
Sharpsburgh
Siam
Summit (prior name for Lenox;
     also in Taylor County)
Windsor

Union County
Alaska
Bismark
Coelo
Edinburg
Highland
Kings
Lee
McDill
Monette
Mt. Pisgah

Myers
New Hope
Olio
Olivet
Patriot
Petersville
Philo
Pisgah
Platt
Shepard
Spaulding
Talmage
Tingley
Union City
West Union
Zalia

Van Buren County
Alexandria
Black Hawk City
Boyer
Boyers Station
Business Corner
Columbus
Des Moines City
Dogtown
Douds Leando
Douds Station
Doud's Station
Gainesorough
Harrisburg
Harrisburgh
Hedrolante

Hickory
Home
Independent
Indian Prairie
Iowa City
Iowaville
Kilbourn
Lena
Lexington
Lick Creek
Longview
McVeigh
Mechnicsburg
Meek's Mills
Mt. Zion
Napoleon
New Lexington
New Market
Niles
North Bentonsport
Oak Point
Oakland
Palestine
Pameko
Parkersville
Philadelphia
Pierceville
Pleasant Hill
Plymouth
Portland
Portoro
Rising Sun
Rochester

Salubria
Sheridan
South Bentonsport
South Keosauqua
Stumptown
Summit
Union
Union Corners
Upton
Van Buren
Van Meter
Vernon
Watertown
Willits
Wilsonville
Winchester
Wood Mills
Zanesville

Wapello County
Agency City
Alpine
Alpine City
Amador
Amsterdam
Appanoose
Ashland (also known as Ashlind Crossing)
Ayersville
Bearcreek
Bidwell
Bladensburg
Blakesburgh

Bryson
Burton
Christianburgh
Cleonville
Cliffland
Columbia
Commons
Competine
Comstock
Coopersville
Cynthiana
Dahlonega
Defiance
Dudley
Fairplay
Fountain Springs
Godfrey
Green
Greene
Happy Hollow
Keb
Kirkville Station
Louisville
Marion
Marysville
Mechanicsburg
Midlothian
Morton
Munterville
Nanisee
Opposition
Ormanville
Palestine

Phillips
Pickwick
Pleasant Lane
Point Isabelle
Point Pleasant
Port Richmond
Richmond
Sac and Fox Agency
Sailorville
Shock's Station
Sickles
Tunis
Village
Willard
Williamsburgh
Yampa

Warren County
Banner
Bellemont
Belmont Center
Clarkson
Conger
Cool
Derrough
Dorrville
Dudley
Economy
Ellendale
Felix
Ford
Ft. Plain
Friend's Grove

Green Bush
Hackney's Grove
Hammondsburgh
Handsome View
Irish Grove
Latimer
Lawrenceburgh
Liberty Centre
Lida
Loretto
Lothrop
Lynn
Medford
Medora
Montpelier
Motor
Orillia
Oswego
Planeville
Pyra
Rose Mount
Rosemount
Sandyville
Schonberg
Sharon
Sutton
Taunton
Three Rivers
Trenton
Twelve Mile Grove
Union Hill
Westford
White Oak Point

Wilmington
Wisconsin

Washington County
Amboy
Astoria
Bethel
Cedarville
Center Hill
Clay
Dairy
Davis Creek or Davis' Creek
Dayton
Daytonville
Dublin
Dutch Creek
Eureka
Grace Hill
Gracehill
Harrisburg
Haskins
Havre
Juan
Lahart
Lake
Lexington
Marcellus
McCoid
McJunkin
Middleburg
Mills
New Haven
Nira

Noble
Paris
Pilotburg
Pottsville
Seventy Six Centre
Slaughter
Titus
Valley
Verdi
Vincent
Wassonville
Wellston
White Ash
Yatton

Wayne County
Aetna
Bentonville
Bethlehem
Big Spring
Bigspring
Bridgeport
Cambria
Clinton Center
Clinton Centre
Confidence
Genoa
Grainville
Grand River
Happy Hollow
Harvard
Hodge
Kniffen

Kniffin
Lewisburg
Lewisburgh
Lucerne
Milerton
New York
Orlando
Ovid
Peoria
Samville
Saxon
Selma
South Fork
Una
Warsaw
Wayne Cross Roads

Webster County
Alisburg
Badger Creek
Badger Mound
Belleville
Border Plains
Brushy
Buchanan
Carbon
Carbon Junction
Casady
Casady's Corner or Cassaday's
    Corners
Clayworks
Craig's Hollow
Crooks

Dakota or Dekota
De Kota or Da Kota
Dekota or Dakota
Evanston
Flugstad
Frankfort
Greenside
Gypsum
Haskalia
Hesperian
Industry
Jackson Centre
Judd
Kalo Junction
Kentuck Grove
Kesho
Lackawana
Latham
Linnburg
Lundgren
Lunds
McGuire
McLaughlin Grove
Nebraska
Newark
Otho
Palmgrove
Porters
Roelyn
Shady Oak
Slabtown
Slifer
Tara

Tyson's Mills
Vesper
West Dayton

Winnebago County
Amund
Benson Grove
Benson Grove Station
Deering
Delano
Grytte
Hollandale
Lelandsburgh
Lime Creek
Mt. Valley
Nasheim
Neils
Norman
Ratna
Saylorville
Steen
Tweten
Vinje

Winneshiek County
Agency
Alba
Aquilla Grove
Big Canoe
Burr Oak Springs
Byrne
Canoe
Clifton

Conover
Counover
Cupid
Eide
Franklin Prairie
Freeport
Hyde
Isted
Jamestown
Lewiston
Locust
Locust Lane
Marysville
Moneek
Morgan
Nasset
Navan
New Alba
Nordness
Old Mission
Orlean
Plymouth Rock
Rattletrap
Sampson
Sattre
Springwater
Thoten
Trout River
Twin Spring
Twin Springs
Washington Prairie
Willimantic
Winneshiek

Woodside
Woodville

Woodbury County
Annetta
Barlow Hall
Browns Settlement
Burr Oak Grove
Crawford
Discord
Dodds
Floyd's Bluff
Friendlings Tavern
Gale
German City
Glenellen
Glenn Ellen
Grange
Grove
Hamlin
Hoskins
Idell
Lakeport
Leeds
Linndale
Listonville
Lozier
Lucky Valley
Luckyvalley
Midway
Morris
New Buffalo
Odd

Owego
Pamelia
Peiro
Penrose
Rock Branch
Rockbranch
Sergeant
Sergeant's Bluff
Slaunsville
Smithtown
Snyder's Grove
Thompsontown
Wolfdale
Woodbury

Worth County
Bristol
Cornelia
Deer Creek
Deercreek
Elk Creek
Elkcreek
Fern
Fontanelle
Glade
Glenmary
Gulbrand
Hanson
Hartland
Hirondelle
Lansrud
Lark
Lena

Leni

Manly Junction

Meltonville

Norland

Oakvale

Polo Station

Shell Rock

Silver Lake

Silverlake

Somber

Tenold

Wales

Westfield

Wright County

Aldrich

Bach Grove

Bruce

Crown Point

Drew

Dry Lake

Eagle Grove

Eagle Grove Junction

Eagleville

Empire

Fryeburg

Galtville

Grant

Lena

Liberty

Luni

Montgomery

Morhain

Moscow

Norwich

Olaf

Orsego

Otisville (also in Franklin
County)

Otsego

Palsville

Rosedale

Thrall

Waterman

Williams Point

Williamsburg

Woolstock

Sources

Dilts, Harold E. *From Ackley to Zwingle*. 2nd ed. Ames: Iowa State University Press, 1993.

Ghost Towns of Iowa. http://www.iowaghosttowns.com (accessed July 2006).

Gue, Benjamin F. *History of Iowa from the Earliest Times to the Beginning of the 20th Century*. Vol. 3. New York: Century History, 1903.

Mott, David Charles. *Abandoned Towns, Villages and Post Offices of Iowa*. Council Bluffs, Iowa: J. W. Hoffman and S. L. Purington, 1973.

Patera, Alan H. *Iowa Post Offices, 1833–1986*. Lake Oswego, Ore.: Depot, 1986.

Stennett, William H. *A History of the Origin of the Place Names Connected with the Chicago and North Western and Chicago, St. Paul, Minneapolis and Omaha Railways*. Chicago, 1908.

SOURCES

1. "Abandoned Allamakee Co. Towns." http://www.rootsweb.com/
   ~iaallama/history4/abandoned.htm (accessed April 27, 2006).
2. "About Hiawatha." http://www.hiawatha-iowa.com/about.htm
   (accessed April 26, 2006).
3. "About Us." http://www.whittemoreiowa.com/about.htm
   (accessed May 1, 2006).
4. "Adair County." http://www.iowacounties.org/About%20Us/
   AboutCoGov/County%20Pages/Adair.htm (accessed May 3,
   2006).
5. "Adams County." 2002. http://www.iowacounties.org/About%
   20Us/AboutCoGov/County%20Pages/Adams.htm (accessed
   May 3, 2006).
6. Adel Public Library. Information furnished to the author, June
   2005.
7. Administrative Services Coordinator. E-mail, October 5, 2005.
8. Alexander, W. E. *History of Chickasaw and Howard Counties Iowa.*
   Decorah, Iowa: Western, 1883.
9. Alexander, W. E. *History of Winneshiek and Allamakee Counties, Iowa.*
   Sioux City, Iowa: Western, 1882.
10. Algona Public Library. Information furnished to the author,
    summer 2005.
11. "Algona-St. Benedict." http://www.catholicglobe.org/parhist/
    NE/algonastben.htm (accessed April 29, 2006).
12. "Allamakee County." http://www.iowacounties.org/About%
    20Us/AboutCoGov/County%20Pages/Allamakee.htm (accessed
    May 3, 2006).
13. *Allamakee County, Iowa History, 1989.* Waukon, Iowa: Allamakee
    County, Iowa Heritage Book Committee, 1990.
14. Allamakee County Historical Museum. Information furnished to
    the author, summer 2005.

15. Allamakee County Historical Society. Information furnished to the author, summer 2005.

16. Allen, William G. *A History of Story County Iowa*. Des Moines, Iowa: Iowa Printing Company, 1887.

17. Alta Vista Public Library. Information furnished to the author, summer 2005.

18. Altoona Public Library. E-mail, July 13, 2005.

19. Amana Heritage Society. "The History of Amana." http://www.amanaheritage.org/history.html (accessed April 6, 2006).

20. Anamosa Public Library. E-mail, July 13, 2005.

21. Andreas, A. T. *Illustrated Historical Atlas of the State of Iowa 1875*. Des Moines: State Historical Society of Iowa, 1970.

22. Andrews, H. F., ed. *History of Audubon County Iowa*. Indianapolis: B. F. Bowen, 1915.

23. Ankeny Area Historical Society. "History of Ankeny." http://www.ankenyhistorical.org/pages/history.shtml (accessed April 5, 2006).

24. Antrobus, Augustine M. *History of Des Moines County, Iowa*. Vol. 1. Chicago: S. J. Clarke, 1915.

25. "Appanoose County." http://www.iowacounties.org/About%20Us/AboutCoGov/County%20Pages/Appanoose.htm (accessed May 3, 2006).

26. *Appanoose County, Iowa*. Appanoose County Historical Society, compiled 1984–1985.

27. Arlington City Hall. Information furnished to the author, summer 2005.

28. Armstrong Public Library. E-mail, July 18, 2005.

29. "Athelstan, Taylor County, Iowa History from Bedford Times Press, Nov. 7, 1974." http://www.rootsweb.com/~iataylor/towns/athelstan.htm (accessed April 28, 2006).

30. Atlantic Public Library. E-mail, July 8, 2005.

31. "Audubon County." http://www.iowacounties.org/About%20Us/AboutCoGov/County%20Pages/Audubon.htm (accessed May 3, 2006).

32. Auen, Norma E. *A Brief Early History of Ida County: In Honor of Iowa's Sesquicentennial.* N.p.: Ida County Sesquicentennial Committee, 1996.

33. Bailey, Edwin C. *Past and Present of Winneshiek County Iowa.* Vol. 1. Chicago: S. J. Clarke, 1913.

34. Baker, Chris D. *In Retrospect: An Illustrated History of Wapello County.* Virginia Beach, Va.: Donning, 1992.

35. Baker, William R. *Villages and Towns of Yesteryear: In Jefferson County, Iowa.* Fairfield, Iowa: Fairfield Ledger, 1982.

36. Baldwin, Clarence W. *Historical Sketches: A Collection of Articles Prepared for Presentation to Various Clubs and Organizations and Now Assembled in Book Form.* N.p.: self-published, 1982.

37. Battin, William, and F. A. Moscrip. *Past and Present of Marshall County Iowa.* Vol. 1. Indianapolis: B. F. Bowen, 1912.

38. Beltman, Daryl. E-mail, November 10, 2005.

39. "Benton County." http://www.iowacounties.org/About%20Us/AboutCoGov/County%20Pages/Benton.htm (accessed May 3, 2006).

40. "Benton County, Iowa Benton Development Group Van Horne 52346." 2004. http://www.bentoncountyiowa.com/Atkins/Belle_Plaine/Blairstown/Garrison/Shellsburg/van_horne.htm (accessed April 15, 2006).

41. Betenbender Mfg., Inc. E-mail, August 1, 2005.

42. *Biographical and Historical Record of Carroll County Iowa.* Reprint, n.p.: Carroll County Genealogy Society, 1997.

43. *Biographical and Historical Record of Clarke County, Iowa.* Chicago: Lewis, 1886.

44. *Biographical and Historical Record of Ringgold and Decatur Counties, Iowa.* Chicago: Lewis, 1887.

45. *Biographical and Historical Record of Ringgold and Union Counties.* Reprint, n.p.: Union County Genealogical Society, 1997.

46. *Biographical and Historical Record of Wayne and Appanoose Counties, Iowa.* Chicago: Interstate, 1886.

47. Birdsall, B. P., ed. *History of Wright County Iowa.* Indianapolis: B. F. Bowen, 1915.

48. "Black Hawk County." http://www.iowacounties.org/About%20Us/AboutCoGov/County%20Pages/BlackHawk.htm (accessed May 3, 2006).

49. Bondurant City Hall. Information furnished to the author, April 26, 2006.

50. "Boone County." http://www.iowacounties.org/About%20Us/AboutCoGov/County%20Pages/Boone.htm (accessed May 3, 2006).

51. Boone County Recorder. E-mail, June 1, 2005.

52. *Bouton Centennial.* N.p., [1981?].

53. "Bradgate History." http://www.bradgateiowa.com/8401.html (accessed April 12, 2006).

54. Bremer County. http://www.iowacounties.org/About%20Us/AboutCoGov/County%20Pages/Bremer.htm (accessed May 3, 2006).

55. "A Brief History of Beaman." http://www.beaman.lib.ia.us/History.html (accessed July 16, 2005).

56. Brooklyn Library. E-mail, July 13, 2005.

57. Brown, Dana. "Jefferson County Town Celebrates History, Ottumwa Courier, November 29, 1999, pages 1, 2." http://www.rootsweb.com/~iajeffer/Towns/Pleasant_Plain.html (accessed April 25, 2006).

58. Brueckel, H. W. *History of Jerico and Jacksonville Township.* Waucoma, Iowa: Sentinel-Echo, [1952?].

59. "Buchanan County." http://www.iowacounties.org/About%20Us/AboutCoGov/County%20Pages/Buchanan.htm (accessed May 3, 2006).

60. *Buchanan County, Iowa*. Independence, Iowa: Buchanan County Genealogical Society, 1986.

61. *Buchanan County, Iowa*. Independence, Iowa: Buchanan County Genealogical Society, 1991.

62. "Buck Grove." Crawford County.rootsweb.com (accessed July 17, 2005).

63. "Buena Vista County." http://www.iowacounties.org/About%20Us/AboutCoGov/County%20Pages/BuenaVista.htm (accessed May 3, 2006).

64. Buena Vista County Historical Society. E-mail, July 21, 2005.

65. Burlington Public Library. E-mail, July 11, 2005.

66. Burlington Public Library. E-mail, July 29, 2005.

67. Butcher, Sally, Palmer Public Library. E-mail, July 18, 2005.

68. "Butler County." http://www.iowacounties.org/About%20Us/AboutCoGov/County%20Pages/Butler.htm (accessed May 3, 2006).

69. Butler County Genealogical Society. Information furnished to the author, summer 2005.

70. Butler County Recorder's Office. Information furnished to the author, summer 2005.

71. Caldwell, J. R., ed. *History of Tama County, Iowa*. Vol. 1. Chicago: Lewis, 1910.

72. "Calhoun County." http://www.iowacounties.org/About%20Us/AboutCoGov/County%20Pages/Calhoun.htm (accessed May 3, 2006).

73. "Carroll County." http://www.iowacounties.org/About%20Us/AboutCoGov/County%20Pages/Carroll.htm (accessed May 3, 2006).

74. Carroll County Historical Museum. E-mail, July 20, 2005.

75. "Cass County." http://www.iowacounties.org/About%20Us/AboutCoGov/County%20Pages/Cass.htm (accessed May 3, 2006).

76. "Cedar County." http://www.iowacounties.org/About%20Us/ AboutCoGov/County%20Pages/Cedar.htm (accessed May 3, 2006).

77. *Cedar County Historical Review*. Tipton, Iowa: Cedar County Historical Society, 1981.

78. Cedar Rapids Public Library. E-mail, July 18, 2005.

79. *Celebrating Our 100th Year, Murray, Iowa: 1868–1968*. N.p., 1968.

80. *The Centennial 1851–1951: Harmony Evangelical and Reformed Church, Zwingle, Iowa*. Zwingle, Iowa, [1951?].

81. *The Centennial History of Bedford, Iowa 1953*. Bedford, Iowa, [1953?].

82. *A Century of Memories, Ellston, Iowa, 1881–1981*. Mt. Ayr, Iowa: Mt. Ayr Record-News, [1981?].

83. "Cerro Gordo County." http://www.iowacounties.org/About% 20Us/AboutCoGov/County%20Pages/CerroGordo.htm (accessed May 3, 2006).

84. Cerro Gordo County Recorder. Information furnished to the author, summer 2005.

85. Chapell, Harry Church, and Katharyn Joella Chapell. *History of Buchanan County Iowa and Its People*. Vol. 1. Chicago: S. J. Clarke, 1914.

86. "Cherokee County." http://www.iowacounties.org/About% 20Us/AboutCoGov/County%20Pages/Cherokee.htm (accessed May 3, 2006).

87. Cherokee Public Library. E-mail, July 14, 2005.

88. "Chickasaw County." http://www.iowacounties.org/About%20Us/AboutCoGov/ County%20Pages/Chickasaw.htm (accessed May 3, 2006).

89. Chickasaw County Recorder. Information furnished to the author, summer 2005.

90. City Clerk, Alleman. Information furnished to the author, summer 2005.

91. City Clerk, Ames. E-mail, June 24, 2005.

92. City Clerk, Andover. Information furnished to the author, summer 2005.

93. City Clerk, Blanchard. Information furnished to the author, summer 2005.

94. City Clerk, Charlotte. Information furnished to the author, summer 2005.

95. City Clerk, Clermont. E-mail, June 20, 2005.

96. City Clerk, Donnellson. E-mail, June 20, 2005.

97. City Clerk, Elk Run Heights. Information furnished to the author, summer 2005.

98. City Clerk, Elliott. Information furnished to the author, summer 2005.

99. City Clerk, Everly. Information furnished to the author, summer 2005.

100. City Clerk, Hills. Information furnished to the author, summer 2005.

101. City Clerk, Humboldt. E-mail, October 7, 2005.

102. City Clerk, Inwood. E-mail, November 1, 2005.

103. City Clerk, Keystone. Information furnished to the author, July 2005.

104. City Clerk, Lamont. Information furnished to the author, summer 2005.

105. City Clerk, Minburn. E-mail, June 21, 2005.

106. City Clerk, Mitchellville. E-mail, June 20, 2005.

107. City Clerk, Oyens. Information furnished to the author, January 2006.

108. City Clerk, Persia. Information furnished to the author, summer 2005.

109. City Clerk, Pleasant Hill. E-mail, September 15, 2005.

110. City Clerk, Reasnor. E-mail, November 1, 2005.

111. City Clerk, Rolfe. E-mail, October 7, 2005.

112. City Clerk, Sharpsburg. E-mail, November 9, 2005.

113. City Clerk, Springville. E-mail, October 13, 2005.

114. City Clerk, Stanwood. Information furnished to the author, summer 2005.
115. City Clerk, Sully. Information furnished to the author, summer 2005.
116. City Clerk, University Heights. E-mail, June 20, 2005.
117. City Clerk, University Park. Information furnished to the author, summer 2005.
118. City Clerk, Urbandale. Information furnished to the author, summer 2005.
119. City Clerk, Van Wert. Information furnished to the author, summer 2005.
120. City Clerk, Wahpeton. Information furnished to the author, summer 2005.
121. City Clerk, Walnut. E-mail, June 20, 2005.
122. City Clerk, Webster. Information furnished to the author, summer 2005.
123. City Clerk, Wyoming. E-mail, June 21, 2005.
124. City Hall, Oskaloosa. Information furnished to the author, summer 2005.
125. "City of Alburnett Home Page." http://www.alburnett.com/ (accessed April 6, 2006).
126. City of Clive, library staff. E-mail, July 13, 2005.
127. City of Cumberland. E-mail, June 14, 2005.
128. City of Essex. Information furnished to the author, summer 2005.
129. City of Ft. Dodge. E-mail, June 20, 2005.
130. City of Livermore. Information furnished to the author, summer 2005.
131. City of Marquette. Information furnished to the author, summer 2005.
132. Clarion Library. E-mail, July 19, 2005.

133. "Clarke County." http://www.iowacounties.org/About%20Us/
AboutCoGov/County%20Pages/Clarke.htm (accessed May 3,
2006).

134. "Clay County." http://www.iowacounties.org/About%20Us/
AboutCoGov/County%20Pages/Clay.htm (accessed May 3,
2006).

135. Clay County Recorder. E-mail, June 7, 2005.

136. "Clayton County." http://www.iowacounties.org/About%20Us/
AboutCoGov/County%20Pages/Clayton.htm (accessed May 3,
2006).

137. "Clinton County." http://www.iowacounties.org/About%20Us/
AboutCoGov/County%20Pages/Clinton.htm (accessed May 3,
2006).

138. Clyde, Jefferson F., and H. A. Dwelle, eds. *History of Mitchell and
Worth Counties, Iowa*. Vol. 1. Chicago: S. J. Clarke, 1918.

139. Coggon Library. E-mail, July 15, 2005.

140. Colo Library. Information furnished to the author, July 2005.

141. Conrad Public Library. E-mail, July 20, 2005.

142. Corbit, R. M., ed. *History of Jones County, Iowa, Past and Present*.
Vol. 1. Chicago: S. J. Clarke, 1910.

143. Council Bluffs Public Library. E-mail, July 14, 2005.

144. "Crawford County." http://www.iowacounties.org/About%
20Us/AboutCoGov/County%20Pages/Crawford.htm (accessed
May 3, 2006).

145. Crawford County Recorder. Information furnished to the
author, summer 2005.

146. Crystal Lake Library. Information furnished to the author,
summer 2005.

147. Cunningham, John R. "1903 Roseville 2003." Floyd County
Historical Society. *Floyd County Heritage* 32, no. 2 (April 2003).

148. "Dallas County." http://www.iowacounties.org/About%20Us/
AboutCoGov/County%20Pages/Dallas.htm (accessed May 3,
2006).

149. Davenport Library. Information furnished to the author, summer 2005.

150. "Davis County." http://www.iowacounties.org/About%20Us/AboutCoGov/County%20Pages/Davis.htm (accessed May 3, 2006).

151. Davis County Recorder. Information furnished to the author, summer 2005.

152. De Groote—Johnson, Karen. "Welcome to Webster County History and Facts Page." http://www.rootsweb.com/%7Eiawebste/history.htm (accessed April 6, 2006).

153. "Decatur City." http://www.rootsweb.com/~iadecatu/earlydecDocs/edDecaturCity.htm (accessed April 25, 2006).

154. "Decatur County." http://www.iowacounties.org/About%20Us/AboutCoGov/County%20Pages/Decatur.htm (accessed May 3, 2006).

155. Decorah Public Library. E-mail, October 28, 2005.

156. "Delaware County." http://www.iowacounties.org/About%20Us/AboutCoGov/County%20Pages/Delaware.htm (accessed May 3, 2006).

157. Delores Tillinghast Memorial Library. E-mail, July 11, 2005.

158. *Delphos (Iowa)*. Delphos Centennial Book Committee. Delphos Centennial, 1880–1980. N.p., 1980.

159. Denver Public Library. Information furnished to the author, summer 2005.

160. "Des Moines County." http://www.iowacounties.org/About%20Us/AboutCoGov/County%20Pages/DesMoines.htm (accessed May 3, 2006).

161. "Dickinson County." http://www.iowacounties.org/About%20Us/AboutCoGov/County%20Pages/Dickinson.htm (accessed May 3, 2006).

162. "Did You Know." *Franklin County Historical Society Newsletter* 20, no. 3, August 2004.

163. Dilts, Harold E. *From Ackley to Zwingle: The Origins of Iowa Place Names*. 2nd ed. Ames: Iowa State University Press, 1993.

164. Dimwiddie, James C. *History of Iowa County Iowa*. Chicago: S. J. Clarke, 1915.

165. Dixon, J. M., ed. *Centennial History of Polk County, Iowa*. Des Moines, Iowa: State Register, 1876.

166. *Don Berry Trail Scenic and Historic Driving Tour of Warren County*. N.p.: Warren County Conservation Board, n.d.

167. *Donnan at the Crossroads*. Donnan, Iowa: Centennial Committee, 1978.

168. Donnellson Public Library. E-mail, July 18, 2005.

169. Downer, Harry E. *History of Davenport and Scott County, Iowa*. Vol. 1. Chicago: S. J. Clarke, 1910.

170. Drake Library. E-mail, July 11, 2005.

171. Dubuque Carnegie-Stout Public Library. E-mail, July 19, 2005.

172. "Dubuque County." http://www.iowacounties.org/About%20Us/AboutCoGov/County%20Pages/Dubuque.htm (accessed May 3, 2006).

173. "Early History of Aspinwall from 1882." http://www.rootsweb.com/~iacrawfo/aspinwallhist.html (accessed April 25, 2006).

174. "Early History of Van Wert." http://www.rootsweb.com/~iadecatu/earlydecDocs/edVanWert.html (accessed April 25, 2006).

175. "Early Sabula Settlement." http://www.east-central.k12.ia.us/sabula/ms/sabulatown/PioneersandSettlers.html (accessed April 28, 2006).

176. "Edgewood." http://www.rootsweb.com/~iaclayto/1882/chapter_XXXII.htm (accessed April 27, 2006).

177. Eldon Library. Information furnished to the author, summer 2005.

178. Eldridge, Mary Beth. "Abandoned Towns, Post Offices or Settlements of Black Hawk County, Iowa." 1998. http://

www.iagenweb.org//state/places/blackhaw.htm (accessed April 30, 2006).

179. "Elk Run Heights." *Red Cedar Journal*, April 2004.

180. Elkader Public Library. Information furnished to the author, summer 2005.

181. Ellston City Hall. Information furnished to the author, summer 2005.

182. "Ellsworth, Iowa—Founded in 1880." http://showcase.netins .net/web/marjned/ells.html (accessed April 27, 2006).

183. "Emmet County." http://www.iowacounties.org/About% 20Us/AboutCoGov/County%20Pages/Emmet.htm (accessed May 3, 2006).

184. *Emmett County Iowa "United by Spirit" American Revolution Bicentennial 1776 to 1976*. N.p., [1976?].

185. Ericson Public Library. E-mail, July 21, 2005.

186. Essex Public Library. Information furnished to the author, summer 2005.

187. "Estherville" http://www.rootsweb.com/~iaemmet/ twnp.htm#ESTHERVILLE (accessed April 27, 2006).

188. "Fayette County." http://www.iowacounties.org/About%20Us/ AboutCoGov/County%20Pages/Fayette.htm (accessed May 3, 2006).

189. Fayette County Historical Society and Fayette County Genealogical Society. *Heritage of Fayette County Iowa 1996*. West Union, Iowa, 1996.

190. Fayette County Recorder's Office. Information furnished to the author, summer 2005.

191. Field, Homer H., and Joseph R. Reed. *History of Pottawattamie County, Iowa, to 1907*. Vol. 1. Chicago: S. J. Clarke, 1907.

192. Flickinger, Robert E. *The Pioneer History of Pocahontas County, Iowa*. Fonda, Iowa: Times, 1904.

193. "Floyd County." http://www.iowacounties.org/About%20Us/ AboutCoGov/County%20Pages/Floyd.htm (accessed May 3, 2006).

194. Fonda City Hall. Information furnished to the author, summer 2005.

195. "The Forming of Carter Lake." http://www.cityofcarterlake .com/history_forming.html (accessed April 28, 2006).

196. Ft. Dodge Public Library. E-mail, July 14, 2005.

197. Foster, J. E. *Franklin County History, 1852–1970.* Hampton, Iowa: Franklin County Historical Society, 1970.

198. "Franklin County." http://www.iowacounties.org/About% 20Us/AboutCoGov/County%20Pages/Franklin.htm (accessed May 3, 2006).

199. "Fremont County." http://www.iowacounties.org/About% 20Us/AboutCoGov/County%20Pages/Fremont.htm (accessed May 3, 2006).

200. Fremont County Recorder's Office. Information furnished to the author, summer 2005.

201. "Frenchtown—er, Gilbertville Celebrates Rich Irish Heritage." *Red Cedar Journal,* April 2004.

202. "From a Chicken Coop City Hall to Modern Suburb." http://evansdale.govoffice.com/index.asp?Type=B_BASIC&SEC ={E0BB08C2-ADCF-40A7-9A2B-3F90879D365F} (accessed April 27, 2006).

203. Fruitland City Hall. Information furnished to the author, summer 2005.

204. Fulton, Charles. *History of Jefferson County Iowa.* Vol. 1. Chicago: S. J. Clarke. 1914.

205. George, Allaire. Information furnished to the author, summer 2005.

206. "Gilbertville's Name." *Red Cedar Journal,* June 2004.

207. Glenwood Library. E-mail, July 19, 2005.

208. *Golden Jubilee: The Brunsville Story in Prose, Poetry, Picture, 1911–1961.* N.p., 1961.

209. *Golden Jubilee of Our Lady of Lourdes Parish, Howard County, Iowa, Silver Jubilee of Our Lady of Lourdes Church.* N.p., 1926.

210. Goldthwait, N. E. *History of Boone County Iowa.* Vol. 1. Chicago: Pioneer, 1914.

211. Grand Junction Public Library. E-mail, July 18, 2005.

212. Granger City Hall. Information furnished to the author, summer 2005.

213. "Grant Township Westward Ho." http://iagenweb.org/montgomery/histories/cavalcade/cavalcadepg30.htm (accessed April 13, 2006).

214. "Green Castle Township List of Towns, Post Offices, Landmarks, etc." 2002. http://www.rootsweb.com/~iamarsha/twpntowninfo/Greencastletwp/Greencastletowninfo.htm (accessed April 25 and 27, 2006).

215. "Greene County." http://www.iowacounties.org/About%20Us/AboutCoGov/County%20Pages/Greene.htm (accessed May 3, 2006).

216. Greene County Auditor's Office. E-mail, July 19, 2005.

217. Greenfield, Maria, Douds Lanman, and Clay Lanman. *History of Douds-Selma.* Keosaqua, Iowa: Keosaqua Van Buren County Register, 1968.

218. "Greetings from Linn Grove." http://www.linngroveiowa.org/index.html April 3, 2006 (accessed April 12, 2006).

219. "Grundy County." http://www.iowacounties.org/About%20Us/AboutCoGov/County%20Pages/Grundy.htm (accessed May 3, 2006).

220. *Grundy County Remembers: People, Places, Things.* Bristow, Iowa: PenDragon Press, 1977.

221. Gue, Benjamin. *History of Iowa from the Earliest Times to the Beginning of the 20th Century.* Vol. 3. New York: Century History, 1903.

222. "Guthrie County." http://www.iowacounties.org/About%
20Us/AboutCoGov/County%20Pages/Guthrie.htm (accessed
May 3, 2006).

223. "Guthrie County History." http://panora.org/museum/
history.html (accessed April 27, 2006).

224. Guttenberg Library. E-mail, July 14, 2005.

225. Hagen, Jo Anne. "Gilbert, Iowa, 1879–1979 Historical
Perspectives." http://www.gilbertgazette.com/about_
gilbert/history1879–1979.htm (accessed April 27, 2006).

226. Hamburg Library. Information furnished to the author,
summer 2005.

227. "Hamilton County." http://www.iowacounties.org/About%
20Us/AboutCoGov/County%20Pages/Hamilton.htm (accessed
May 3, 2006).

228. Hamilton County Historical Society. *The History of Hamilton
County, Iowa*. Webster City, Iowa: Radio Station KQWC and
Hamilton County Historical Society, 1985.

229. *The Hampton Story, 1870–1970*. N.p., 1970.

230. Hancock, Ellery M. *Past and Present of Allamakee County, Iowa*.
Vol. 1. Evansville, Ind.: Unigraphics, 1975.

231. "Hancock County." http://www.iowacounties.org/About%
20Us/AboutCoGov/County%20Pages/Hancock.htm (accessed
May 3, 2006).

232. "Hardin County." http://www.iowacounties.org/About%20Us/
AboutCoGov/County%20Pages/Hardin.htm (accessed May 3,
2006).

233. Harlan Library. Information furnished to the author, summer
2005.

234. "Harrison County." http://www.iowacounties.org/About%
20Us/AboutCoGov/County%20Pages/Harrison.htm (accessed
May 3, 2006).

235. Hart, William H. *History of Sac County, Iowa*. Indianapolis: H. F.
Bowen, 1914.

236. Hartman, John C., ed. *History of Black Hawk County and Its People*. Chicago: S. J. Clarke, 1915.

237. Hastie, Eugene V. *Hastie's History of Dallas County, Iowa*. Des Moines, Iowa: Wallace-Homestead, 1938.

238. *Haverhill Iowa Centennial 1882–1982*. N.p., 1982.

239. Hazelton Mayor's Office. Information furnished to the author, summer 2005.

240. "Henry County." http://www.iowacounties.org/About% 20Us/AboutCoGov/County%20Pages/Henry.htm (accessed May 3, 2006).

241. Henry County Historical Preservation Society. Information furnished to the author, summer 2005.

242. *Heritage of Hancock County, Iowa*. N.p.: Hancock County Genealogical Society, Curtis Media, 1993.

243. Heusinkveld, Harriet. *Coal Mining Days in Marion County*. Pella, Iowa: H. Heusinkveld, 1995.

244. Hickenlooper, Frank. *An Illustrated History of Monroe County, Iowa*. Albia, Iowa, 1896.

245. *Highlights of Henry County, Iowa, History, 1833–1976*. Burlington, Iowa: Doran and Ward Lithographing, 1977.

246. Hill, Luther B., ed. *History of Benton County Iowa*. Vol. 1. Chicago: Lewis, 1910.

247. "History." http://www.westfieldiowa.com/history.htm (accessed April 19, 2006).

248. "History. 2001." http://www.cityoflowden.org/history.html (accessed April 28, 2006).

249. *History of Adair County, Iowa*. N.p.: Adair County Historical Society, 1976.

250. *History of Adams County Iowa*. Corning, Iowa: Corning Departmental Club and Civic Dept., 1984.

251. "History of Appanoose County (1878)—Iconium—Chariton. Twp." http://iagenweb.org/boards/appanoose/documents/ index.cgi?read=27378 (accessed April 28, 2006).

252. *History of Bremer and Butler Counties, Iowa*. Springfield, Ill.: Union, 1883.

253. *History of Bremer County*. N.p.: Bremer County History Book Committee, 1985.

254. *History of Butler County, Iowa*. Bowie, Md.: Union, Heritage Books, 1999.

255. "History of Calhoun County Courthouse." http://www .calhouncountyiowa.com/history.htm (accessed April 28, 2006).

256. "The History of Carson, Iowa." http://www.carsonia.com/ history.htm 2003 (accessed April 12, 2006).

257. *History of Cass County, Iowa, History of Iowa*. Springfield, Ill.: Continental Historical Company, 1884.

258. *History of Cedar County, Iowa*. Chicago: Western Historical Company, 1878.

259. *History of Chester, Iowa 1858–1958 Centennial Celebration*. N.p., 1958.

260. *The History of Clay County, Iowa*. Dallas: Curtis Media, 1984.

261. *History of Clayton County, Iowa*. Chicago: Inter-State, 1882.

262. *History of Clinton County, Iowa, 1976: A Bicentennial 1976 Project*. N.p.: Clinton County Historical Society, 1978.

263. *The History of Dallas County, Iowa*. Des Moines, Iowa: Union Historical Company, 1879.

264. *History of Davis County*. Des Moines: Iowa Historical Company, 1882.

265. "The History of Donnellson." http://www.donnellsoniowa .com/About/History.html (accessed April 25, 2006).

266. *The History of Dubuque County, Iowa*. Chicago: Western Historical Company. 1880.

267. "History of Dyersville." 2003. http://www.dyersville.org/ pages/cominfo/cominfohis.html (accessed May 2, 2006).

268. *History of Emmet County and Dickinson County Iowa*. Chicago: Pioneer, 1917.

269. *History of Fayette County, Iowa*. Chicago: Western Historical Company, 1878.

270. *History of Franklin and Cerro Gordo Counties, Iowa*. Springfield, Ill.: Union, 1883.

271. *History of Guthrie and Adair Counties, Iowa*. Springfield, Ill.: Continental Historical Company, 1884.

272. *History of Hardin County, Iowa*. Springfield, Ill.: Union, 1883.

273. *The History of Henry County, Iowa*. Chicago: Western Historical Company, 1879.

274. *The History of Henry County, Iowa*. Henry County Bicentennial Commission. Dallas: National ShareGraphics, 1982.

275. *The History of Humboldt County with a History of Iowa Illustrated*. Chicago: Historical Publishing, 1901.

276. *History of Jackson County, Iowa 1900–1989*. Hampton, Iowa: Jackson County Historical and Genealogical Societies, 1989.

277. *The History of Jefferson County, Iowa*. Chicago: Western Historical Company, 1879.

278. *History of Johnson County*. Iowa City, Iowa, 1883.

279. *The History of Keokuk County, Iowa, 2001*. N.p.: Keo-Mah Genealogical Society, [2001?].

280. *History of Kossuth and Humboldt Counties, Iowa*. Springfield, Ill.: Union, 1884.

281. *The History of Lee County, Iowa*. Chicago: Iowa Western Historical Society, 1879.

282. *The History of Linn County, Iowa*. Chicago: Western Historical Company, 1878.

283. *History of Lucas County, Iowa*. Lucas County Genealogical Society. Marceline, Mo.: Walsworth, 1978.

284. "A History of Manilla's Beginning Railroad History." 2004. http://manillaia.com/history1.htm (accessed April 28, 2006).

285. *History of Marshall County, Iowa*. Chicago: Western Historical Company, 1878.

286. *History of Mitchell County, Iowa*. Dallas: Curtis Media, 1989.

287. *History of Monona County, Iowa*. Reprint, Evansville, Ind.: Unigraphics, 1974.

288. *The History of Muscatine County, Iowa*. Chicago: Western Historical Company, 1879.

289. *The History of Polk County, Iowa*. Des Moines, Iowa: Union Historical Company, 1880.

290. *The History of Poweshiek County, Iowa*. Des Moines, Iowa: Union Historical Company, 1880.

291. *History of Scott County, Iowa*. Chicago: Inter-state, 1882.

292. *The History of Tama County, Iowa 1987*. Dallas: Curtis Media, 1987.

293. *History of Taylor County, Iowa*. Des Moines, Iowa: State Historical Company, 1881.

294. *History of the Counties of Woodbury and Plymouth, Iowa*. Chicago: A. Warner, 1890–1891.

295. *History of the Farrar United Methodist Church 1889–1989*. Farrar, Iowa, 1989.

296. *History of Twin Springs (Festina)*. [Festina, Iowa?]: Sigre, 1979.

297. *The History of Van Buren County, Iowa*. Van Buren County American Revolution Bicentennial Commission. Marceline, Mo.: Walsworth, 1976.

298. *History of Wapello County, Iowa*. Chicago: Western Historical Society, 1878.

299. *History of Washington County, Iowa*. Des Moines, Iowa: Union Historical Company, 1880.

300. "History of West Burlington." http://www.westburlington.org/ (accessed April 30, 2006).

301. "History of West Des Moines." http://www.wdm-ia.com/asp/ administrative/history.asp?deptid=13 (accessed May 1, 2006).

302. *History of Western Iowa, Its Settlement and Growth*. Sioux City, Iowa: Western, 1882.

303. *History of Winnebago County and Hancock County, Iowa*. Chicago: Pioneer, 1917.

304. *The History of Woodbury County, Iowa*. Dallas: National ShareGraphics, 1984.

305. Houlette, Leota. "New Virginia about Our Town." http://www.newvirginia.com/about.html (accessed April 29, 2006).

306. "How It Got Its Name." http://www.rootsweb.com/%7Eiawebste/names.htm (accessed April 28, 2006).

307. "How the Towns in Wayne County Got Their Names." http://freepages.history.rootsweb.com/%7Erkross/wayne_town_names.html (accessed April 26, 2006).

308. "Howard County." http://www.iowacounties.org/About%20Us/AboutCoGov/County%20Pages/Howard.htm (accessed May 3, 2006).

309. Howard County Economic Development Commission. E-mail, June 20, 2005.

310. Howard County Genealogical Society. Information furnished to the author, summer 2005.

311. "Humboldt County." http://www.iowacounties.org/About%20Us/AboutCoGov/County%20Pages/Humboldt.htm (accessed May 3, 2006).

312. Hunt, Charles W. *History of Harrison County, Iowa*. Indianapolis: B. F. Bowen, 1915.

313. Hutchison, Mike. Information furnished to the author, August 2005.

314. "Ida County." http://www.iowacounties.org/About%20Us/AboutCoGov/County%20Pages/Ida.htm (accessed May 3, 2006).

315. Indianola Public Library. Information furnished to the author, summer 2005.

316. *Inwood's First 100 Years, 1884–1984*. Dallas: National ShareGraphics, 1984.

317. Ionia Community Library. E-mail, July 26, 2005.

318. *Iowa: A Guide to the Hawkeye State*. Federal Writers Project of the Works Progress Administration for the State of Iowa and the State Historical Society of Iowa. New York: Viking Press, 1938.

319. "Iowa County." http://www.iowacounties.org/About%20Us/ AboutCoGov/County%20Pages/Iowa.htm (accessed May 3, 2006).

320. Iowa Department of Transportation. Information furnished to the author, July 2005.

321. "Iowa Ghost Towns Bremer County." http://www .iowaghosttowns.com/bremercounty.html (accessed April 18, 2006).

322. "Jackson County." http://www.iowacounties.org/ About%20Us/AboutCoGov/County%20Pages/Jackson.htm (accessed May 3, 2006).

323. Jackson County Historical Society. E-mail, July 19, 2005.

324. Janesville Library. E-mail, July 19, 2005.

325. "Jasper County." http://www.iowacounties.org/About% 20Us/AboutCoGov/County%20Pages/Jasper.htm (accessed May 3, 2006).

326. "Jefferson County." http://www.iowacounties.org/About% 20Us/AboutCoGov/County%20Pages/Jefferson.htm (accessed May 3, 2006).

327. Jefferson County Recorder's Office. Information furnished to the author, summer 2005.

328. "Jefferson Township List of Towns, Post Offices, Landmarks, etc." 2002. http://www.rootsweb.com/~iamarsha/ twpntowninfo/Jeffersontwp/Jeffersontowninfo.htm (accessed April 26, 2006).

329. "Johnson County." http://www.iowacounties.org/About% 20Us/AboutCoGov/County%20Pages/Johnson.htm (accessed May 3, 2006).

330. Johnson County Historical Society. E-mail, July 7, 2005.

331. *Johnson County History*. N.p.: Iowa Writers Program of the Works Projects Administration, 1941.

332. "Johnson County Iowa Place Names." 2004. http://www
.rootsweb.com/~iajohnso/place_names.htm (accessed April 29,
2006).

333. Johnston Historical Society. Information furnished to the
author, summer 2005.

334. "Jones County." http://www.iowacounties.org/About%20Us/
AboutCoGov/County%20Pages/Jones.htm (accessed May 3,
2006).

335. Kaufmann, Jeff, Cedar County Historical Society. Information
furnished to the author, summer 2005.

336. Keith, T. L. "Van Buren County Iowa." American Guide Series.
Farmington, Iowa: Writers Program, Iowa, 1940.

337. *Kellogg Historical Booklet*. Kellogg Camp Fire Association. N.p.,
1974.

338. "Keokuk County." http://www.iowacounties.org/About%
20Us/AboutCoGov/County%20Pages/Keokuk.htm (accessed
May 3, 2006).

339. Keo-Mah Genealogical Society and the Mahaska Historical
Society. *History of Mahaska County, Iowa 1984*. Dallas: Curtis
Media, 1984.

340. Kershaw, W. L. *History of Page County, Iowa*. Vol. 1. Chicago: S. J.
Clarke, 1909.

341. *Keswick, 1879–1979*. N.p., 1979.

342. *Kimballton, Iowa, 1883–1983*. Kimballton, Iowa, 1983.

343. "Kossuth County." http://www.iowacounties.org/About%
20Us/AboutCoGov/County%20Pages/Kossuth.htm (accessed
May 3, 2006).

344. Krapfl, Julia. "Town Descriptions, Old Towns of Dubuque
County." http://www.rootsweb.com/~iadubuqu/towns/
towndesc.html (accessed April 7, 2006).

345. Krotz, Robert. "A Town Named Paris (Bunch)." *Des Moines
Register*, September 14, 1969.

346. Kruse, Arlys Lindaman. *Little Rock, Iowa, 1869–1984, Those By-gone Years*. Little Rock, Iowa: [Little Rock Centennial Committee?], 1984.

347. La Porte City Hall. Information furnished to the author, summer 2005.

348. Lamb, Hiram. "Hopeville History." http://www.rootsweb .com/~iaclarke/hishopelamb.html (accessed April 28, 2006).

349. Lambs Grove City Hall. Information furnished to the author, summer 2005.

350. Lary, Veronica. "Massena Township." http://www.rootsweb .com/~iacass/history/twps-CCGS-pubs.htm#Benton (accessed April 27, 2006).

351. Laurel City Hall. Information furnished to the author, summer 2005.

352. Lease, Lester. *History of Wesley: One Hundred Years, Wesley, Iowa, as It Was and as It Is Now*. N.p., 1972.

353. LeCompte Memorial Library. E-mail, October 20, 2005.

354. "Lee County." http://www.iowacounties.org/About%20Us/ AboutCoGov/County%20Pages/Lee.htm (accessed May 3, 2006).

355. Lesan, B. M. *Early History of Ringgold County, 1844–1937*. Mt. Ayr, Iowa, 1937.

356. Lester City Hall. Information furnished to the author, summer 2005.

357. "Liberty Township List of Towns, Post Offices, Landmarks, etc." 2002. http://www.rootsweb.com/~iamarsha/twpntowninfo/ Libertytwp/Libertytowninfo.htm (accessed April 28, 2006).

358. Libertyville City Hall. Information furnished to the author, summer 2005.

359. Lied Public Library. Information furnished to the author, summer 2005.

360. "Linby." 2001. http://www.rootsweb.com/~iajeffer/Towns/ Linby.html (accessed April 26, 2006).

361. Lingenfelter, L. *History of Fremont County Iowa*. St. Joseph, Mo.: Steam Printing, 1877.

362. "Linn County." http://www.iowacounties.org/About%20Us/ AboutCoGov/County%20Pages/Linn.htm (accessed May 3, 2006).

363. Linn County Auditor's Office. Information furnished to the author, summer 2005.

364. Linn Grove Library. E-mail, October 19, 2005.

365. "A Little Bit of History." 1999. http://www.netins.net/ricweb/ community/urbana/urbana.htm (accessed April 18, 2006).

366. "Logan Township List of Towns, Post Offices, Landmarks, etc." 2002. http://www.rootsweb.com/~iamarsha/twpntowninfo/ Logantwp/Logantowninfo.htm (accessed April 28, 2006).

367. "Louisa County." http://www.iowacounties.org/About%20Us/ AboutCoGov/County%20Pages/Louisa.htm (accessed May 3, 2006).

368. Louisa County Historical Society. E-mail, June 23, 2005.

369. Lucas, Alfred E. *Kent Next Four Exits 1840's to 1983*. Creston, Iowa: Union County Genealogical Society, 1999.

370. "Lucas County." http://www.iowacounties.org/About%20Us/ AboutCoGov/County%20Pages/Lucas.htm (accessed May 3, 2006).

371. Lund, Dave. Information furnished to the author, spring 2005.

372. "Lyon County." http://www.iowacounties.org/About%20Us/ AboutCoGov/County%20Pages/Lyon.htm (accessed May 3, 2006).

373. Maclean, Paul. *History of Carroll County Iowa*. Vol. 1. Chicago: S. J. Clarke, 1912.

374. "Madison County." http://www.iowacounties.org/About% 20Us/AboutCoGov/County%20Pages/Madison.htm (accessed May 3, 2006).

375. *Madison County, Iowa*. Winterset, Iowa: Madison County Genealogical Society, 1984.

376. Madison County Historical Society. E-mail, July 21, 2005.

377. "Maharishi Vedic City, Iowa." http://www.maharishivediccity .com/ (accessed April 28, 2006).

378. "Mahaska County." http://www.iowacounties.org/About% 20Us/AboutCoGov/County%20Pages/Mahaska.htm (accessed May 3, 2006).

379. *Maloy, Iowa Centennial History*. Committee for Maloy Centennial Books. Mt. Ayr, Iowa, [1987?].

380. Manchester Library. Information furnished to the author, summer 2005.

381. "Maple Hill. 1998–2006." http://www.rootsweb.com/~ iaemmet/twnp.htm#Maple%20Hill (accessed April 28, 2006).

382. Marengo Public Library. E-mail, July 21, 2005.

383. "Marion County." http://www.iowacounties.org/About% 20Us/AboutCoGov/County%20Pages/Marion.htm (accessed May 3, 2006).

384. Marion County Genealogical Society. E-mail, July 25, 2005.

385. Marion County Historical Society. Information furnished to the author, summer 2005.

386. "Marion Township List of Towns, Post Offices, Landmarks, etc." 2002. http://www.rootsweb.com/~iamarsha/ twpntowninfo/Mariontwp/Mariontowninfo.htm (accessed April 11, 2006).

387. "Marshall County." http://www.iowacounties.org/About% 20Us/AboutCoGov/County%20Pages/Marshall.htm (accessed May 3, 2006).

388. Mason City Public Library. E-mail, July 13, 2005.

389. Mauer, William. "The Early Years." http://www.readlyn.com/ history2.htm (accessed April 28, 2006).

390. Maurer, JoAnne. Information furnished to the author, spring 2005.

391. Mayor of Coppock. Information furnished to the author, July 2005.

392. Mayor of Gladbrook. E-mail, June 21, 2005.

393. Mayor of Hazelton. Information furnished to the author, summer 2005.

394. Mayor of Le Roy. Information furnished to the author, summer 2005.

395. Mayor of Luxemburg. E-mail, July 19, 2005.

396. Mayor of West Okoboji. Information furnished to the author, summer 2005.

397. Mayor of Westwood. E-mail, July 17, 2005.

398. McCarty, Dwight G. *History of Palo Alto County, Iowa*. Cedar Rapids, Iowa: Torch Press, 1910.

399. *McCausland, Iowa, Centennial: 1882–1982*. N.p., 1982.

400. McCleary, Dorothy Sprague. Information furnished to the author, summer 2005.

401. McCulla, Thomas. *History of Cherokee County Iowa*. Vol. 1. Chicago: S. J. Clarke, 1914.

402. Melbourne Public Library. E-mail, July 15, 2005.

403. Merritt, W. W., Sr. *A History of the County of Montgomery*. Red Oak, Iowa: Express, 1906.

404. Merry, John F. *History of Delaware County, Iowa*. Vol. 1. Chicago: S. J. Clarke, 1914.

405. Messerly, Lila. *Over 100 Years in and around Finchford*. Finchford, Iowa: Finchford Community Bible Church Ladies' Aid, 1954.

406. Meyer, Connie, Franklin County Historical Society. Information furnished to the author, April 6, 2006.

407. Meyers, F. W. *History of Crawford County, Iowa*. Vol. 1. Chicago: S. J. Clarke, 1911.

408. "Mills County." http://www.iowacounties.org/About%20Us/AboutCoGov/County%20Pages/Mills.htm (accessed May 3, 2006).

409. *Mills County, Iowa: 1985*. Glenwood, Iowa: Committee, 1985.

410. *Milo Centennial, 1880–1980: Including Belmont and Otter Townships.* N.p.: Walsworth, 1980.

411. "Minerva Township List of Towns, Post Offices, Landmarks etc." February 14, 2002. http://www.rootsweb.com/~iamarsha/twpntowninfo/Minervatwp/Minervatowninfo.htm (accessed April 13, 2006).

412. "Mitchell County." http://www.iowacounties.org/About%20Us/AboutCoGov/County%20Pages/Mitchell.htm (accessed May 3, 2006).

413. Mitchellville Public Library. E-mail, July 15, 2005.

414. Modlin, Mari. "Hardin County Towns." 2001–2004. http://www.rootsweb.com/~iahardin/html/towns.html (accessed April 6, 2006).

415. "Monona County." http://www.iowacounties.org/About%20Us/AboutCoGov/County%20Pages/Monona.htm (accessed May 3, 2006).

416. "Monroe County." http://www.iowacounties.org/About%20Us/AboutCoGov/County%20Pages/Monroe.htm (accessed May 3, 2006).

417. Monroe County Genealogical Society. E-mail, July 21, 2005.

418. "Montgomery County." http://www.iowacounties.org/About%20Us/AboutCoGov/County%20Pages/Montgomery.htm (accessed May 3, 2006).

419. "Montour! Early History, Business Prospects, etc. The Toledo Chronicle, Toledo, Tama County, Iowa. July 1, 1875." http://www.rootsweb.com/~iatama/montour.html (accessed April 27, 2006).

420. "Montrose: A Look into the Past." http://freepages.genealogy.rootsweb.com/~montrose/ (accessed April 29, 2006).

421. *Mormontown Centennial, 1861 to 1961, Blockton, Iowa, August 23, 24, 25, 26, 1961.* Bedford, Iowa: Centennial Committee, [1961?].

422. Morris, Kent, and Kathy Morris. "Noble Township." 2004. http://www.rootsweb.com/~iacass/history/twps-CCGS-pubs.htm#Noble2 (accessed April 28, 2006).

423. Mott, David C. "Abandoned Towns, Villages and Post Offices of Iowa." *Annals of Iowa* 17, no. 6 (October 1930).

424. Mueller, Herman A., ed. *The History of Madison County, Iowa.* Vol. 1. Chicago: S. J. Clarke, 1915.

425. Mullinix, Rosalie. Information furnished to the author, summer 2005.

426. Mullinix, Rosalie Sweeden. *History of Hiteman: A Mining Town.* N.p.: R. Mullinix, 1983.

427. "Muscatine County." http://www.iowacounties.org/About%20Us/AboutCoGov/County%20Pages/Muscatine.htm (accessed May 3, 2006).

428. Muscatine County Recorder's Office. Information furnished to the author, summer 2005.

429. Nevada Public Library. E-mail, August 19, 2005.

430. "New Albin Named for Youth." *Annals of Iowa* 30, no. 7 (January 1951).

431. "Newhall—52315." http://www.bentoncountyiowa.com/Atkins/Belle_Plaine/Blairstown/Garrison/Shellsburg/newhall.htm (accessed April 29, 2006).

432. Newhall Library. Information furnished to the author, summer 2005.

433. Nieuwenhuis, Nelson G. *Siouxland: A History of Sioux County, Iowa.* Orange City, Iowa: Sioux County Historical Society, 1983.

434. *1984 History of Clayton County Iowa.* Elkader, Iowa: Griffith Press, 1984.

435. North East Iowa Genealogical Society. *Cedar Tree* 17. Black Hawk County, Iowa, Eagle Township edition, 1986.

436. Northwood Library. E-mail, August 2, 2005.

437. "O'Brien County." http://www.iowacounties.org/About%
20Us/AboutCoGov/County%20Pages/Obrien.htm (accessed
May 3, 2006).

438. Office of the Iowa Secretary of State. Information furnished to
the author, 2004–2005.

439. *100 Years, Morley's First Century of History, 1873–1973*. Morley,
Iowa: Morley Centennial Book Committee, 1973.

440. "125 Years Garrison, Iowa." http://www.rootsweb.com/~
iabenton/garrison.htm (accessed April 27, 2006).

441. *125 Years of Dow City-Arion History 1869–1994*. N.p., [1994?].

442. Orange City Public Library. E-mail, July 25, 2005.

443. Orient Bank of Memories. E-mail, June 9, 2005.

444. Orono Public Library. Information furnished to the author,
summer 2005.

445. Osage City Hall. Information furnished to the author, summer
2005.

446. "Osceola County." http://www.iowacounties.org/About%
20Us/AboutCoGov/County%20Pages/Osceola.htm (accessed
May 3, 2006).

447. Oskaloosa Public Library. E-mail, August 12, 2005.

448. Ossian City Hall. Information furnished to the author, summer
2005.

449. *An Overview of the History of Winnebago County from 1855*. N.p.,
1970s.

450. "Page County." http://www.iowacounties.org/About%20Us/
AboutCoGov/County%20Pages/Page.htm (accessed May 3,
2006).

451. *Page County History*. Page County, Iowa: Page County
Genealogical Society, 1984.

452. "Palo Alto County." http://www.iowacounties.org/About%
20Us/AboutCoGov/County%20Pages/PaloAlto.htm (accessed
May 3, 2006).

453. *Panama, Pages of Time*. Panama, Iowa: [Panama Centennial Committee?], 1984.

454. *Parnell Centennial 1885–1985: 100 Years in Little Ireland*. Deep River, Iowa: Brennan-Printing, 1987.

455. *Past and Present of Buena Vista County, Iowa*. Chicago: S. J. Smith, 1909.

456. *Past Harvests: A history of Floyd County to 1996*. Charles City, Iowa: Floyd County Historical Society, 1996.

457. Pastor, Lanyon Church. E-mail, August 18, 2005.

458. Patera, Alan H. *Iowa Post Offices, 1833–1986*. Lake Oswego, Ore.: Depot, 1986.

459. Pecinovsky, Bradley J. *Howard County History*. N.p.: Howard County Commission for Iowa Sesquicentennial, n.d.

460. Peck, John Lucinius Everett. *Past and Present of O'Brien and Osceola Counties, Iowa*. Vol. 1. Indianapolis: B. F. Bowen, 1914.

461. "Pekin, 2001." http://www.rootsweb.com/~iajeffer/Towns/Pekin.html (accessed April 28, 2006).

462. Perkins, D. A. W. *History of Osceola County, Iowa*. Sioux Falls, S.Dak.: Brown and Saenger, 1892.

463. "Picturesque Nottinghamshire Villages Linby." http://www.ashfield-dc.gov.uk/hiddenvalleys/linby_and_papplewick.shtml (accessed April 18, 2006).

464. Pioneer Association of Lyon County. *Compendium of History Reminiscence and Biography of Lyon County, Iowa*. Chicago: George A. Ogle, 1904–1905.

465. Plover Library. E-mail, July 19, 2005.

466. "Plymouth County." http://www.iowacounties.org/About%20Us/AboutCoGov/County%20Pages/Plymouth.htm (accessed May 3, 2006).

467. "Pocahontas County." http://www.iowacounties.org/About%20Us/AboutCoGov/County%20Pages/Pocahontas.htm (accessed May 3, 2006).

468. "Polk County." http://www.iowacounties.org/About%20Us/ AboutCoGov/County%20Pages/Polk.htm (accessed May 3, 2006).

469. Pomeroy City Hall. Information furnished to the author, summer 2005.

470. "Pottawattamie County." http://www.iowacounties.org/About% 20Us/AboutCoGov/County%20Pages/Pottawattamie.htm (accessed May 3, 2006).

471. Pottawattamie County Genealogical Society. E-mail, November 25, 2005.

472. Powers, J. H. *Historical and Reminiscences of Chickasaw County, Iowa*. Des Moines, Iowa: Iowa Printing Company, 1894.

473. "Poweshiek County." http://www.iowacounties.org/About% 20Us/AboutCoGov/County%20Pages/Poweshiek.htm (accessed May 3, 2006).

474. *Poweshiek County Heritage*. N.p.: Poweshiek County Historical and Genealogical Society, 1991.

475. Pratt, H. M. *History of Fort Dodge and Webster County, Iowa*. Vol. 1. Chicago: Pioneer, 1913.

476. Price, Donald A. *History of Ira*. Des Moines, Iowa: self-published, 1976.

477. Prill, Mary. "Towns-Post Offices-Rail Stops of Jefferson County, 1967." http://www.rootsweb.com/~iajeffer/Towns/ Abington.html (accessed July 15, 2005).

478. Print, Margaret. *History of Raymond*. N.p., 1975.

479. "Projected Railroads Plentiful in Those Early Days." Washington County, Iowa, Centennial Issue, 1936. http:// members.aol.com/ntgen/hrtg/waiarr.html (accessed April 27, 2006).

480. "Protivin Iowa." 2001. http://www.howard-county.com/ protivin/index.html (accessed April 29, 2006).

481. "A Quiet Bedroom." 2005. http://www.teammahaska.org/ cities/keomah.html (accessed April 27, 2006).

482. Rake Public Library. E-mail, July 15, 2005.

483. Randall, William D. "Under Many Flags." In *Little Known Stories of Muscatine*. Vol. 1. Muscatine, Iowa: Friends of the Musser Public Library, 1980.

484. Randall, William D. "Why Muscatine?" In *Little Known Stories of Muscatine*. Vol. 1. Muscatine, Iowa: Friends of the Musser Public Library, 1980.

485. Randall City Hall. Information furnished to the author, summer 2005.

486. Rathbun, Bill. E-mail, July 11, 2005.

487. Reddick, Andy. "Country Facts and Folklore, Van Buren's 70 Villages." http://www.rootsweb.com/~iavanbur/ FactsAndFolklore/Villages_1_26.htm (accessed July 15, 2005).

488. "Redding Will Celebrate the Centennial of Its Incorporation on July 10 and 11 of This Year." *Ringgold Roots*, vol. 3, January 1982, Ringgold County Genealogical Society, Mt. Ayr, Iowa.

489. Reinbeck Library. E-mail, October 7, 2005.

490. Riceville Library. E-mail, July 22, 2005.

491. Richland Public Library. E-mail, July 18, 2005.

492. Richman, Irving B., ed. *History of Muscatine County, Iowa*. Vol. 1. Chicago: S. J. Clarke, 1911.

493. Ricketts Senior Center. Information furnished to the author, summer 2005.

494. Riley, Glenda. *Cities on the Cedar*. Parkersburg, Iowa: Mid-Prairie Books, 1988.

495. Ringberg, Alice, Shannon City United Methodist Church treasurer. Information furnished to the author, summer 2005.

496. "Ringgold County." http://www.iowacounties.org/About% 20Us/AboutCoGov/County%20Pages/Ringgold.htm (accessed May 3, 2006).

497. *Ringgold County History, Iowa*. Mt. Ayr, Iowa, 1942.

498. "Ringgold Roots Salutes Ellston Formerly Wirt." *Ringgold Roots*, vol. 2, April 1981, Ringgold County Genealogical Society, Mt. Ayr, Iowa.

499. Rippey Public Library. E-mail, July 8, 2005.

500. Robert W. Barlow Memorial Library. E-mail, July 19, 2005.

501. Rockwell City Public Library. E-mail, July 12, 2005.

502. Royal City Hall. Information furnished to the author, summer 2005.

503. "Sac County." http://www.iowacounties.org/About%20Us/ AboutCoGov/County%20Pages/Sac.htm (accessed May 3, 2006).

504. St. Luke Church. E-mail, July 22, 2005.

505. Sanchez, Sandra. "1870 Linn County, Iowa Census Surname Index. 2001–2003." http://www.usgennet.org/usa/ia/county/ linn/census/1870censusindexcd.htm#c (accessed April 18, 2006).

506. Scheidel, Lon. Information furnished to the author, summer 2005.

507. Schultz, Gerard, and Don L. Berry. *History of Warren County*. Indianola, Iowa: Record and Tribune, 1953.

508. "Scott County." http://www.iowacounties.org/About% 20Us/AboutCoGov/County%20Pages/Scott.htm (accessed May 3, 2006).

509. *Scott County Heritage*. Davenport, Iowa: Scott County Heritage Book Committee, 1991.

510. Scott County Library. E-mail, August 4, 2005.

511. Scott County Library. Information furnished to the author, summer 2005.

512. *Settlement to Centennial: History of the Saint Anthony Area from Time of Earliest Settlement, 1849–1982*. N.p., 1982.

513. *1776–1876 Jefferson County, Iowa Centennial History*. By Authority of Board of Supervisors, under the direction of S. M. Boling, C. W. Slagle, W. W. Junkin, J. F. Wilson, Charles Negus, and I. D.

Jones, Citizens Committee, Charles H. Fletcher, Historian, Fairfield, Iowa, 1876.

514. "Shelby County." http://www.iowacounties.org/About%20Us/ AboutCoGov/County%20Pages/Shelby.htm (accessed May 3, 2006).

515. "Shelby County Iowa Towns." 2001. http://www.rootsweb.com/ ~iashelby/towns.htm (accessed April 30, 2006).

516. Shipley, Dixie. Information furnished to the author, summer 2005.

517. Simon, Cindi. "Early Dow City History from 1851." http:// www.rootsweb.com/~iacrawfo/dowhist.html (accessed April 25, 2006).

518. "Sioux County." http://www.iowacounties.org/About%20Us/ AboutCoGov/County%20Pages/Sioux.htm (accessed May 3, 2006).

519. Sloat, Jerry. *Pictorial History of Lee County Iowa.* Virginia Beach, Va.: Donning, 1993.

520. Smith, Celesta. "Some Early History of Gravity." *Gravity Independent,* Gravity, Iowa, May 17, 24, and 31, 1934. http:// www.rootsweb.com/~iataylor/tci25.htm (accessed April 26, 2006).

521. Smith, R. A. *A History of Dickinson County, Iowa.* Des Moines, Iowa: Kenyon Printing and Manufacturing, 1902.

522. Somers City Hall. Information furnished to the author, summer 2005.

523. *Southwest Iowa's Heritage: History of Page and Fremont Counties.* Shenandoah, Iowa: World, 1973.

524. Spirit Lake Public Library. E-mail, July 12, 2005.

525. Spoon, Betty Jane. *Lucas, Iowa, 125 Years 1868–1993.* Indianola, Iowa: Publishing House, 1993.

526. Springer, Arthur. *History of Louisa County, Iowa.* Vol. 1. Chicago: S. J. Clarke, 1912.

527. *Stanton, Iowa Centennial, June 21–28, 1970.* Stanton, Iowa: Stanton Area Centennial Corporation, 1970.

528. Stennett, William E. *A History of the Origin of the Place Names Connected with the Chicago and North Western and Chicago, St. Paul, Minneapolis and Omaha Railways.* Chicago, 1908.

529. Sterling, Ruth. Information furnished to the author, summer 2005.

530. Stickle, Harry F. *Grimes: One Hundred Years.* Woodward, Iowa: Northeast Dallas County Record, 1980.

531. Stillman, Edwin B. *Past and Present of Greene County, Iowa.* Chicago: S. J. Clarke, 1907.

532. Stonebraker, Beaumont E. *Past and Present of Calhoun County, Iowa.* Chicago: Pioneer, 1915.

533. "Story County." http://www.iowacounties.org/About%20Us/ AboutCoGov/County%20Pages/Story.htm (accessed May 3, 2006).

534. "Story County Towns and Post Offices." 1998–1999. http:// www.rootsweb.com/~iastory/towns.htm (accessed April 18, 2006).

535. Swisher City Hall. E-mail, June 20, 2005.

536. "Tama County." http://www.iowacounties.org/About%20Us/ AboutCoGov/County%20Pages/Tama.htm (accessed May 3, 2006).

537. Taylor, L. L., ed. *Past and Present of Appanoose County Iowa.* Vol. 1. Chicago: S. J. Clarke, 1913.

538. "Taylor County." http://www.iowacounties.org/About%20Us/ AboutCoGov/County%20Pages/Taylor.htm (accessed May 3, 2006).

539. Taylor County Recorder's Office. Information furnished to the author, summer 2005.

540. Thayer City Hall. Information furnished to the author, summer 2005.

541. Thompson, Cliff. Information furnished to the author, December 2005.

542. *Those Were the Days: Elma, Iowa 1886–1986*. Lake Mills, Iowa: Elma Centennial Committee, 1986.

543. Todd, David. Information furnished to the author, summer 2005.

544. "Town History." http://www.titonka.com/history.htm (accessed April 18, 2006).

545. Townsend, W. A. *Standard Historical Atlas of Mills and Fremont Counties*. Chicago: Anderson, 1910.

546. "Treaty with the Yankton Sioux, 1858." http://digital.library .okstate.edu/kappler/Vol2/treaties/yan0776.htm (accessed April 30, 2006).

547. "Treaty with the Yankton Sioux, 1858." http://www.usd.edu/ iais/siouxnation/treaty1858.html (accessed April 28, 2006).

548. Truckenmiller, Bob. *Osceola County Sesquicentennial History 1996*. Sibley, Iowa: Osceola County Sesquicentennial Commission, 1996.

549. "Union County." http://www.iowacounties.org/About%20Us/ AboutCoGov/County%20Pages/Union.htm (accessed May 3, 2006).

550. Union County Recorder's Office. Information furnished to the author, summer 2005.

551. *The Urbana Bicentennial*. Urbana Bicentennial Committee, August 13–14, 1976.

552. Urbandale Public Library. E-mail, July 11, 2006.

553. *Ute History, One Hundred Years: 1884–1984*. N.p., 1984.

554. "Valeria." valeriaiowa.com/history.html (accessed July 15, 2005).

555. Valeria City Hall, interview with the mayor, fall 2005.

556. "Van Buren County." http://www.iowacounties.org/About% 20Us/AboutCoGov/County%20Pages/VanBuren.htm (accessed May 3, 2006).

557. Van der Zee, Jacob. *Hollanders of Iowa*. Des Moines, Iowa: Iowa Printing Company, 1894.

558. Van Horne Library. E-mail, July 25, 2005.

559. Vasiliev, Irina. "U.S. Places Called Moscow." Department of Geography, Syracuse University. 1996. http://www.uwec.edu/geography/Ivogeler/w111/moscow.htm (accessed April 14, 2006).

560. *Vincent's First 100 Years, 1887–1987: The Official Vincent, Iowa Centennial Book*. Vincent, Iowa, 1987.

561. Vogel, Virgil J. *Iowa Place Names of Indian Origin*. Iowa City: University of Iowa Press, 1983.

562. Waller, Randy. E-mail, August 24, 2005.

563. Walsh, Dennis. "Magnolia Township Excerpts from the 1891 History of Harrison County Iowa." http://www.rootsweb.com/~iaharris/twp/twpmagno.htm (accessed April 28, 2006).

564. "Wapello County." http://www.iowacounties.org/About%20Us/AboutCoGov/County%20Pages/Wapello.htm (accessed May 3, 2006).

565. Warren County. http://www.iowacounties.org/About%20Us/AboutCoGov/County%20Pages/Warren.htm (accessed May 3, 2006).

566. Warren County Historical Society. Information furnished to the author, summer 2005.

567. "Washington County." http://www.iowacounties.org/About%20Us/AboutCoGov/County%20Pages/Washington.htm (accessed May 3, 2006).

568. Washington County Genealogical Society. E-mail, July 14, 2005.

569. Washington County Genealogical Society. Information furnished to the author, summer 2005.

570. Waterloo Public Library. Information furnished to the author, summer 2005.

571. "Wayne County." http://www.iowacounties.org/About%20Us/AboutCoGov/County%20Pages/Wayne.htm (accessed May 3, 2006).

572. Wayne County Historical Society. *Pictorial Review of Wayne County.* N.p., [1974?].

573. Weaver, James E. *Past and Present of Jasper County Iowa.* Vol. 1. Indianapolis: B. F. Bowen, 1912.

574. "Webster County." http://www.iowacounties.org/About%20Us/AboutCoGov/County%20Pages/Webster.htm (accessed May 3, 2006).

575. "Welcome to . . ." http://www.lawtoniowa.com/lawton_web_page_001.htm (accessed April 26, 2006).

576. "Welcome to Buckeye, Iowa." 2002–2006. http://hardincountyonline.com/buckeye/ (accessed April 19, 2006).

577. "Welcome to Coalville." http://www.wccta.net/gallery/coalville/ (accessed April 13, 2006).

578. "Welcome to Montezuma, Iowa!" http://www.montezuma.org/backgrnd.htm (accessed April 20, 2006).

579. "Welcome to Steamboat Rock Iowa." http://hardincountyonline.com/steamboatrock/ (accessed April 27, 2006).

580. "Welcome to Traer, Iowa." http://www.traer.com/ (accessed April 18, 2006).

581. "Welcome to Whitten, Iowa." http://hardincountyonline.com/whitten/ (accessed April 27, 2006).

582. *Weldon Centennial, 1880–1980.* Weldon, Iowa: Book Committee, [1980?].

583. Wells, John G. *Wells' Pocket Hand-Book of Iowa.* New York: John G. Wells, 1857.

584. West Des Moines Library. Information furnished to the author, summer 2005.

585. *Westgate Memory Lane 1886–1986.* Westgate, Iowa: Westgate Centennial Committee, 1986.

586. "Westside History. 2001–2005." http://www.rootsweb.com/~iacrawfo/westsidehist.html (accessed April 30, 2006).

587. White, Edward S. *Past and Present of Shelby County, Iowa.* Vol. 1. Indianapolis: B. F. Bowen, 1915.

588. "Willey." http://www.rootsweb.com/~iacarrol/towns/towns_willey.htm (accessed May 1, 2006).

589. "Winnebago County." http://www.iowacounties.org/About%20Us/AboutCoGov/County%20Pages/Winnebago.htm (accessed May 3, 2006).

590. "Winneshiek County." http://www.iowacounties.org/About%20Us/AboutCoGov/County%20Pages/Winneshiek.htm (accessed May 3, 2006).

591. Wolfe, P. B., ed. *Wolfe's History of Clinton County Iowa.* Vol. 1. Indianapolis: B. F. Bowen, 1911.

592. "Woodbury County." http://www.iowacounties.org/About%20Us/AboutCoGov/County%20Pages/Woodbury.htm (accessed May 3, 2006).

593. "Worth County." http://www.iowacounties.org/About%20Us/AboutCoGov/County%20Pages/Worth.htm (accessed May 3, 2006).

594. Wright, John W. *History of Marion County and Its People.* Vol. 1. Reprint, LaCrosse, Wis.: Brookhaven Press, 2001.

595. "Wright County." http://www.iowacounties.org/About%20Us/AboutCoGov/County%20Pages/Wright.htm (accessed May 3, 2006).

596. Wyoming Public Library. E-mail, July 15, 2005.

597. "Ye' Old Post Offices Grundy County, IA." 2004. http://iagenweb.org/grundy/oldpostoffices.htm (accessed April 29, 2006).

598. Yori, Raymond. Information furnished to the author, spring 2005.

OTHER BUR OAK BOOKS OF INTEREST

A Bountiful Harvest
The Midwestern Farm Photographs
of Pete Wettach, 1925–1965
By Leslie A. Loveless

Buxton
A Black Utopia in the Heartland
By Dorothy Schwieder, Joseph
Hraba, and Elmer Schwieder

Central Standard
A Time, a Place, a Family
By Patrick Irelan

Harker's Barns
Visions of an American Icon
Photographs by Michael P. Harker
Text by Jim Heynen

An Iowa Album
A Photographic History, 1860–1920
By Mary Bennett

Iowa Stereographs
Three-Dimensional Visions of the Past
By Mary Bennett and Paul C. Juhl

Letters of a German American Farmer
Jürnjakob Swehn Travels to America
By Johannes Gillhoff

Neighboring on the Air
Cooking with the KMA
Radio Homemakers
By Evelyn Birkby

Nothing to Do but Stay
My Pioneer Mother
By Carrie Young

Picturing Utopia
Bertha Shambaugh and the
Amana Photographers
By Abigail Foerstner

Prairie Cooks
Glorified Rice, Three-Day Buns,
and Other Reminiscences
By Carrie Young
with Felicia Young

Prairie Reunion
By Barbara J. Scot

Sarah's Seasons
An Amish Diary and Conversation
By Martha Moore Davis

Weathering Winter
A Gardener's Daybook
By Carl H. Klaus

The Wedding Dress
Stories from the Dakota Plains
By Carrie Young

A Dictionary of Iowa Place-Names is set in Bitstream Iowan Old Style. This contemporary text typeface was drawn by Iowa sign painter John Downer. It owes much of its identity to specific regional characteristics, which are derived from the sign painting and stone cutting of eastern Iowa. ¶ Mr. Downer was born in 1951 and began training as a sign painter while he was in high school. He finished his apprenticeship after receiving a BA in fine art, then started graduate studies at the University of Iowa, where he received MA and MFA degrees in painting. He currently lives in Iowa City and lectures throughout the United States and Europe.